THE
PRESENT STATE
OF
MUSIC
IN
GERMANY,
THE NETHERLANDS,
AND
UNITED PROVINCES.

OR,

The JOURNAL of a TOUR through those Countries, undertaken to collect Materials for

A GENERAL HISTORY OF MUSIC.

By CHARLES BURNEY, Muſ. D.

IN TWO VOLUMES.

VOL. I.

Auf Virtuoſen ſey ſtolz, Germanien, die du gezeiget;
In Frankreich und Welſchland ſind gröſſere nicht.

Zachariä.

LONDON,

Printed for T. BECKET and Co. Strand; J. ROBSON, New Bond-Street; and G. ROBINSON, Paternoſter Row. 1773.

This is a facsimile of Charles Burney's The Present State of Music in Germany, the Netherlands, and the United Provinces, or, The Journal of a Tour through those Countries, undertaken to collect Materials for a General History of Music. London: Printed for T. Becket and Co. in the Strand; J. Robson, New Bond Street; and G. Robinson, Paternoster Row. 1773. This was the first edition. A second edition was published in 1775.

This work was published in two volumes which have been republished here as a single book containing both the original volumes.

Dr. Charles Burney, Mus. D. (1726-1814), organist, composer and music historian.

Music related books written by Dr. Burney include:
1771: The Present State of Music in France and Italy or, The Journal of a Tour through those Countries, undertaken to collect Materials for a General History of Music. London: Printed for T. Becket and Co. (Second edition 1773)
1771: A Letter from the Late Signor Tartini to Signora Maddalena Lombardini (now Signora Sirmen). Published as an Important Lesson to Performers on the Violin. Translated by Dr. Burney. (Also 1779)
1773: The Present State of Music in Germany, the Netherlands, and the United Provinces, or, The Journal of a Tour through those Countries, undertaken to collect Materials for a General History of Music. London: Printed for T. Becket and Co. 2 vols. (Second edition 1775)
1776-1789: A General History of Music from the Earliest Ages to the Present Period, to which is prefixed, a Dissertation on the Music of the Ancients. 4 vols. (Vol 1 reprinted in 1789).
1779 Account of an Infant Musician. [William Crotch.]
1785: An account of Mademoiselle Theresa Paradis.
1785: An Account of the Musical Performances in Westminster-Abbey, and the Pantheon, May 26th, 27th, 29th; and June the 3rd, and 5th, 1784. In Commemoration of Handel.

Standard works on the life of Dr. Burney include:
BURNEY, Frances ['Fanny', Madame d'Arblay, his daughter], Memoirs of Dr. Burney. (1832)
SCHOLES, Percy A.: The Great Dr. Burney: His Life, His Travels, His Works, His Family and His Friends.. (OUP, 1948)
LONSDALE, Roger: Dr. Charles Burney: A Literary Biography: (OUP, 1965)
More information, and fuller bibliography, can also be found in The New Grove Dictionary of Music and Musicians (Macmillan / OUP)

This facsimile is based on digitised camera scanning of the original book, so as to reproduce the original as closely as possible. While efforts are made to reduce distortions, there may be some distortion from the curve in the margin of the original. Any material in colour has been reproduced in black and white. Larger pages, such as inserts, may have been reduced to fit the page size of the facsimile.

Reprinted 2008 Travis & Emery,
17 Cecil Court, London, WC2N 4EZ,
England.
(+44) 20 7240 2129
neworders@travis-and-emery.com
Bibliography – Travis & Emery ©2008
Hardback: ISBN: 1-904331-57-2. ISBN13 978-1-904331-57-5
Paperback: ISBN: 1-904331-58-0. ISBN13 978-1-904331-58-2

THE

PRESENT STATE

OF

MUSIC

IN

GERMANY,

THE NETHERLANDS,

AND

UNITED PROVINCES.

OR,

The JOURNAL of a TOUR through those Countries, undertaken to collect Materials for

A GENERAL HISTORY OF MUSIC.

By CHARLES BURNEY, Muſ. D.

IN TWO VOLUMES.

VOL. I.

Auf Virtuoſen ſey ſtolz, Germanien, die du gezeiget;
In Frankreich und Welſchland ſind gröſſere nicht.

Zachariä.

LONDON,

Printed for T. BECKET and Co. Strand; J. ROBSON, New Bond-Street; and G. ROBINSON, Paternoſter Row. 1773.

THE
INTRODUCTION.

IT is well known that such merchandize as is capable of adulteration, is seldom genuine after passing through many hands; and this principle is still more generally allowed with respect to intelligence, which is, perhaps, never pure but at the source.

Music has, through life, been the favourite object of my pursuit, not only with respect to the practice of it as a profession, but the history of it as an art; and that my knowledge might be free from such falshood and error as the plainest and simplest facts are known to gather up in succeffive relations, I have made a second tour on the continent, taking nothing upon report, of which I could procure better testimony, and, accumulating the most authentic memorials of the times that are past; and as I have, in a late publication, endeavoured to do justice to the talents and attainments of the present musicians of France and Italy, I shall now make the same attempt with respect to those of Germany, hoping that the testimony of one who has himself been witness of the particulars he relates, will have a weight which integrity itself cannot give to hear-say evidence, and that the mind of the reader will be more entertained, in proportion as it is more satisfied of the truth of what is written. For if *knowledge* be *medicine for the soul*, according to the famous inscription on the Alexandrian Library *, it seems as much to concern us to obtain it genuine, as to procure unadulterated medicine for the body.

* ψυχῆς ἰατρεῖον.

Travelling for information concerning the transactions of remote countries, was much more practised by the writers of antiquity than it has been by those of later times, who have found it more convenient to compile books at their own fire-side, from books which have been compiled before, than to cross seas, mountains, and deserts, in foreign countries, to seek for new and authentic materials. But Homer, Herodotus, Plato, Plutarch, and Pausanias, who were great travellers, either lived in times when there were few books to consult, or, if they were not possessed of more wealth than modern authors, must have met with more than modern hospitality; for long voyages, however necessary, would otherwise have been scarcely practicable.

For my part, who have travelled without these advantages, and who pretend not to the character of *sage*, if it be said, that the object of my pursuit is by no means

means equivalent to my labour and expence; I can only anfwer, that though I am unwilling to allow the knowledge of a fcience which diffufes fo much blamelefs pleafure, through a circle of fuch vaft extent, to be of fmall importance, yet I moft fincerely wifh that I could have procured it upon eafier terms, and have vifited remote countries after the deliberate and parfimonious manner of Afclepiades, who, according to Tertullian, made the tour of the world on a cow's back, and lived upon her milk.

It is however certain, that whatever will juftify my rambling through France and Italy after the *materia mufica*, or apologize for it, may with the fame force and propriety be pleaded for my having vifited Germany; for though Italy has carried *vocal* mufic to a perfection unknown in any other country, much of the prefent excellence of *inftrumental* is certainly owing to the natives of Germany,

many, as wind and keyed inftruments have never, perhaps, in any age or country, been brought to a greater degree of refinement, either in conftruction or ufe, than by the modern Germans.

The notice and affiftance with which I was honoured by feveral perfons of diftinction on the continent, are acknowledged in the courfe of my narrative; but to avoid repetitions in my book, and to follow an impulfe of gratitude, perhaps not unmixed with vanity, I muft here declare, that for thefe and many other advantages which my journey produced, I am principally indebted to the patronage of the Earl of Sandwich, who, to affift me in calling the attention of the public to the hiftory of his favourite art, and in recording the talents of its moft illuftrious profeffors in remote countries, was pleafed to honour me with recommendatory letters, in his own hand, to every nobleman and gentleman of this country who refided in a public character in the feveral cities through which I paffed; the influence of which was fo powerful as to gain me eafy accefs to thofe who were not only the moft able, but whom I was fo fortunate as to find the moft willing to forward my undertaking.

THE PRESENT STATE OF MUSIC, &c.

St. OMERS.

I Muſt confeſs, that my appetite for French muſic was not very keen when I now landed on the continent, July 6th, 1772. However, being detained at St. Omers a day longer than I expected, I viſited ſome of the churches there, as well as the theatre; but heard nothing in either which inclined me to change my ſentiments concerning the national taſte of France, for muſic.

A company of strolling players, from Dunkirk, acted, on the night of my arrival, a tragedy and a comedy. I went to the playhouse, which I found small and dirty; and though the tragedy was half over when I arrived, there was no other company in the boxes, than two or three English families, and a few of the officers of the garrison. It is impossible for Englishmen to judge, accurately, of French acting, and declamation; but these performers seemed much more at their ease, and appeared more like the characters they were to represent, than those on the English stage, who, except a few of the principal actors, are generally so aukward and unnatural, as to destroy all illusion.

At the cathedral of St. Omer there is a very fine sixteen feet organ, which is played in a masterly, but old style, by a priest, father Thomas, who teaches the harpsichord to many English people, as well as other inhabitants of that city.

But

But the most considerable instrument there, in figure and grandeur, is the organ at the abbey of St. Bertin: it was built but five years ago, by a country mechanic, who could neither write, read, nor play on his instrument when it was made. I had, as yet, seen nothing so elegant and magnificent as the case and ornaments of this organ; the stops are numerous, and the movements light and tolerably quiet; there are pedals, but there is no swell, or great variety in the solo stops, nor do I think the tone so sweet as that of the cathedral. But the best organ in this part of the world, for sweetness of tone, is an old one at the monastery of Clairmarais, about a league from St. Omers. The organist there is a friar; and that of the abbey of St. Bertin is a nephew and scholar of father Thomas.

There is a little organ, called a *positif*, consisting of four stops only, in the chancel of the abbey, which is used on common occasions; it is nearly such a one as I remember to have seen and heard Colista play upon, to accompany the voices, at the church of St. John Lateran, at Rome, in 1770.

At mounting guard in the *Grande Place* of St. Omer, I observed that the *serpent* was used in the military band, as a double base to a great number of bassoons, horns, and hautboys, and had a very good effect.

L I S L E.

To persons who stay but a short time in French garrisoned towns, the military affords considerable amusement; there are not at present above four battalions, or two thousand men, quartered in the city; though it is usual for the garrison to consist of ten thousand. The mounting guard upon the *Grande Place,* or square, is, in itself, a gay and entertaining sight; yet it always gives me a melancholy, and painful sensation, to see the people out-numbered by the military. So many stout and robust fellows kept from the plough, and from manufactures, must be a great burden upon the community, and totally useless in time of peace, to any thing but ambitious and oppressive views.

Having visited this city, in quest of musical information, so lately as the year 1770, I expected to find nothing new, that was very interesting; however, I attended to the military music, which is much changed here since I was last in France. The marches, as well as musicians, are chiefly German. The *crotolo* is used here as I had seen it at Florence; it serves very well to mark the time in marching, though it has only one tone, like that of a side drum: it is the same instrument as that which the ancients called the *cymbalum*. The Turks were the first among the moderns who used it in their troops; the form is that of a bafon, or the cover to a difh; there is one for each hand. It is made of brafs, but the vibration is fo ftopt by its being in contact with the hand, that it cannot be called fonorous, it is rather a clafhing than a founding inftrument of percuffion; however, its effect in marking the time is fo powerful as to be diftinctly heard through the ftunning noife of forty drums.

In fpeaking of military mufic, it feems not unworthy of remark, that drums, *monotonous* as they are, frequently play in *two parts*. I obferved to-day, at mounting guard, that, of forty drums which began to beat together ifochronous, or in equal time, one half continued to beat the march, and the other half accompanied them with a continual roll for feveral bars: the effect of this is admirable, as it contributes to animate the troops, without deftroying or altering the divifion of time, by which they are to meafure their fteps.

In

In other music, during a long note, which is either simply sustained in a swell, or *diminuendo*, or has a continued shake, the time is wholly unmarked, unless its accents and proportions are pointed out and regulated by some other part; a single drum, while one hand rolls, has frequently the time marked by the single strokes of the other, given at stated periods. The use of music, in marching, as well as in dancing, is more to mark the steps than delight the ear; and the best instruments, perhaps, for both purposes, are the drum and tabor, neither of which has more than one sound.

After Moliere's *Ecole des Maris*, I heard here *l'Amitié à l'Epreuve*, taken from one of the *Contes Moraux* of Marmontel, by Favart, with *ariettes* by Gretry: the music is full of pretty things, and it is an honour to the French to admire the compositions of this ingenious composer, who seems, in gratitude,

gratitude, to conform, as much as he can, to the national taſte; though his melodies are more frequently Italian than French, and his modulation and accompaniments are new and pleaſing. To criticiſe the execution of this pretty opera would be firing at carrion crows, not worth powder and ſhot. But in this ſevere cenſure I muſt diſtinguiſh the actors from the ſingers, and the voices from the corruption and abuſe of them.

Both the pieces were well acted; but, as to *ſinging*, nothing could be more offenſive; and yet there was not one bad voice among the performers: one of the young actreſſes had, indeed, a voice that was ſweetly toned, and of great compaſs; but the ſongs were too difficult for her execution, and ſhe joined to the national falſe direction of voice, to forcing, ſcreaming, and bad taſte, that incurable and inſufferable expreſſion, which is equally diſguſting to the learned and the ignorant of other countries.

In

In travelling through French Flanders, I could not help obferving that the finging of the common people is ftrongly tinctured with the *plain-chant*, which they hear fo frequently at church. All the labouring people and *bourgeois* go to matins as foon as it is light on common days, and on Sundays and feftivals two or three times in the courfe of the day; fo that by their conftantly hearing the priefts, and finging with them, they acquire that kind of melody and expreffion which is ufed in the church, and apply it to their fongs, in their work-fhops, and in the ftreet.

Though I omitted no opportunity of hearing all the inftruments and performers I could, in my way through French Flanders, yet they furnifhed no new ideas or reflections concerning either the tafte, or ftyle, of French muficians. To defcribe them, therefore, would be only to repeat what I have already faid on the fubject, in my former mufical tour
through

through this country. I muft, however allow, and it would difcover a total want of candour to be filent on the fubject, that upon keyed inftruments, particularly the harpfichord, the French, in point of neatnefs, precifion, and brilliancy of execution, are not excelled by the people of any other country in Europe; and it is but juft to obferve likewife, that the French military mufic is now not only much better in itfelf, but better performed than it was a few years ago: and a very intelligent Englifh officer, who was with me on the parade, remarked the fame improvement in the difcipline, drefs, and appearance of the French troops in the fame fpace of time. The men are now felect, the manœuvres fhortened, and there is fome appearance both of the gentleman and the foldier, even in the common men.

COURTRAY.

When I arrived at this place, which is the first considerable town in the Austrian Netherlands, I found a remarkable change in the language, manners, and music of the people. It is very embarrassing to a stranger to find within the compass of a hundred English miles, four languages very different from each other: French, Flemish, Walloon, and Low Dutch. At Courtray, the common people speak the Walloon language: I accosted several in the streets, in French, but they did not understand me; so that the Abbé du Bos' assertion, and the consequence he draws from it, that French is the universal language of the Flemings, fall to the ground, for it is a common thing, even at Lisle, for two people to converse in two different languages; the inhabitant of Lisle asks the country-man, who comes to market, the price of his commodities in French, and is anfwered in Flemifh; and both underftand each other's dialect, though unable to fpeak it.

In the town of Courtray, the organ, at the collegiate church of *Notre Dame*, is difpofed of in a very fingular manner; it is placed in a gallery at the weft end of the building; but, in order to preferve the window, which was neceffary to light the body of the church, the organ is divided in two parts, one of which is fixed on one fide of the window, and one on the other; the bellows run under the window, and communicate with both parts of the inftrument, which is a large one of fixteen feet, with pedals, and feems to have been but lately erected. The keys are in the middle, under the window, but not to be feen below; the choir is accompanied, even when the organ does not play, with a *ferpent*, as at Paris, and a double bafe, as at Rome. It was in
this

this town that I firſt perceived the paſ
ſion for *carillons*, or chimes, which is
ſo prevalent throughout the Netherlands. I happened to arrive at eleven
o'clock, and half an hour after the
chimes played a great number of chearful tunes, in different keys, which awakened my curioſity for this ſpecies of muſic
ſo much, that, when I came to

GHENT,

I determined to inform myſelf, in a
particular manner, concerning the *carillon* ſcience. For this purpoſe, I mounted
the town belfrey, from whence I had a
full view, not only of the city of Ghent,
which is reckoned one of the largeſt in
Europe, but could examine the mechaniſm of the chimes, as far as they are
played by clock-work, and likewiſe ſee
the *Carilloneur* perform with a kind of
keys communicating with bells, as thoſe
of the harpſichord and organ do with
ſtrings and pipes.

I ſoon

I soon found that the chimes in these countries had a greater number of bells than those of the largest peal in England; but, when I mounted the belfrey, I was astonished at the great quantity of bells I saw; in short, there is a complete series or scale of tones and semitones, like those on the harpsichord and organ. The *Carilloneur* was literally *at work*, and *hard* work indeed it must be; he was in his shirt with the collar unbuttoned, and in a violent sweat. There are pedals communicating with the great bells, upon which, with his feet, he played the base to several sprightly and rather difficult airs, performed with the two hands upon the upper species of keys. These keys are projecting sticks, wide enough asunder to be struck with violence and velocity by either of the two hands edge ways, without the danger of hitting the neighbouring keys. The player has a thick leather covering

for

for the little finger of each hand, otherwise it would be impossible for him to support the pain which the violence of the stroke necessary to be given to each key, in order to its being distinctly heard throughout a very large town, requires.

The *carillons* are said to be originally of Aloft, in this country, and are still here, and in Holland, in their greatest perfection. It is certainly a Gothic invention, and perhaps a barbarous taste, which neither the French, the English, nor the Italians have imitated or encouraged. The *Carilloneur*, at my request, played several pieces very dexterously, in three parts, the first and second treble with the two hands on the upper set of keys, and the base with the feet on the pedals.

The *Carilloneur* plays four times a week, Sunday, Monday, Wednesday, and Friday, from half an hour past eleven till twelve o'clock: it is constant employment

employment for a watch or clock-maker to attend the works of the common chimes; here he has an apartment under the belfrey, and it is by him that the *Carilloneur* is paid. This place and Antwerp are, according to the inhabitants, the moſt celebrated cities in the Netherlands, and perhaps in the world, for carillons and chimes.

The great convenience of this kind of muſic is, that it entertains the inhabitants of a whole town, without giving them the trouble of going to any particular ſpot to hear it; but the want of ſomething to ſtop the vibration of each bell, at the pleaſure of the player, like the valves of an organ, and the red cloth in the jacks of a harpſichord, is an intolerable defect to a cultivated ear: for by the notes of one paſſage perpetually running into another, every thing is rendered ſo inarticulate and confuſed as to occaſion a very diſagreeable jargon. As to the

the clock-work chimes, or those worked by a barrel, nothing, to my thinking, can be more tiresome; for, night and day, to hear the same tune played every hour, during six months, in such a stiff and unalterable manner, requires that kind of patience, which nothing but a total absence of taste can produce.

As Ghent was the first town which I had been in, that had a German garrison in it, or, rather, troops in the pay, and under the discipline of Germany, I was curious to hear the military music. I found two Walloon regiments here; and though no general officer was on the spot, yet there were two bands attending every morning and evening, on the *Place d'Armes*, or parade. The one was an extra-band of professed musicians, consisting of two hautbois, two clarinets, two bassoons, and two French horns; the other were enlisted men and boys, belonging to the regiments; the number of these amounted to twenty. There were four trumpets,

pets, three fifes, two hautbois, two clarinets, two *tambours de basque*, two French horns, one *crotolo*, or cymbal, three side-drums, and one great kettle-drum. All these sonorous instruments, in the open air, have a very animating and pleasing effect.

I soon found, in visiting the churches of this country, that splitting an organ in twain, in order to preserve a window, was no uncommon thing. At the Jesuit's church, for Jesuits have still an existence here, there is a small organ, for this country, placed in a gallery at the west window, divided in that manner. I found but one set of keys, from C, to G, no pedals, and but few stops, the tone was coarse and noisy when heard near, but, by the size and construction of the building, it was so softened and meliorated, as to sound very agreeably, at a distance.

At the great church of St. Bavo, two *serpents* and a double base accompany the chant,

chant, when sung in parts, even when the organ is not played. The organ here is placed under the arch of the left-side aile, at the entrance into the choir, in order to preserve the center, or broad aile, from being intersected with an organ-loft, which frequently destroys all the symmetry and proportions of a building; as an organ, when placed over the west door, frequently darkens the whole church, by shutting up a principal window, originally intended for other purposes, by the architect, than mere external ornament.

I did not quit Ghent without visiting the principal libraries there, in hopes of meeting with ancient manuscript music, which might ascertain the assertion of Lod. Guicciardini, that counter-point took its rise, and was first cultivated in Flanders; but I neither found at the abbey of St. Peter (the oldest and richest in Flanders) nor at the Augustines, or

Dominicans, where the libraries are very confiderable, any thing to my purpofe.

ALOST.

Here I found, in the church of St. Martin, a noble organ, built by Van Petigham, and fon, of Ghent, but five years fince, which fills the whole weft end of the church; its form is elegant, and the ornaments are in a good tafte. It has fifty-three ftops, three fets of keys, great organ, choir organ, and echo, down to F, on the fourth line in the bafe [*]. The touch is not fo heavy as might be expected from the great refiftance of fuch a column of air as is neceffary for fo confiderable a number of ftops. The reed ftops are well toned, the diapafons well voiced, and the effect of the whole chorus rich and noble: I was the more particular in my obfervations upon this inftrument, in order to enable myfelf to compare its contents with thofe of the large organs

[*] The pedals went down two octaves lower.

organs which I expected to see hereafter in Holland and Germany. The French organ-builders are much esteemed by the Germans themselves, for the simplicity of their movements, and the mechanism of the whole; but the variety which these stops afford is not proportioned to their number; we have frequently more solo stops in an English organ of half the size and price; however, Silbermann, the most celebrated organ-builder in Germany, who died not long ago, resided and worked many years in France, from whence he brought several improvements in the construction of organs, that he afterwards applied to those which he erected in his own country.

The voices in the church at Aloft are accompanied, besides the organ, with six or eight instruments every day, and on festivals by a great band; and the musical taste here, as far as I could judge by the performance of the organist and his son, is more Italianised, or at least Germanised, than in any of the churches of France.

BRUSSELS.

The theatre in this city is one of the most elegant I ever saw, on this side the Alps; it is constructed in the Italian manner; there are five rows of boxes, nineteen in each, which, severally, contain six persons in front. There are seats in the pit, five or six of which are railed off for the accommodation of strangers, who, otherwise, would be in danger of obtaining no good places, as the boxes are usually let to subscribers, and there are no galleries.

The orchestra of this theatre is celebrated all over Europe. It is, at present, under the direction of M. Fitzthumb, a very active and intelligent *maestro di capella*, who beats the time, and is indefatigable

fatigable in preferving good difcipline, and M. Vanmaldere, brother of the compofer of that name, whofe fymphonies are well known in England. M. Vanmaldere, fince the death of his brother, plays the principal violin, though the violoncello is his inftrument.

The piece that was performed to night, July 15th, 1772, was *Zemire* and *Azor*, a fpecies of *Comedie larmoyante*, written by M. Marmontel, and fet by M. Gretry; it is interfperfed with airs and dances. As the drama is French, the performance was after the French manner, and confequently fubject to much criticifm. As an opera, it might be divided into the following conftituent parts: *Poetry, Mufic, Singing, Acting, Dancing, Orcheftra, Theatre, Scenes,* and *Decorations*; and, it is but juftice to fay, that, of thefe, a great majority were good; however, let us difcriminate, for to judge a performance of this kind in the grofs, by faying that the whole was very good, bad, or indifferent,

different, would be unjuſt as well as taſteleſs. The ſubject of the *Poetry* is a fairy tale, which is wrought into an intereſting drama with great art, taſte, and genius; and is wholly worthy of its elegant and refined author. If it were, however, permitted to doubt of the perfection of particular parts of the production of ſo able a writer, it might perhaps be ſaid that ſome of the ſongs contain too many words and ideas for a ſimplicity of air, if compared with thoſe of Metaſtaſio, the true model of perfection in this particular; it alſo ſtruck me, as an impropriety, for the daughter of a great Perſian merchant to ſing two or three duets with her father's ſlave. Several parts of the piece too are made to be ſung, which ſhould, in this kind of drama, be declaimed, particularly in the laſt ſcene of the firſt act.

The *Muſic* of this opera, is, in general, admirable; the overture is ſpirited and full of effects; the ritornels, and other pieces

pieces of symphony, are full of new ideas and imagery; now and then, indeed, with the assistance of the singing, the airs bordered too much on the old style of French music. However, the melody is more frequently Italian than French, and the accompaniments are both rich, ingenious, and transparent, if I may be allowed the expression, by which I mean, that the air is not suffocated, but can be distinctly heard through them.

The *Singing* may be pronounced to have been but indifferent: there were three male and three female voices employed, no one of which was good, and out of the whole number, not one had either a shake, or the faculty of singing in tune; at best, they would have been called in England, only pretty ballad-singers. One of the females, Defoix, who performed the part of *Zemire*, had something like execution, and a compass of voice; yet, with these advantages, her performance was unsteady and unfinished.

The

The *Acting* was, in general, charming, full of propriety and grace.

The *Dancing* was below criticism.

The *Orchestra* was admirably conducted, and the band, taken as a whole, was numerous, powerful, correct, and attentive: but, in its separate parts, the horns were bad, and out of tune; which was too discoverable in the capital song of the piece, when they were placed at different distances from the audience, to imitate an echo, occasioned by the rocks, in a wild and desert scene. The first clarinet, which served as a hautboy, was, though a very good one, too sharp the whole night; and the bases, which were all placed at one end of the orchestra, played so violently, that it was more like the rumbling reverberation of thunder, than musical sound. The four double bases, employed in this band were too powerful for the rest of the instruments. There was no harpsichord, which, as there were but two pieces of recitative, and those accompanied, was perhaps not wanted.

The

The *Theatre* has been described above, and I have only to add, that it is lofty and noble; but though constructed much after the Italian model, it is far inferior in size to most of the theatres of Italy. The *Scenes* and *Decorations* were rich, ingenious, and elegant.

July 16. This evening, after a pretty comedy, by Boiffy, called *le Mercure Galant*, the *Huron* was very well acted, though poorly sung. However, the little Defoix, who did the part of Zemire last night, was much more at her ease now, as all her songs were such as suited her powers. She is rather less French in her manner of singing than the rest; but she is ignorant of music, and a Frenchwoman, no trivial objections to her singing well.

The method of playing the march in this piece had a very fine effect, by the judicious use of the *Crescendo* and *Diminuendo*. It was begun behind the scenes, at the end of the stage, so soft as to be scarcely

scarcely heard; and after the band had gradually approached the audience, and were arrived at the greatest degree of force, they retired in the same slow manner, insensibly diminishing the sound to the last audible degree of *Piano*.

ANTWERP.

It was in this city, that I expected to meet with materials the most important to the history of counter-point, or music in different parts, as it was here, according to Lodovico Guicciardini, and, after him, several others, who took the fact upon trust, that most of the great Flemish musicians, who swarmed all over Europe in the sixteenth century, were bred. I arrived here Friday evening, July 17th: it is a city that fills the mind with more melancholy reflections concerning the vicissitudes of human affairs, and the transient state of worldly glory, than any other in modern times: the exchange, which

which served as a model to Sir Th. Gresham, when he built that of London, and which, though still intire, is as useless to the inhabitants, as the *Coloseo* at Rome: The Town-house, constructed as a tribunal, for the magistrates, at the head of two hundred thousand inhabitants, which are now reduced to less than twenty thousand: the churches, the palaces, the squares, and whole streets, which, not two hundred years ago, were scarce sufficient to contain the people for whom they were designed, and which are now almost abandoned: the spacious and commodious quays, the numerous canals, cut with such labour and expence, the noble river Schelde, wider than the Thames at Chelsea-reach, which used to be covered with ships from all quarters of the world, and on which now, scarce a fishing boat can be discovered: all contribute to point out the instability of fortune, and to remind us that, what Babylon,

Carthage, Athens, and Palmyra now are, the moſt flouriſhing cities of the preſent period, muſt, in the courſe of time, inevitably become!

The cathedral of *Notre Dame*, except the choir, was deſtroyed by fire, in the year 1533, as a great part of Rome was in 1527, which renders it difficult to find any manuſcript muſic of anterior times, in either of theſe cities.

It was rebuilt again the year following, more beautifully than ever, and is eſteemed ſuperior to all the Gothic buildings of this country, eſpecially the ſteeple, which is extremely light and elegant. The church was, however, pillaged and much defaced in 1560 by the *Iconoclaſts*, or image breakers, as the Dutch rebels, or heretics, are called; but ever ſince the year 1584, when it was taken by the duke of Parma, it has continued to be enriched with ſuperb altars and monuments, together with paintings by the firſt maſters;

ters; it is five hundred feet long, two hundred and forty wide, and three hundred and sixty high, and is supported by a hundred and twenty-five pillars; it was first built in the thirteenth century. The emperor Charles V. laid the first stone of the present choir. In 1521 the chapter of canons was instituted by Godfrey of Boulogne, king of Jerusalem; their number at first was only twelve, but it is now twenty-four; there are eight minor canons, with a number of chaplains, &c. which altogether form an assembly in the choir, to the amount of seventy beneficed clergy. There are three organs in this church, one very large, on the right hand side, at the west end of the choir, and a small one in a a chapel on each side the broad aile.

The organist at present is M. Vanden Bosch, he is a spirited and masterly player. The chanting here, as in other churches of this country, is accompanied

by

by the double base and *serpent;* an excellent service was sung on Saturday afternoon, July, 18th, out of a printed book, which had for title, *Octo Cantica Divæ Mariæ Virginis, secundum Octo Modos, Auctore Arturo Aux-Couteaux,* Parisiis, 1641.

At the Jesuit's college, I was treated with great politeness, and assisted in my researches by the learned father Gesquiere, together with father Newton and brother Blithe, two Englishmen of that college. The former shewed me a manuscript treatise on music, which, from the kind of writing, is judged to be nine hundred years old; and a fine ancient manuscript of our famous *Magna Charta*; both of which seem to have come from England, or at least to have been in the possession of an Englishman, as there is the signature of *John Cotton* in both.

At the Dominicans church, there are two organs, which are esteemed the best in the town; the one is very large, with pedals, fifty-four stops, and three entire sets of keys, from C to c; it was built in 1654. I found the pipes of these instruments well toned, but so miserably out of tune, as to give more pain than pleasure to the hearer. One of the four monkish organists who attended me in a very obliging manner, pleaded poverty upon this occasion, and said, they could afford to have their instruments put in order but seldom, on account of the expence.

As no picture worth looking at here, is shewn to a stranger, without a *Schelling* or two, a curtain being placed before each, which *Simony* only can draw, I asked, not indeed with much expectation that it would be taken, whether I might venture to tender any thing to the venerable person abovementioned, and, upon an answer in the affirmative, I made my humble offering, which was, as elsewhere, received with great good nature and condescension.

D   Sunday,

Sunday, 19th. I this morning at seven o'clock attended the firſt maſs. There were a few violins, two baſſoons, and a double baſe placed with the voices in the organ-loft, over the weſt door of the choir; but before theſe were employed, a conſiderable part of the ſervice was chanted in *Canto Fermo*, with only a *ſerpent*, and two baſſoons in accompaniment; and, afterwards, the voices and inſtruments in the organ-loft performed the uſual ſervices in three or four parts, I mean voice parts, with inſtruments. However, the ſmall number of violins, in ſo large a building, and thoſe not of the firſt claſs, had but a mean effect.

At nine o'clock high maſs began, and continued upwards of two hours. I attended this in the choir, in different parts of the church, and in the organ-loft, to hear the muſic, and its effects, at different diſtances, and in different ſituations; but I found none which pleaſed me. The performances to which I had been accuſtomed in Italy,

Italy, and, indeed, in the choirs of London, were greatly superior to this. Whatever merit the Antwerpians may have had, in surpassing the rest of Europe, in arts, sciences, and commerce, two hundred years ago, they certainly have no claim to pre-eminence now; no part of their ancient grandeur is visible at present, but in the church: there, indeed, riches, splendor, and expence are still as conspicuous as ever, though but a small part of this expence is appropriated to music. The church revenues are applied to the maintenance of the several orders of the clergy; to that almost innumerable quantity of wax-lights, for ever burning, and to those sumptuous vestments, and tawdry ornaments, with which they dazzle the eyes of the multitude; but as for music, they have been so long accustomed to inaccurate and slovenly execution, that they seem to have lost all distinction. I did not meet with one single organ in the whole town that was in tune; and as to the few violins employed in the church, they are mere fcrapers. The baffoons, players in common ufe, are worfe than thofe nocturnal performers, who, in London, walk the ftreets during winter, under the denomination of *Waits*; and for the *ferpent*, it is not only over-blown, and deteftably out of tune, but exactly refembling in tone, that of a great hungry, or rather angry, Effex calf.

Before the fervice in the choir began with the organ, the canons and boys marched in proceffion round the church, with each a lighted taper in his hand, chanting the pfalms, in four parts, with the two baffoons, and *ferpent* above-mentioned; but all was fo diffonant and falfe, that notwithftanding the building is immenfe, and very favourable to found, which it not only augments, but meliorates, and in fpite of two or three fweet and powerful voices among the boys, the whole was intolerable to me, who remained in the choir, from whence I expected to
enjoy

enjoy the natural *Diminuendo* and *Crescendo*, of a large body of found retreating and advancing by such slow degrees.

While that part of the service, which succeeded this procession, was performing, I went up into the organ-loft, and was very politely treated by the organist, M. Vanden Bosch, who is a man of considerable merit in his profession; his style of playing is modern, and he is very dexterous in the use of the pedals *. This instrument of *Notre Dame*, contains upwards of fifty stops, and has a full compass; it has been built about a hun-

* When I use the epithets *old* and *new*, I mean neither as a term of reproach, or stigma, but merely to tell the reader in what style a piece is conceived, or written; and he will suppose it to be better or worse, as he pleases. In Italy, though an old opera is as useless and neglected as an almanac of last year, yet an old composition, if it be the best of the time in which it was made, I shall always speak of with respect; but as to *Performance*, an old fashioned manner, whether the consequence of ignorance or obstinacy, will not, perhaps, be treated with equal indulgence.

dred and fifty years, and would be well toned, if it were in tune.

After church, I went home with M. Vanden Bofch, who was fo obliging as to fhew me his inftruments and books. Several compofitions for the harpfichord of this mafter, have been engraved at Paris; he has a very good tafte, and great fire, both in writing and playing.

In my refearches after old mufic in this place, I was directed to Monf. ―― the finging mafter of St. James's church, a Frenchman. Indeed, I was obligingly conducted to his houfe, by one of the canons, and upon my acquainting him with my errand, and afking him the queftion I had before put to all the muficians, and men of learning that I had met with in France and Italy, without obtaining much fatisfaction, " *where, and* " *when did counter-point, or modern har-* " *mony begin?*" the Abbé's anfwer was quick, and firm. " O Sir, counter-point " was certainly invented in France."

" But,

" But, said I, L. Guicciardini, and the
" Abbé du Bos, give it to the Flamands."
This made no kind of impression on my
valiant Abbé, who still referred me to
France for materials to ascertain the fact.
" But, Sir, said I, What part of France
" must I go to; I have already made all
" possible enquiry in that kingdom, and
" had the honour of being every day
" permitted to search in the *Bibliotheque*
" *du Roi*, at Paris, for more than a
" month together, in hopes of finding
" something to my purpose, but in vain;
" and as you were in possession of the
" old manuscript music belonging to your
" church, I was inclined to believe it
" possible, that you could have pointed
" out to me some compositions, which,
" if not the *first* that were made in
" counter-point, would at least, be more
" ancient than those which I had found
" elsewhere." " *Mais, Monsf. soyez sure que
" tout cela étoit inventé en France.*" This
was all the answer I could get, and upon

my preffing him to tell me where I might be furnifhed with proofs of this affertion, *Ah, ma foi, je n'en fais rien,* was his whole reply. I had been for fome time preparing for a retreat from this ignorant coxcomb, by fhuffling towards the door, but after this I flew to it as faft as I could, firft making my bow, and affuring him, fincerely, that I was extremely forry to have given him fo much trouble.

In the afternoon I attended vefpers at the church of our Lady; there were rather more inftrumental performers than in the morning, but all of the fame kind, as to excellence. The refponfes in the cathedral here, and indeed in all the other churches of Flanders, where inftruments are employed, are made in four vocal parts; but the inftrumental performers flourifh and fcrape with as much violence as at our theatre, when Richard the Third enters, or the king of Denmark caroufes; which, in my opinion, betrays a barbarous tafte, and total want of decency. The only

only entertainment I received from the whole mufic, was that which the long voluntary afforded me, which M. Vanden Bofch was fo obliging as to play, at my requeft, after church, in which he difplayed great abilities.

After this I went to a very large building on a quay, at the fide branch of the Scheld, which is called the *Oofters Huys*, or Eafterlings houfe; it was formerly ufed as a ware-houfe by the merchants trading to Lubec, Hamburg, and the Hanfeatic towns; it is a very handfome ftructure, and has ferved, in time of war, as a barrack for two thoufand men. I fhould not have mentioned my vifiting this building, if I had not found in it a large quantity of mufical inftruments of a peculiar conftruction. There are between thirty and forty of the commonflute kind, but differing in fome particulars; having, as they increafe in length, keys and crooks, like hautbois and baffoons; they were made at Hamburg,

and

and are all of one sort of wood, and by one maker; CASPER RAVCHS SCRATENBACH, was engraved on a brass ring, or plate, which encircled most of these instruments; the large ones have brass plates pierced, and some with human figures well engraved on them; these last are longer than a bassoon would be, if unfolded*; The inhabitants say, that it is more than a hundred years since these instruments were used, and that there is no musician, at present, in the town who knows how to play on any one of them, as they are quite different from those now in common use. In times when commerce flourished in this city, these instruments used to be played on every day, by a band of musicians who attended the merchants, trading to the Hans towns, in procession to the exchange; they now hang on pegs in a closet, or rather press, with folding doors,

* The long trumpet, played lately in London, seems only to have been an ordinary trumpet straitened.

made

made on purpose for their reception; though in the great hall there still lies on the floor, by them, a large single case, made of a heavy and solid dark kind of wood, so contrived, as to be capable of receiving them all; but which, when filled with these instruments, requires eight men to lift it from the ground; it was of so uncommon a shape, that I was unable to divine its use, till I was told it.

At six o'clock this evening a splendid procession passed through the streets, in honour of some legendary saint; consisting of a prodigious number of priests, who sung psalms in *canto fermo,* and sometimes in counter-point, all the way to the church, with wax tapers in their hands, accompanied by French horns, and *serpents*; a large silver crucifix, and a *Madonna* and child, as big as the life, of the same metal, decorated this solemnity.

The Spaniards have left this good people a large portion of pride and superstition; the former is shewn by the dress and inactivity of the nobles, and the latter by the bigotry and lively faith of the rest; there are more crucifixes and virgins, in and out of the churches here, than I ever met with in any other Roman catholic town in Europe.

The procession above mentioned seemed to have been as much the occasion of riot and debauchery, among the common people, as the *beer* and *liberty* with which an English mob is usually intoxicated on a rejoicing night in London; there were bonfires all over the town, and the huzzas, rockets, squibs, and crackers, were so frequent, and so loud, all night, in the *Place de Mer*, where I lodged, that it was impossible to sleep; and at two o'clock in the morning the mob was so vociferous and violent, that I thought all the inhabitants of the town had fallen together by the ears; and yet, on other nights, no one of the citizens is allowed to walk in the streets later than half an hour after ten, without a particular permission from the governor.

This morning, at seven o'clock, I attended the singing master of St. Andrew's church, M. Blaviere, a Liegeois, in whose possession I expected, in old manuscript music, to meet with examples of the early progress made in counter-point by the Flamands. I found him to be very rational, intelligent, and well read in musical authors, of which he shewed me several; but there was only one among them which I had not seen before, and that was a treatise in Italian, by Francesco Penna, Bolognese, printed at Antwerp, in 1688. He likewise shewed me several of his own compositions, for the church, which convinced me that he had studied hard, and was an able contra-puntist.

I spent the rest of the morning in the Jesuit's library, with father Newton, and father Gesquiere, who were indefatigable in ferreting out books and manuscripts

scripts that were likely to furnish any thing necessary to my work; the latter is one of several Jesuits who have been long employed in writing the lives of the saints, as they are placed in the Romish calender of each month of the year; it is the intention of those authors to purge the lives they are writing, of all the fables which have crept into the legendary accounts of saints: upwards of fifty volumes in folio are already printed, and more than twenty are still behind. The work is written in Latin, and has for title, *Acta Sanctorum a Johanne Bollando, S. I. Collegi felicita cæpta a Godfredo Henschenio, et Daniele Pabebrochio, aucta, digesta, & illustrata.* Antwerpiæ, 1768. I consulted several articles in the volumes already printed, for information concerning the first establishment of chanting in the church, its reformation by pope Gregory the Great, with other particulars relative to the history of church music; in some of these I obtained more satisfaction than other books, which I had frequently

quently read on the subject, had afforded me.

The famous harpsichord makers, of the name of Ruckers, whose works have been so much, and so long admired all over Europe, lived in this city: there were three, the first, and the father of the other two, was *John Ruckers*, who flourished at the beginning of the last century. His instruments were the most esteemed, and are remarkable for the sweetness and fullness of their tone. On the left hand of the sound-hole, in the bellies of these instruments, may be seen a large H, the initial of Hans, which, in the Flemish Language, means John. *André*, the eldest of John's sons, distinguished his work, by an A, n the sound-hole. His large harpsichords are less esteemed than those made by any one of that name; but his small work, such as spinets, and virginals, are excellent. *Jean*, the youngest son's harpsichords, though not so good as those of the father, are very much esteemed

teemed for the delicacy of their tone; his inſtruments may be known by the letter I, in the ſound hole. The harpſichord-maker of the greateſt eminence, after them, was J. Dan. Dulcken; he was a Heſſian. At preſent there is a good workman at Antwerp, of the name of Bull, who was Dulcken's apprentice, and who ſells his double harpſichords for a hundred ducats each, with only plain painted caſes, and without ſwell or pedals; the work too of Vanden Elſche, a Flamand, has a conſiderable ſhare of merit; but, in general, the preſent harpſichords, made here after the Rucker model, are thin, feeble in tone, and much inferior to thoſe of our beſt makers in England.

I cannot quit this city, without mentioning a particular mark of attention, with which I was honoured by father Geſquiere, the night before my departure. In the morning he had communicated to me a very ancient Latin manuſcript upon muſic; but though the writing proved it to be of great antiquity, we could not exactly fix the date of it; there were likewise some letters of the alphabet, used as musical characters in it, which were not easy to determine, as it was difficult to distinguish an A from an O, or a D, on account of the great resemblance of these letters in the manuscript; but by a note written in elegant Latin, with which he favoured me at night, I found that these difficulties had occupied his mind the whole day; indeed he seemed entirely to have spent it in trying to clear up the first, and offered his future service in removing the last.

BRUSSELS.

At my return hither, from Antwerp, I employed myself in visiting churches, as I had before only been at the theatre. On the day after my second arrival, there was a mass, in music, performed in the little, but neat and elegant, church of Mary Magdalen; here are a few good pictures,

pictures, with some excellent sculpture in wood; and the portraits of the Apostles are boldly represented in relief, or medallions, at the sides of this church. The band of musicians, on occasion of the festival, to day, was but small; however, the organ was played in a masterly manner, by M. Straze, who is esteemed the best performer upon keyed instruments in Brussels; and several symphonies were well executed by the whole band, during the course of the service. Some pieces of Italian church music were sung, not indeed so well as they would have been in their own country; but the voices here were far from contemptible. Two boys, in particular, sung a duet very agreeably; but there is generally a want of steadiness in such young musicians, which makes it to be wished that females were permitted in the church, to take the *soprano* part, which is generally the principal, as the voices of females are more permanent than those of boys, who are almost

always

always deprived of theirs before they know well how to use them.

From this little church I went to the cathedral of St. Gudula, where high mass was likewise performing, by a considerable band of voices and instruments. This is the largest church in Brussels, the pillars are too massive, but, upon the whole, it is a neat and noble building; all the best pictures, and some very fine tapestry, were exposed on occasion of this festival, which, on common days, cannot be seen; it is rather loaded with tawdry ornaments, and too much begilded, as is the case of most of the Brabant churches, which the inhabitants think they can never make fine enough.

There is some admirable old painting upon glass, in this church, with figures, as large as the life, well preserved; these paintings were by Rogiers, cotemporary with Holbens; they were presents from several princes of those times, particularly John, king of Portugal, Mary, queen of Hungary, Francis the first, of France, Ferdinand, brother to the emperor Charles the fifth, and by Charles the fifth himself.

The *maestro di capella*, who directed the band here, was M. Van Helmont. The music had no great effect, as the instruments were too few for so large a building; but there was a performer with a tenor voice, who sung several Latin *motets*, composed by Italian masters, reasonably well; his voice was good, and he sung in tune. The singing in the churches here is less French than at the theatre, as the words are always Latin, and less likely to corrupt the voice, and the taste of the performer, than French words and French music.

In the evening I heard two musical pieces, at the theatre, in the Flemish language; both were translated from the French; the one was *le Tonnelier*, originally set to music by M. Duni, and the other, *Toinon et Toinetti*, set by M. Gossec;

the natives seemed highly diverted by these performances, which, as dramas, have great merit, in the original. The music of messrs. Duni and Goffec, was preserved entire, except in a very few places, which had been altered for the accommodation of the Flemish poetry, by M. Fitzthumb.

In hearing this performance, I could not help reflecting how easy it was to adapt Italian music to any language, however rough and barbarous; that of the pieces in question, is, for the most part, certainly composed of passages taken from Italian songs and symphonies, though grafted on French words; all the present composers of French comic operas imitate the Italian style, and many of them pillage the *buffe* operas of Italy, without the least scruple of conscience, though they afterwards set their names to the plunder, and pass it on the world as their own property. I wish this may not, sometimes, be the case in England; but, however that may be, it is certainly an irrefragable proof of the superiority of that melody which is become the common musical language of all Europe: not like the French tongue, by conquest, or policy, but received every where, by the common consent of all who have ears susceptible of pleasure from sound, and who give way to their own feelings.

Indeed, the French seem now the only people in Europe, except the Italians, who, in their dramas, have a music of their own. The serious opera of Paris is still in the trammels of Lulli and Rameau, though every one who goes thither, either yawns or laughs, except when roused, or amused, by the dances and decorations. As a *Spectacle*, this opera is often superior to any other in Europe; but, as *Music*, it is below our country psalmody, being without time, tune, or expression, that any but French ears can bear: indeed the point is so much given up, by the French themselves, that nothing but a kind of national pride, in a few individuals, keeps the dispute alive;

the

the rest frankly confess themselves ashamed of their own music; and those who defend it, must soon give way to the stream of fashion, which runs with too much rapidity and violence to be long stemmed.

July 23d. Prince Charles, and the principal personages of his court, were at the play to night. The *Gageur*, a French comedy, written by Sedaine, was admirably played, in which Mad. Verteil, an excellent actress, did the principal part; after which, I heard, for the first time, *Les deux Miliciens*, a comic opera, set by Gretry; the music was worthy of that fertile and ingenious composer*. The instrumental parts were extremely well

---

* This author, in his scores, is however sometimes negligent of the most common rules of counter-point, which may proceed from writing with too much rapidity; as it is hardly to be conceived that a man of such acknowledged genius should have studied seven or eight years, in a Conservatorio at Naples, without acquiring a competent knowledge of musical grammar, and the mechanism of his art.

executed; great effects were produced in the ritornels, and the poetry was much heightened by the rich and varied colouring of the orchestra. In a musical drama, it frequently happens that a numerous and well disciplined band, has the power of imagery, of awakening ideas, and describing the passions, more than a single voice, or even a chorus of many voices can attempt, with propriety; indeed the little opera of to-night nearly approached perfection in all its parts, as it was well written, well set, well spoken, well acted; and, with respect to the instrumental parts, was well played: how sorry I am that truth will not allow me to add, that it was *well sung!*

During my residence at Bruffels, I had the pleasure, of being made acquainted with M. Girard, secretary to the literary society in this place. He is now employed, in arranging and cataloguing the books and manuscripts of the Burgundy library, which have been more than two centuries

ries here; but they have so long remained in obscurity and disorder, that it is not yet known, what they all contain. It was by the zeal and good offices of prince Starhemberg, that these books had a new room built for their reception, and that they will soon form a public library.

The manuscripts are the best, and most beautiful, in point of illuminations, which I ever saw: most of them were brought to Brussels from Burgundy, and are very ancient. It it even wonderful, to what a degree of perfection miniature painting has been carried in some of them, particularly in one transcribed and illuminated at Florence, in 1485: it was a present from Matthias Corvinus, king of Hungary, to the duke of Burgundy.

The arms of Burgundy are pasted in all these ancient manuscripts, which are divided into there classes; theology, history and arts, poetry and romances. In the two first, I found several curious and interesting particulars, relative to my work.

In

In 1745, at which time the French were in poffeffion of Bruffels; the commiffaries, and even fome of the officers, took away books and manufcripts from the Burgundy library, notwithftanding the cartel; fome of them were, indeed, returned, after the peace, upon being claimed, particularly, fuch as had been carried to the king's library, at Paris; but many others of great value, are now in the Sorbonne, and in other private hands, and cannot be recovered.

I was very politely treated by M. Girard, who attended me at the library at fix o'clock every morning, and afforded me all poffible affiftance, even to the helping me to make extracts. He likewife favoured me with a vifit at my lodgings, and gave me a letter to the elector Palatine's librarian at Manheim, and all from a very flight acquaintance, brought about by means of a note, written by M. Needham, celebrated for his
micro-

microscopic discoveries, and his difference with M. de Voltaire.

At Brussels I heard a young lady play extremely well on the harp with pedals, some pretty pieces composed by Godecharle, a German, who likewise plays a good violin, and accompanied the young lady in these pieces; she is his scholar: the harp is very much played on by the ladies here, and at Paris. It is a sweet and becoming instrument, and, by means of the pedals for the half notes, is less cumbrous and unwieldy than our double Welsh harp. The compass is from double Bb to f in *altissimo*; it is capable of great expression, and of executing whatever can be played on the harpsichord; there are but thirty-three strings upon it, which, except the last, are the mere natural notes of the diatonic scale; the rest are made by the feet *.

* This method of producing the half-tones on the harp, by pedals, was invented at Brussels, about fifteen years ago, by M. Simon, who still resides in that city. It is an ingenious and useful
con-

In attending the high mass at the collegiate church of St. Gudula, on Sunday 26, I again heard the performance of a considerable band of voices and instruments; and I was glad to find among the former two or three women, who, though they did not sing well, yet their being employed, proved that female voices might have admission in the church, without giving offence or scandal to piety, or even bigotry. If the practice were to become general, of admitting women to sing the *soprano* part in the cathedrals, it would, in Italy, be a service to mankind, and in the rest of Europe render church-music infinitely more pleasing and perfect; in general, the want of treble voices, at least of such as have had sufficent time to be polished, and rendered steady, destroys the effect of the best compositions, in which, if

contrivance, in more respects than one: for, by reducing the number of strings, the tone of those that remain, is improved; as it is well known, that the less an instrument is loaded, the more freely it vibrates.

the principal melody be feeble, nothing but the fubordinate parts, meant only as attendants, and to enrich the harmony of the *whole*, can be heard.

LOVAIN.

This is the laft confiderable city of the Netherlands, in the emprefs queen's dominions, eaft of Bruffels; it has a univerfity, in which the youth of the ten catholic provinces are educated, as Leyden has for the other feven. It was founded by John the Fourth, duke of Brabant, in 1425; at prefent the number of ftudents is faid to amount to upwards of two thoufand. I remained but a fhort time in this place, as I was informed, that the library, which is faid to be very rich in manufcripts, was in fuch great diforder, that it would be difficult to find any one to my purpofe, without a longer refidence than the work which I had allotted myfelf in Germany would allow. I therefore contented myfelf, with gaining what information I could, relative to the state of modern music in that city; and I found, that M. Kennis is the most remarkable performer on the violin, in point of execution, not only of Lovain, but of all this part of the world. The solos he writes for his own instrument and hand, are so difficult, that no one hereabouts attempts them but himself, except M. Scheppen, the *Carilloneur*, who lately, piqued by the high reputation of M. Kennis, laid a wager, that he would execute upon the bells one of his most difficult solos, to the satisfaction of judges, appointed to determine the matter in dispute; and he gained not only his wager, but great honour by his success, in so difficult an enterprize. This circumstance is mentioned in order to convey some idea to my English readers, of the high cultivation of this species of music in the Netherlands. For there, the inhabitants of every city think it an indispensible point of honour, to tell

every

every stranger, that their *carillons* are better than all others. At Lovain, M. Vandengheim, the organist, has the care of the chimes, and M. Scheppen plays them, by his appointment.

LIEGE.

This city has lately produced several good musicians, which I had met with in the Low Countries; but I found in it little worthy of remark. The organ in the cathedral is small, and divided into two parts, placed on each side the choir. There is a theatre here for Flemish plays, and sometimes for comic operas; but it was not open while I continued at Liege. The organist of the cathedral is likewise *Carilloneur,* as is often the case in the Netherlands; but here the passion for chimes begins to diminish.

MAESTRICK.

Here I visited the collegiate church, belonging to the catholics, and found in it a very large organ, but it was out of tune; and the organist, M. Houghbrach, who is likewise *Carilloneur*, is no conjurer. There was a Hessian regiment, in the Dutch service, quartered in this city, which had an excellent band of music, consisting of hautbois, clarinets, *cymbala*, or *bassins*, great drum, side-drums, and triangles; and at the time of beating *la retraite*, I heard them play a considerable time on the *Place d'Armes*; at the inn too, where I lodged, I was entertained on the *dulcimer*, by a strolling boy, who seemed to have a musical genius, far superiour to his instrument and situation.

AIX LA CHAPELLE.

It was here that I first remarked the High Dutch, or German language, to be spoken by the common people, and 𝕲𝖔𝖙𝖍𝖎𝖈 letters to be used by printers.

Where the English acquired their pronunciation of *th*, I know not: it was natural to suppose that they had it from their

their Saxon anceſtors, and to expect to find it in Germany; but it is as much a *Shibboleth* to the inhabitants of that country, as to thoſe of all the reſt of Europe. In words where this combination of letters is uſed in orthography, it has no other effect in pronunciation, than if the words were written without the H. Werth, which ſignifies worth, in Engliſh, is pronounced *wert*; Thron, a throne, *Trone*; and Theologus, a theogiſt, *Teologus*. It is no leſs difficult to trace our peculiar ſound of the vowel I; and as to thoſe guttural graces of pronunciation in the *ch* and *g*, of the German language, which are ſo difficult to deſcribe, and to learn, they are ſtill retained here, and regarded as indubitable proofs of the high antiquity of the Teutonic dialect, though nearly loſt in her daughter the Engliſh.

As to muſic, my expectations from this city were by no means anſwered. I could find neither books nor muſicians worthy

worthy of much attention. M. Kuckelkorn, organist of the famous cathedral where Charlemagne, and several succeeding emperors, were crowned, accompanies the church service very judiciously, but has no hand for extemporary playing. M. Wenzlaer has, however, a great hand on the violin; but he is a wild, half mad character, and not a deep theorist.

The passion for *carillons*, and chimes, seems here at an end; however, in the streets, through which a procession had lately passed, there were hung, to festoons and garlands, a great number of oblong pieces of glass, cut and tuned in such a manner, as to form little peals of four and five bells, all in the same key, which were played on by the wind. In walking under them, I was some time unable to discover from whence the sounds I heard proceeded; they are hung so near each other, as to be put in contact by the most gentle breeze, which may truly be called the *Carilloneur*.

JULIERS.

In my way through this town, to Cologn, I was entertained at the post-house, while I changed horses, by two vagabonds, who, in opposite corners of the room, imitated, in dialogue, all kinds of wind instruments, with a card and the corner of their hats, so exactly, that if I had been out of their sight, I should not have been able to distinguish the copy from the original; particularly in the clarinet, French horn, and bassoon, which were excellent. After this they *took off* the bellowing noise of the Romish priests, in chanting, so well, that I was quite frightened; for, being in a catholic town, where the inhabitants are very zealous for the honour of their religion, I thought it might be imagined that this *ludere sacrâ*, was at the instigation of the English heretic.

COLOGN.

I have but little to say concerning the music of this place. There was no public exhibition during the time I remained in it; however, I visited the great church, or cathedral, which is built upon the model of the *Duomo* at Milan, but of common stone; whereas, that at Milan is of white marble. There is a similarity likewise in the fate of these two famous churches, as both have remained many ages unfinished. The plan of that at Cologn is not above half completed; perhaps it is owing to this, that the choir appears much more lofty than that at Milan. What was intended as the approach to the choir is very low, and arched over with bricks.

In a very small chapel, behind the altar, I was shewn the famous shrine, in which, it is said, are the entire skulls of the three kings, who came with offerings to our Saviour, immediately after his birth; it has been said that every great town has a

lion

lion to shew to strangers, and this *shrine* is the *lion* of Cologn: it is immensely rich in gold, sculpture, jewels, antique gems, intaglios, and cameos.

The organ in this cathedral is of the most noble and beautiful form I ever saw; its front is flat, and spreads from pillar to pillar, over the nave of the church; it has three columns, or rather compartments, of great pipes on each side; in the middle are three ranks of small pipes over each other, which form three complete and elegant buffets, and which, separately, would be regarded as complete fronts to small organs; the choir organ is placed below all these, at the back of the player.

Mr. Westmann is at present the organist. I only heard him accompany the choir in the first service, which was begun when I entered the church; the second was chanted in *canto fermo*, without instruments. It is very difficult in Roman catholic countries, to hit upon a proper time for trying an organ, or hearing an organist, as the several services continue from five o'clock in the morning, till twelve at noon; and, afterwards, from two, till near night; and even during the small recess from duty, the servants of the church are either at dinner, or from home upon their own concerns; so that, except during the time of divine service, I could hardly ever get an opportunity of hearing an organist or an organ.

In the church of St. Cecilia, I heard a nun play the organ, to the coarse singing of her sisters; her interludes would have been thought too light for the church in England: I soon discovered that they were not extemporary; however, they were pleasing, and well executed.

B O N N.

The elector of Cologn was not here, so that I heard no music in this city; however, during winter, his highness has a comic opera, at his own expence, performed in his palace. Most of his musicians ficians were now at Spa, they are all Italians, and the *maeſtro di capella* is Signor Lucchese, who is a very pleaſing compoſer; when I was in Italy, I heard Manſoli ſing a *Motet* of his compoſition, in a church near Florence, which was charming.

I had the honour of being very well received by Mr. Creſſener, his majeſty's miniſter plenipotentiary at this court, who, not only countenanced me during my ſhort ſtay at Bonn, but kindly furniſhed me with recommendatory letters to ſeveral perſons of diſtinction in my route.

COBLENTZ.

Italian operas are frequently performed at this court. The elector has a good band, in which M. Ponta, the celebrated French horn from Bohemia, whoſe taſte and aſtoniſhing execution were lately ſo much applauded in London, is a performer.

The princess Cunegonde, sister to the elector of Treves, and youngest daughter of Augustus, king of Poland, is a very great harpsichord player. There is likewise a most extraordinary performer on the double base at this court, who plays solos on it, even worth hearing. The *maestro di capella* of this court is Signor Sales, of Brescia.

FRANKFORT upon the Main.

In travelling on the banks of the Rhine, from Cologne to Coblentz, I must own, that I was astonished and disappointed, at finding no proofs of that passion for music, which the Germans are said to possess, particularly along the Rhine; but even at Coblentz, though it was Sunday when I arrived there, and the streets and neighbourhood were crowded with people walking about for their recreation, I heard not a single voice or instrument, as is usual in most other Roman catholic countries; I had

had therefore a mind to try another part of Germany, and crossing the Rhine, and the terrible mountains of Wetteravia, arrived at Frankfort on the Main, much more fatigued than I was formerly after passing mount Cenis. Here indeed, I found a little of that disposition for music, which I expected; and though I met no great performer vocal or instrumental, music, such as it was, might be heard in all parts of the town.

The great church of St. Bartholomew, famous for being the place where the emperors are crowned, was not furnished with singers of great talents, but yet there were a number of girls, who, though the service was that of the Roman catholics, were many of them Lutherans or Calvinists, that chanted with the priests and canons, without the organ *.

* Though the Catholics have the great church here, yet the Lutherans are in possession of the steeple, upon which they constantly keep a guard. A precaution, which, in peaceable times, *is said to be used in order to give the alarm, in case of fire;* but, in war, they make no scruple to confess, that

In the streets, at noon, there was likewise a number of young students singing Hymns in three or four parts, attended by a chaplain; these are poor scholars designed for the church, who in this manner excite the benevolence of passengers, that contribute towards their cloathing.

At the inn, called the Roman Emperor, where I lodged, after dinner there was a band of street musicians, who played several symphonies reasonably well, in four parts. All this happened on a day which was not a festival, and therefore it is natural to believe, that the practice is common.

The organist of the cathedral is one of the vicars, and much in years; the instrument is not ill toned, but, like most of the others which I had heard in my route, miserably out of tune, and the touch so heavy, that the keys, like those of a *carillon*, severally required the weight of the whole hand, to put them down.

it is to watch the motions of the catholics, from whom they are in fear of a massacre.

The labels of some stops in this instrument excited my curiosity; such as the *Posaun, Solicional, Cymbel, Suavial, Violon,* &c. in the great organ, and in the choir organ, the *Grosgedukt, Kleingedukt, Violdgamba,* &c. but, from being out of order, they were totally unfit to be played, as solo stops. I could just discover that the *suavial* was meant for that sweet stop in Mr. Snetzler's organs, which he calls the *Dulcian*; and the *Violon*, for the *Violona,* or double base; it is a half stop, which goes no higher than the middle C.

There *has* been a contrivance in this organ for transposing half a note, a whole note, or a flat third, higher; but it is now useless: the instrument was built many years ago by Meyer, and repaired, with an addition of new stops, six or seven years ago, by Grosswald, of Hanau. But an organ whose foundation is not good, is generally rendered worse by attempts at mending it; and I remember Mr. Snetzler honestly telling some church-wardens, who asked him, what he he thought an old organ, which they wanted to have repaired, was worth, and what would be the expence of mending it: he appraised it at one hundred pounds, and said, if they would lay out another hundred upon it, perhaps it would then be worth fifty.

The first instrument I heard during my stay at Frankfort, was the organ, at the Dominicans church; it was better toned, and more in tune than the rest, but it was not so good as many I have heard in England, nor was the *Vox humana* remarkably sweet, or like the human voice, though it is much admired here.

This organ has an arch cut through it, to let the light into the church from the west window; it is in a handsome case, the ornaments over the arch are in a good taste, and the side columns are well disposed. The keys are on the right hand *side* of the instrument, over which there is a small front; the compass is

from

from C to C, the pedals have an Octave below double C.

The principal muficians in this city are, at prefent, M. Sarrazin on the violin, M. Pfeil, a gentleman performer on the harpfichord, and M. Haueifen, organift to the Calvinifts of Frankfort, at their church at Berkenheim, a little diftance from the city, in which they are not allowed a place of public worfhip.

DARMSTADT.

In paffing through this place to Manheim, I was fo fortunate, as to alight from my chaife juft as the landgrave's guards were coming on the parade. I never heard military mufic that pleafed me more; the inftruments were, four hautboys, four clarinets, fix trumpets, three on each fide the hautboys and clarinets, and thefe were flanked by two baffoons on each fide; fo that the line confifted of eighteen muficians; in the rear of thefe were cornets and clarions.

The whole had an admirable effect, it was extremely animating, and though trumpets and clarions are usually too thrill and piercing, when heard in a small place, yet here, the parade or square where they mounted guard is so spacious that the sound has room to expand in all directions, which prevents the ear from being hurt by too violent a shock.

Before I proceed further in my musical narrative, I must make two or three memorandums concerning the villainous and rascally behaviour of postmasters and postilions, in this part of the world; the effects of which it is impossible to escape. In going over the mountains of Wetteravia, under the pretence of bad roads, *three* horses were tied to the hurdle, called a post-chaise, and after I had once submitted to this imposition, I never was allowed to stir with less. At Frankfort I tried hard, but in vain, though the inn-keeper and his guests, who were natives, all assured me, that they never had more than two horses,
when

when they travelled *extra post*; yet here, though no mountains were to be crossed, the sands were made a plea, notwithstanding the roads from Frankfort to Manheim are, in every particular, the least bad of any that I had yet travelled in Germany.

The women, among the common people in the country, are miserably ugly, not, perhaps, so much in feature, as from dress, and a total neglect of complexion. They entirely hide their hair, by a kind of a skull-cap, usually made of tawdry linen or cotton; they are hardly ever seen with shoes and stockings, though the men are furnished with both, such as they are.

I could wish to speak of these people with candour and temper, in despight of the bile which every stranger, travelling among them must feel at work within him; but, as I neither mean to abuse or flatter them, I must say, that the numberless beggars, clamorously importunate, though often young, fat, robust,

bust, and fit for any labour; the embarrassments of perpetual change and loss of money; the extortion, sullenness, and insolence of postmasters and postilions, are intolerably vexatious.

MANHEIM.

The first music I heard here was military. I lodged on the *Place d'Armes*, or parade; the *retraite* had only drums and fifes; and in the morning there was nothing worth listening to. If I had had an inclination to describe, in a pompous manner, the effects of wind instruments in martial music, there had been no occasion to quit London; for at St. James's, and in the Park, every morning, we have now an excellent band; and hitherto, as I had not seen more soldier-like men in any service than our own, so the music and musicians, of other places, exceeded ours in nothing but the number and variety of the instruments; our military music at present must seem to have made great and hasty strides towards perfection,

tion, to all such as, like myself, remember, for upwards of twenty years, no other composition made use of in our foot-guards, than the march in Scipio, and in our marching regiments, nothing but side-drums.

The expence and magnificence of the court of this little city are prodigious; the palace and offices extend over almost half the town; and one half of the inhabitants, who are in office, prey on the other, who seem to be in the utmost indigence.

The Jesuits house, built by the present Elector, close to the palace, has thirty windows in front, apart from the church, which is the most superb in the city; the front of the theatre, which is only a small wing of the palace, has likewise thirty windows.

The town itself is more neat, beautiful, and regular, than any which I had yet seen; its form is oval; the streets, like those of Lisle, are *tireés au cordeau*, running in strait lines from one

G   end

end to the other. There is a great number of squares; it contains about 1548 houses, and in the year 1766, its inhabitants amounted to 24190.

Thursday, August 6th. In the evening I went to the public theatre in this town, where Zemire and Azor, translated into German, and accommodated to the pretty music of Mr. Gretry, was performed; it was the first dramatic exhibition at which I was present in Germany.

In summer the Elector Palatine resides at Schwetzingen, three leagues from Manheim; and during that time a strolling company is allowed to entertain the citizens. The performance was in a temporary booth, erected in the square of the great market-place. Yet, though nothing better than deal boards appear without, the stage was well decorated, and the scenes and dresses were not without taste or elegance.

I was curious to hear a German play, but still more curious to hear German singing:
and

and I muſt own, that I was aſtoniſhed to find, that the German language, in ſpite of all its claſhing conſonants, and gutturals, is better calculated for muſic than the French. I am ſorry to return again to the charge; but I muſt ſay, that the great number of naſal ſounds and mute ſyllables in the French language, ſeem to corrupt and vitiate the voice, in its paſſage, more than the defect of any other language, of which I have the leaſt knowledge.

The girl who played the part of Zemire had not a great voice, but her manner of ſinging was natural and pleaſing. She had a good ſhake, and never forced her voice, or ſung out of tune; there were two of the men who had reaſonable good voices, and whoſe *portamento* and expreſſion would not have offended ſuch as had been long converſant with the beſt ſinging of Italy.

Upon the whole, I was more pleaſed with this ſinging, than with any which I had heard since my arrival on the continent: indeed the Germans are now so forward in music, and have so many excellent composers of their own country, that it is matter of astonishment to me, that they do not get original dramas for music written in their own language, and set by the natives: or, if they must have translations, why they do not get those translations new set *.

The orchestra here was far inferior to that at Brussels, in number and discipline; for all the great performers of this place were now with the elector at Schwetzingen, so that the singers had no support but their own merit.

August 7. I spent in the public library, which is a very fine room, with

* When I advanced farther into Germany, I found that M. Hiller, of Leipsick, had furnished his countrymen with a great number of comic operas, in which the music was so natural and pleasing, that the favourite airs, like those of Dr. Arne in England, were sung by all degrees of people; and the more easy ones had the honour of being sung in the streets.

fine books, but none very ancient, and few manuscripts, these being all taken away by the Bavarians in the war of 1622, and given to the Pope: they are well known in the Vatican library, by the name of the Heidelberg or Palatine Collection. The present library is said to consist of forty thousand volumes; but though the pompous account in the *Etrennes Palatine*, speaks of manuscripts, and says, that they are kept in a chamber apart, M. Lamey, the librarian, to whom I was favoured with a letter by M. Girard, of Brussels, confessed to me, that the collection had been too short a time in forming to be yet very rich in manuscripts, and that it contained but few of any consequence.

SCHWETZINGEN.

A list only of the performers in the service of his electoral highness, would convey a very favourable idea of the excellence of his band; it consists of near a hundred hands and voices. I shall only mention here, however, some of the principal musicians employed in this orchestra, whose names are already known in England. M. Holtzbauer, is one of the chapel masters. M. Christian Canabich, and Charles Toeschi, are the principal violins; the former leads in the Italian operas, and the latter in the French and German. These three masters are authors of several excellent *symphonies*, some of which have been printed in England. M. J. Baptist Wendling, is the principal flute here, and among the violins are John Toeschi, Frenzel, Fr. and Charles Wendling, and Kramer. This last is reckoned one of the best solo players in Europe; however, I shall say but little about him here, as he is now in England, and my countrymen have an opportunity of judging of his talents for themselves. There are twenty-three vocal performers in this band, several of which deserve to be distinguished, particularly

cularly Mademoiselle Wendling, Mademoiselle Danzy, and Madame Kramer. Signori Roncaglio, Pesarini, and Saporosi.

Many of the performers on the court list, are either superannuated or supernumeraries; but of the former, after having served the elector for a number of years, if by sickness or accident they happen to lose their voice or talents, they have a handsome pension, which they enjoy as long as they live at Manheim; and even if they chuse to retire into their own country, or elsewhere, they are still allowed half their pension.

I wanted very much to come to my principal point of hearing the best of these performers; but nothing can be done precipitately in Germany. *Festine lente* seems here a favourite motto. It was necessary to visit, the first day, and to be visited the second; and, on the third, there was some chance, but no certainty, of obtaining the favour I required.

It has frequently been said, that bluntness, and a thorough contempt of every person and thing, which is not entirely English, mark my honest countryman, *John Bull*, in every part of the world. I am unwilling to indulge national reflections; however, now and then a *single* character certainly appears, which calls to mind, all that has been said of a *whole* people. The French Abbé I met with at Antwerp, was what many would have called a *true Frenchman*; and I met with several afterwards, who would be called *true Germans*, for slow apprehension and inactivity. If, in the morning, I had explained as clearly as I could, the object of my journey, and shewn the general plan of my future work, to a man of letters, a librarian, or a musician, it was common for that individual, in the evening, to say " the History of Music, I think " you are going to write—hum—ay, " the History of Music—hum—well, " and what do you wish I should do for you?"

" you ?" Here I was forced, in a painful *Da Capo*, to tell my story over again, and to beg his assistance.

Travelling is not very common in this country; and people here, like the English, are shy of strangers, and wishing to shake them off. In France, and Italy, the inhabitants are used to do the honours, and do them well. As to my particular enquiries here, which, in fact, concerned their honour more than my own, I gained but little assistance; it was difficult to discover who *could* afford me any, and much more to find those that *would*. I sometimes wished to employ the town cryer, at my first entrance into a German city, to tell the musical inhabitants who I was, and what I wanted; for it frequently happened, where his majesty had no minister, that I was on the point of quitting a place before this was known.

Sunday, 9th August. This evening I was at the representation of *La Contadina na in Corte*, a comic opera, at the Elector's theatre, adjoining to his palace. The music was composed by Signor Sacchini, and was full of that clearness, grace, and elegant simplicity, which characterise the productions of that author. The vocal parts were performed by Signor Giorgietto, an Italian *soprano*, whose voice was but feeble, nor were his abilities very considerable in other particulars. Signora Francesca Danzi, a German girl, whose voice and execution are brilliant; she has likewise a pretty figure, a good shake, and an expression as truly Italian, as if she had lived her whole life in Italy; in short, she is now a very engaging and agreeable performer, and promises still greater things in future, being young, and having never appeared on any stage till this summer. Signor Zonca, an Italian tenor, who was in England some years ago; his highest praise is, that he does not offend; and Signora Allegrante, a young Italian, under the care of M. Holtz-

Holtzbaur, sings in a pretty unaffected manner; and though her voice will not allow her to aspire at the first part in an opera, she seems likely to fill the second in a very engaging manner. There were two dances between the acts, one of which, representing a German fair, was the most entertaining I ever saw; one of the principal dancers here is the daughter of the late celebrated Stamitz, from whose fire and genius the present style of *Sinfonies,* so full of great effects, of light and shade, may in a considerable degree be derived.

The Elector, Electress, and princess royal of Saxony, were present at this performance. The theatre, though small, is convenient; the decorations and dresses ingenious and elegant, and there was a greater number of attendants and figurers than ever I saw in the great opera, either of Paris or London: in the dance, representing a German fair, there were upwards of a hundred persons on the stage at one time; but this opera is very inconfiderable, compared with that at Manheim, in the winter, which is performed in one of the largeft and moft fplendid theatres of Europe, capable of containing five thoufand perfons; this opera begins the fourth of November, and continues generally, twice a week, till Shrove-Tuefday.

I was informed that the mere illuminations of the Manheim theatre, with wax lights, coft the elector upwards of forty pounds, at each reprefentation; and that the whole expence of bringing a new opera on this ftage, amounted to near four thoufand pounds. The great theatre, the enfuing winter, was to be opened with an opera compofed by Mr. J. Bach, who was daily expected here from London, when I was at Manheim.

I cannot quit this article, without doing juftice to the orcheftra of his electoral highnefs, fo defervedly celebrated throughout Europe. I found it to be indeed

indeed all that its fame had made me expect: power will naturally arise from a great number of hands; but the judicious use of this power, on all occasions, must be the consequence of good discipline; indeed there are more solo players, and good composers in this, than perhaps in any other orchestra in Europe; it is an army of generals, equally fit to plan a battle, as to fight it.

But it has not been merely at the Elector's great opera that instrumental music has been so much cultivated and refined, but at his *concerts*, where this extraordinary band has " ample room and verge enough," to display all its powers, and to produce great effects without the impropriety of destroying the greater and more delicate beauties, peculiar to vocal music; it was here that Stamitz first surpassed the bounds of common opera overtures, which had hitherto only served in the theatre as a kind of court cryer, with an " O Yes !" in order to awaken attention, and bespeak
silence,

silence, at the entrance of the fingers. Since the discovery which the genius of Stamitz first made, every effect has been tried which such an aggregate of sound can produce; it was here that the *Crescendo* and *Diminuendo* had birth; and the *Piano*, which was before chiefly used as an echo, with which it was generally synonimous, as well as the *Forte*, were found to be musical *colours* which had their *shades,* as much as red or blue in painting.

I found, however, an imperfection in this band, common to all others, that I have ever yet heard, but which I was in hopes would be removed by men so attentive and so able; the defect, I mean, is the want of truth in the wind instruments. I know it is natural to those instruments to be out of tune, but some of that art and diligence which these great performers have manifested in vanquishing difficulties of other kinds, would surely be well employed in correcting

this

this leaven, which so much sours and corrupts all harmony. This was too plainly the case to-night, with the bassoons and hautbois, which were rather too sharp, at the beginning, and continued growing sharper to the end of the opera.

My ears were unable to discover any other imperfection in the orchestra, throughout the whole performance; and this imperfection is so common to orchestras, in general, that the censure will not be very severe upon this, or afford much matter for triumph to the performers of any other orchestra in Europe.

The Elector, who is himself a very good performer on the German flute, and who can, occasionally, play his part upon the violoncello, has a concert in his palace every evening, when there is no public exhibition at his theatre; but when that happens, not only his own subjects, but all foreigners have admission gratis.

The going out from the opera at Schwetzingen, during summer, into the electoral gardens, which, in the French style, are extremely beautiful, affords one of the gayest and most splendid sights imaginable; the country here is flat, and naked, and therefore would be less favourable to the free and open manner of laying out grounds in English horticulture, than to that which has been adopted. The orangery is larger than that at Versailles, and perhaps than any other in Europe.

His electoral highness's suite at Schwetzingen, during summer, amounts to fifteen hundred persons, who are all lodged in this little village, at his expence.

To any one walking through the streets of Schwetzingen, during summer, this place must seem to be inhabited only by a colony of musicians, who are constantly exercising their profession: at one house a fine player on the violin is heard;

at

at another, a German flute; here an excellent hautbois; there a baffoon, a clarinet, a violoncello, or a concert of feveral inftruments together. Mufic feems to be the chief and moſt conſtant of his Electoral highneſs's amuſements; and the operas, and concerts, to which all his ſubjects have admiſſion, forms the judgment, and eſtabliſhes a taſte for muſic, throughout the electorate.

LUDWIGSBURG.

It is no uncommon thing, in Germany, for a ſovereign prince, upon a difference with his ſubjects, to abandon the ancient capital of his dominions, and to erect another at a ſmall diſtance from it, which, in proceſs of time, not only ruins the trade, but greatly diminiſhes the number of its inhabitants, by attracting them to his new reſidence: among the princes who come under this predicament, are the elector of Cologn, removed to *Bonn*; the Elector Palatine,

removed

removed from Heidelberg, to *Manheim*; and the duke of Würtemberg, from Stutgard to *Ludwigsburg*.

The ground upon which this town is built, is irregular and wild, yet it contains many fine streets, walks, and houses. The country about it is not pleasant, but very fertile, especially in vines, producing a great quantity of what is called Neckar wine.

Though Stutgard is nominally the capital of the dutchy of Würtemburg, it has not, for ten years past, been the residence of its sovereign; and though the operas, and musical establishments of this prince, used, during the seven years direction of Jomelli, to be the best and most splendid in Germany, they are now but the shadow of what they were: indeed the expence so far exceeded the abilities of his subjects to support, that the Germans say the duke of Würtemberg's passion for music was carried to such excess as to ruin both his country and people, and to
oblige

oblige his subjects to remonstrate against his prodigality at the diet of the empire.

At present his highness seems œconomising, having reformed his operas and orchestra, and reduced a great number of old performers to *half* pay : but, as most musicians have too great souls to live upon their *whole* pay, be it what it will, this reduction of their pensions is regarded, by the principal of those in the service of this court, as a dismission; so that those who have vendible talents, demand permission to retire, as fast as opportunities offer, for engaging themselves elsewhere.

The German courts are so much dazzled by their own splendor, 'as to be wholly blind to what is doing at the distance only of a day's journey among their neighbours; hence, I never found, in any of them, exactly what report had made me expect. Upon quitting Schwetzingen, I deviated somewhat from the direct road

road to Vienna, in order to viſit Ludwigſburg, at which place I was told I ſhould
not only find the duke of Würtemburg,
but likewiſe hear fine operas, concerts,
and great performers; but, alas! after
being roaſted alive, and jumbled to death,
in a *wagon*, which the Germans call a
poſt-chaiſe, for fourteen or fifteen hours,
while I travelled ſeventy-five miles;
when I came to Ludwigſburg, I found the
information which I had received ſo far
from exact, that the duke of Wurtemburg
was at Gravenic, thirteen leagues off, and
ſcarce a muſician of eminence left in the
town. However I obtained an exact ſtate
of the preſent muſical eſtabliſhment of
the Wirtemburg court, ſtage, and church.

The firſt *maeſtro di capella*, is Signor
Boroni. The *ſoprano* voices are, Signora
Bonani, and Seeman, Signor Muzio, and
Signor Gurreieri, *Caſtrati*; *Contralti*,
Rubinelli, and Paganelli. Among the
tenors, the duke had laſt winter a great
loſs by the death of the admirable Cav.
Ettori,

Ettori, who was reckoned, by the Italians, the beſt ſinger of his kind on the ſerious opera ſtage: there are eighteen violins, with Signor Lolli at their head, among the reſt, are Curz, and Baglioni; this laſt is a very good player, and of the famous Bolognia family; there are ſix tenors, three violoncellos, and four double baſes; the principal organiſts are, Frederick Seeman, and Schubart; four hautbois, Alrich, Hitſch, Bleſner, and Commeret; flutes, Steinhardt, a very good one, and Auguſtinelli; three horns; two baſſoons, Schwartz, an admirable one, and Bart.

For the *Opera Buffa*, Signore Bonani, Seeman, Liberati, Frigeri: Signori Meſſieri, Roſſi, Coſimi, Liberati, and Righetti.

Dancers, male and female, thirty-two; principals, Balliby, Franchi, and Riva. Upwards of ninety perſons are on the penſion liſt for theſe operas; but many are kept in it long after they become unfit for ſervice; and it is likewiſe ſwelled

with

with the names of perfons of no great importance, fuch as inftrument carriers, copyifts, and bellows-blowers.

This prince had two new ferious operas laſt winter, the one compoſed by Jomelli, and the other by Sacchini. The theatre is immenſe, and is open at the back of the ſtage, where there is an amphitheatre, in the open air, which is ſometimes filled with people, to produce effects in perſpective; it is built, as are all the theatres which I had yet feen in Germany, upon the Italian model.

The duke of Würtemburg, who is ſo expenſive in the muſic of his court and theatre, has no other inſtruments among his troops, that I heard, than trumpets, drums, and fifes. The moſt ſhining parts of a German court, are uſually its *military*, its *muſic*, and its *hunt*. In this laſt article the expence is generally enormous; immenſe forefts and parks, ſet apart for a prince's amuſement, at the expence of agriculture, commerce, and, indeed,

indeed, the neceſſaries of life, keep vaſt tracts of land uncultivated, and his ſubjects in beggary.

The ſoldiery of this prince's preſent capital are ſo numerous, conſiſting never of leſs than ſix thouſand in time of peace, that nothing like a gentleman can be ſeen in the ſtreets, except officers. The ſoldiers ſeem diſciplined into clock-work. I never ſaw ſuch mechanical exactneſs in animated beings. One would ſuppoſe that the author of " *Man a Machine*," had taken his idea from theſe men: their appearance, however, is very formidable; black whiſkers, white peruques, with curls at the ſides, ſix deep; blue coats, patched and mended with great ingenuity and diligence. There are two ſpacious courts, one before, and one within the palace, full of military.

This prince, who is himſelf a good player on the harpſichord, had, at one time, in his ſervice, three of the greateſt performers on the violin in Europe, Ferari,

rari, Nardini, and Lolli; on the hautbois, the two Plas, a famous baſſoon, Schwartz, who is ſtill here; and Walther, on the French horn; with Jomelli to compoſe; and the beſt ſerious and comic ſingers of Italy. At preſent, indeed, his liſt of muſicians is not ſo ſplendid; however, his œconomy is, I believe, more in appearance than reality; for at *Solitude*, a favourite ſummer palace, he has, at an enormous expence, eſtabliſhed a ſchool of arts, or Conſervatorio, for the education of two hundred poor and deſerted children of talents; of theſe a great number are taught muſic, and from theſe he has already drawn ſeveral excellent vocal and inſtrumental performers, for his theatre: ſome are taught the learned languages, and cultivate poetry; others, acting and dancing. Among the ſingers, there are at preſent fifteen Caſtrati, the court having in its ſervice two Bologna ſurgeons, expert in this vocal manufacture. At Ludwigſburg there is likewiſe a Conſervatorio

torio for a hundred girls, who are educated in the same manner, and for the same purposes; the building constructed at *Solitude*, for the reception of the boys, has a front of six or seven hundred feet.

It is the favourite amusement of the duke of Wurtemburg to visit this school; to see the children dine, and take their lessons. His passion for music and shews, seems as strong as that of the emperor Nero was formerly. It is, perhaps, upon such occasions as these, that music becomes a vice, and hurtful to society; for that nation, of which half the subjects are stage-players, fidlers, and soldiers, and the other half beggars, seems to be but ill governed. Here nothing is talked of but the adventures of actors, dancers, and musicians.—In this article I have perhaps gone beyond my *last*.

I can proceed no further in my account of this place, without making my acknowledgements to M. Schubart, organist of the Lutheran church: he was the first real great harpsichord player that

that I had hitherto met with in Germany, as well as the first who seemed to think the object of my journey was, in some measure, a national concern. I travelled not as a musician usually travels, to *get* money, but to *spend* it, in search of musical merit and talents, wherever I could find them, in order to display them to my countrymen. M. Schubart seemed sensible of this, and took all possible pains to please my ears, as well as to satisfy my mind. He is formed on the Bach school; but is an enthusiast, and original in genius. Many of his pieces are printed in Holland; they are full of taste and fire. He played on the Clavichord, with great delicacy and expression; his finger is brilliant, and fancy rich; he is in possession of a perfect double shake, which is obtained but by few harpsichord players.

He was some time organist of Ulm, where he had a fine instrument to play on; but here he has a most wretched one. His

His merit is but little known where he is at prefent planted: the common people think him mad, and the reft overlook him.

We communicated our thoughts to each other in a fingular manner: I was not, as yet, able to keep pace with his ideas, or my own impatience to know them, in German; and he could neither fpeak French nor Italian, but could converfe in Latin very fluently, having been originally intended for the church; and it amazed me to find, with what quicknefs and facility he expreffed whatever he would, in Latin; it was literally, a living language in his hands. I gave him the plan of my Hiftory of Mufic to read, in German; and, to convince me, that he clearly underftood my meaning, he tranflated it, that is, read it aloud to me in Latin, at firft fight. My pronunciation of Latin, if I had been accuftomed to fpeak it, would not have been intelligible to him; but as he underftood Italian,

lian, though he could not speak it, our converfation was carried on in two different languages, Latin and Italian; fo that the queftions that were afked in one of thefe tongues, were anfwered in the other. In this manner we kept on a loquacious intercourfe the whole day, during which, he not only played a great deal on the Harpfichord, Organ, Piano forte, and Clavichord; but fhewed me the theatre, and all the curiofities of Ludwigfburg, as well as wrote down for me, a character of all the muficians of that court and city.

And, in the evening, he had the attention to collect together, at his houfe, three or four boors, in order to let me hear them play and fing *national mufic*, concerning which, I had expreffed great curiofity.

The public library here has not been formed many years, and is as yet not very rich in manufcripts, or ancient books; the hiftory profeffor and librarian

M. Urot, a native of France, was very polite, and took great pains to satisfy my curiosity, particularly, in shewing me a very extraordinary astronomical machine or orrery, which M. Hahn, minister at Onstmettingen, in the bailiwic of Balingen, invented and executed, in the space of eighteen months, and which his serene highness the duke of Würtemburg has purchased for the public library.

It is composed of three parts, that are put in motion by the weights of a common clock, which is wound up every eight days, and whose *pendulum* vibrates seconds.

In the middle part are three dials, placed perpendicularly.

The upper one simply marks hours, and minutes.

The next, in which are fixed the signs of the zodiac, indicates the hours of the day, the days of the week, and the days of the month, without its ever being

being neceffary to regulate the index, for the unequal number of days in different months.

And the laft dial, upon the great circle, on which are diftinguifhed, the centuries of 8000 years, has two principal indices, one of which points out the prefent century, and the other, the prefent year.

Of the two collateral parts of this machine, that on the right hand reprefents the Copernican fyftem; and that on the left, the apparent courfe of the heavenly bodies. Thefe parts are put in motion, by the principal fpring of the clock in the middle, and correfpond fo perfectly, that no variation in their movements, or in the different afpects of the heavenly bodies has ever been difcovered; and both have been found conftantly conformable to the calculations of the moft exact ephemeris.

This whole machine is fo conftructed, that without any rifk of putting it out of order,

order, or spoiling it, the reciprocal positions of the planets and constellations, such as they *will* be in any future minute, or such as they *have* been, in any one that is past, may be seen; so that this machine takes in all time; the past, present, and future; and is, not only an orrery for these times, but a perpetual, accurate, and minute history of the heavens for all ages.

The description of this piece of mechanism, by professor Vischer, librarian of the public library, taken from the writings, and experiments, of the inventor, M. Hahn, will give the public a more perfect idea than I am able to do of this amazing machine, which in Germany, is greatly admired by the learned in astronomy and mechanics *.

---

* This description was published at Stutgard, in the German language, in 1770. It contains twenty-eight pages, in quarto, and has for title, Beschreibung einer Astronomischen Maschine, welche sich in der öffentlichen Herzoglichen Bibliothek zu Ludwigsburg befindet.

U L M.

U L M.

I cannot say much for the beauty of this old city; however, its cathedral is one of the largest, highest, and best preserved Gothic buildings I have seen. Its organ is so much celebrated by travellers, for size and goodness, that it excited in me a great desire to see and examine it; but I was somewhat disappointed in finding it neither so ancient, so large, or so full of stops as I expected. It was built but thirty-eight years ago; the builder, M. Schmahl, is still living, and he and his son, who were cleaning it, were so obliging as to furnish me with an account of its contents.

The Gallery, and ornaments of this instrument, are a hundred and fifty feet high; it contains forty-five stops, three sets of keys, and pedals; the largest pipes are sixteen feet long, and the sum total of pipes amounts to 3442.

The German flute in this organ seems the best of the solo stops, the reed-work is pretty good, but there is no swell.

The prefent organift is not reckoned a great player; and I could not find, upon enquiry, that this city is now in poffeſſion of one capital performer upon any inſtrument.

Ulm uſed to be famous for its company of Minneſängers, or *Laudiſti*, like that at Florence; but it now no longer ſubſiſts.

My neareſt and cheapeſt way, from hence to Vienna, would have been down the Danube, which is a paſſage of 600 miles by water; but I could not reſiſt the deſire of ſeeing Augſburg and Munich, or indeed reconcile to myſelf the neglect of thoſe two cities, which had ſo fair a claim to my notice among the principal places in Germany. I therefore determined to croſs, not deſcend, the Danube, in order to viſit

AUGSBURG.

I arrived here on Saturday morning, the 15th July, about ſeven o'clock, after

I tra-

travelling all night, and luckily went to the cathedral between eight and nine, where I heard part of a German sermon, and a mass, in music, performed by two choirs*; being a festival, the church was very much crowded. It is a small and ordinary building, but richly and tawdrily ornamented; there are, however, two large and elegant organs, one on each side the west end of the choir. One of these was well played, but in a way more masterly than pleasing; the rage for crude, equivocal, and affected modulation, which now prevails generally all over Germany, renders voluntary playing so unnatural, that it is a perpetual disappointment and torture to the ear; which is never to expect any thing that comes, or to have one discord resolved, but by another. A little of this high

* This church is in the possession of the Catholics, one half of the inhabitants of this free city are Protestants, who have not only churches allowed them, but also an equal share in the government.

sauce,

sauce, discreetly used, produces great and surprising effects; but, for ever to be seeking for far-fetched and extraneous harmony, is giving a man that is hungry, nothing but *Chian* to eat, instead of plain and wholesome food.

The music of the mass was in a good style; there was an agreeable mixture of ancient and modern, and some of the vocal parts were pleasingly performed; particularly by two boys and a tenor, whose voices were good, and who had several solo verses and duets given them; and from what I heard this day, I was confirmed in my opinion, that, except the Italian, the German manner of singing is less vicious and vulgar, than that of any other people in Europe. There was a *solo concerto* introduced on the violin, which, though difficult, was neatly executed. The rest of the violins were weak and ordinary.

There was a rude and barbarous flourish of drums and trumpets at the elevation of the Hoft, which was what I had never heard before, except at Antwerp.

Having been told, that M. Seyfurth, the cantor, a celebrated finger, and fcholar of M. C. P. E. Bach, to whom I had letters, was out of town, I ftayed but a fhort time at Augfburg; for, to fay the truth, I was fomewhat tired of going to imperial cities after mufic; as I feldom found any thing but the organ and organift worth attending to, and not always them; for they, like thofe in our country towns, are fometimes good, and fometimes bad. Thefe cities are not rich, and therefore have not the folly to fupport their theatres at a great expence. The fine arts are children of affluence and luxury: in defpotic governments they render power lefs infupportable, and diverfion from thought is perhaps as neceffary as from action. Whoever therefore feeks mufic in Germany, fhould do it at the feveral courts, not in the free imperial cities, which are generally inhabited

habited by poor induſtrious people, whoſe genius is chilled and repreſſed by penury; who can beſtow nothing on vain pomp or luxury; but think themſelves happy, in the poſſeſſion of neceſſaries. The reſidence of a ſovereign prince, on the contrary, beſides the muſicians in ordinary of the court, church, and ſtage, ſwarms with penſioners and expectants, who have however few opportunities of being heard.

Augſburg is a very large and fine old city; ſome of the houſes are whimſically pretty, from the manner in which they are plaiſtered and ornamented, and a few of the ſtreets are rather wide; but the generality of the houſes have their gable ends in front, as in the Netherlands. The town-houſe, with ſome of the ſpires are well worth ſeeing; and at going out on the Munich ſide, there is a very fine building, juſt conſtructed, for the uſe of a cotton manufactory, which is of an immenſe ſize, and in a pleaſing ſtyle of architecture.

The head dress of the women here is very singular; they wear a kind of gold skull-cap; some a broad border of gold lace, and the rest filled up by work in different colours, but mostly all gold embroidery; and here, as well as throughout Bavaria, the Roman catholic women constantly walk the streets with a rosary in their hands, which is a fashion and ornament here as much as an implement of devotion.

I was much distressed during my short stay in this city, by the following adven‑venture. I had sent my servant, and, at present, my interpreter, Pierre, a Lie‑geois, that I had brought with me from Antwerp, to enquire out, while the mass was performing, the habitation of M. Seyfurth, to whom I had been recommended by a friend at Hamburg. I had desired him to return to the church when he had executed his commission, in order to conduct me back to my inn. I waited patiently till ten o'clock, when all the music was over, but no Pierre! I walked about the church,

church, till I was tired, and aſhamed to ſtay any longer, but no Pierre! I walked round the church, and up and down the ſtreets in ſight of it, for I durſt venture no farther, not knowing even the *name* of my inn; and I had, indeed, very little language in which to explain my ſituation to theſe cold, and, in appearance, ſurly people. What could I do, but return to the church and walk about again? this I did till paſt two o'clock, when I feared being ſuſpected as a ſtranger, of a deſign to rob the church of ſome of its treaſures; but no Pierre! at length I was compelled to take courage, and try to make my circumſtances, known: I peruſed every idle countenance to diſcover good nature in it. I accoſted ſeveral in vain, till an old beggar-man applied to me for relief; I gave him two or three *creuzers*, and thought that " one good turn deſerved another." I recollected the having been ſet down by the poſt-wagon, on my arrival, at a poſt-houſe: there are ſeveral in large German cities. Welches iſt der Weg nach dem Poſt=

𝔓𝔬𝔰𝔱𝔥𝔞𝔲𝔰 𝔤𝔲𝔱𝔢𝔯 𝔉𝔯𝔢𝔲𝔫𝔡? here was a gibble-gabble, which ended with, 𝔡𝔦𝔢 𝔅𝔯𝔦𝔢𝔣𝔢? meaning, was it the poſt-houſe for letters? 𝔑𝔢𝔦𝔫, ſaid I, 𝔡𝔢𝔯 𝔓𝔬𝔰𝔱𝔴𝔞𝔤𝔢𝔫 𝔫𝔞𝔠𝔥 𝔘𝔩𝔪 𝔤𝔢𝔥𝔢𝔱 𝔥𝔦𝔢𝔯𝔞𝔟 — 𝔍𝔞, 𝔧𝔞, 𝔦𝔠𝔥 𝔳𝔢𝔯𝔰𝔱𝔢𝔥𝔢 𝔰𝔦𝔢. At length we found this houſe; but then I knew not either what to ſay or do. I blundered out as well as I could, that I wanted the 𝔥𝔞𝔲𝔰 where my baggage had been carried in the morning. But could not recollect the word 𝔚𝔦𝔯𝔱𝔥𝔰, an inn; it turned out to be the Lamb, 𝔡𝔞𝔰 𝔏𝔞𝔪𝔪, and when I found it, my joy was as great as that of a good chriſtian pilgrim would have been in a Pagan country, at the ſight of an *Agnus Dei*. Where ſhould the faithful Pierre, my honeſt Liegeois, have been all this while, but on his bed, comfortably and faſt aſleep? and I did not diſcover, till two months after, that he had never ſought Mr. Seyfurth, to whom I had ſent him, but had deemed it eaſier to find a bed, and to make me believe he was out of town, than to wear out his ſhoes in ſtrolling about a ſtrange place,

place, after a perſon, with whom he had no buſineſs which concerned himſelf. But, in order to make the diſappointment ſomewhat more palatable to me, he ſaid, that the gentleman was only gone to Munich, for a few days, and that I ſhould certainly find him there.

MUNICH.

I was amply rewarded for the trouble I took in viſiting this city, as I not only found in it materials of great importance to my Hiſtory, but a great number of modern muſicians of the firſt claſs, whoſe performance and converſation were delightful and inſtructive. I had likewiſe the honour of being well received, and even aſſiſted in my enquiries, by perſons of all ranks; a happineſs for which I am greatly indebted to the friendly and active zeal of our miniſter at this court, M. de Viſme, whoſe learning, knowledge, and experience, joined to a ſteady benevolence and hoſpitality, all conſpired to

render

render my residence at Munich both profitable and pleasant.

I arrived here on Sunday morning, the 16th August. The first thing I did was to wait on M. de Visme, with my credentials, that is, my recommendatory letters; which having read, and received a more particular information of the object of my journey from myself, he sent immediately to Signor Don Panzachi, an excellent tenor singer, of the Elector of Bavaria's serious opera, who having resided several years in this city, was well qualified to inform me of such persons as were best worth hearing and conversing with; and he gave every day, during my residence here, proofs of his zeal and intelligence. I was likewise indebted to this gentleman for a very particular account of the music of Spain, where he had resided nine years; and he was not only so kind as to lend me many curious Spanish books, on the subject of music, but to sing to me several *Tonadillas* and *Seguidillas*, which

he

he is said, by persons who have been in Spain, to do as well, that is, as truly, as is possible for one not a native of that country.

I was so fortunate as to find here, Signor Guadagni, and Signora Mingotti, who both rendered me very singular services, in the most polite and agreeable manner; and I was the more flattered and pleased by their attention, as they are performers of such high rank, who have seen so much service, and by whose great abilities, in their profession, I have been so frequently delighted in England. They both profess the highest respect, gratitude, and reverence for individuals in England, but make great complaints against the public, with what reason I shall not pretend to determine, as it is not my intention to fight the battles o'er again, of two such able champions: I own myself so partial to talents, wherever I find them, that when they are attacked, I constantly incline to their side.

Gua-

Guadagni complains of illiberal treatment from the public, who, when he sung in the opera of Orfeo, merely to oblige them, and Sir W. W. without fee or reward, hissed him for going off the stage, when he was encored, with no other design than *to return in character*.

Signora Mingotti says too, that she was frequently hissed in England, for having the tooth-ach, a cold, or a fever, to which the good people of England will readily allow every human being is liable, except an actor or a singer. I know that the public are infidels in these matters, and with reason, as their hearts are hardened by repeated imposition; but, however, notwithstanding the many *pseudo* colds and fevers among theatrical performers, it is just possible for these people to have *real* disorders, otherwise they would bid fair for immortality.

Signor Guadagni came to Munich from Verona, with the Electress dowager of Saxony,

Saxony, fister to this Elector, and daughter of the emperor Charles the seventh. This princess is celebrated all over Europe for her talents, and the progress she has made in the arts, of which she is a constant protectress.

Her highness is a poetess, a paintress, and so able a musician, that she plays, sings, and composes, in a manner which *Dilettanti* seldom arrive at. She has, among other things, written in Italian, two operas, which she has herself set to music, *Talestri*, and *il Trionfo della Fedeltà*; both are printed in Score, at Leipsic, and are much admired all over Germany, where they have frequently been performed. This is bringing about a reconciliation between music and poetry, which have so long been at variance, and separated. Among the ancients, the poet and musician were constantly united in the same person; but modern times have few examples of such a junction, except in this princess, and in M. Rousseau, who

was

was not only author of the poetry, but of the music of his little drama, the *Devin du Village*.

Signora Mingotti has not, as I could find, any pension from this court; but she has friends, to whom she is attached, and says that she can live much cheaper here than in England, otherwise she should have spent her small income, and the remainder of her days, there.

The first singer in the serious opera here, is Signor Rauzzini, a young Roman performer, of singular merit, who has been six years in the service of this court; but is engaged to sing in an opera composed by young Mozart, at the next carnival at Milan; he is not only a charming singer, a pleasing figure, and a good actor; but a more excellent contrapuntist, and performer on the harpsichord, than a singer is usually allowed to be, as all kind of application to the harpsichord, or composition, is supposed, by the Italians, to be prejudicial to the voice. Signor Rauzzini

ni has set two or three comic operas here, which have been very much approved; and he shewed and sung to me several airs of a serious cast, that were well written, and in an exquisite taste.

The day after my arrival, I had the pleasure of dining with Guadagni, Rauzzini, and Ravanni, an Italian countertenor, in the service of this court, and after dinner of hearing them sing trios most divinely.

At night I went with them to the comic opera, at the little theatre; at which were the Elector, the Electress, the Electress dowager of Saxony, the Margrave of Baden, and the Duchess of Bavaria; the piece was called *l'Amore senza Malizia*, and was set by Signor Ottane, of Bologna, a scholar of Padre Martini, mentioned in my Italian musical journey. Signora Lodi, who performed the principal woman's part, pleased me much, by the clearness and brilliancy of her voice, as well as by her elegant manner of sing-

ing

ing and acting; if there is any defect in her voice, it is that sometimes it meets with a little obstruction in the throat; and one would wish that she had, as to person, a little less *embonpoint*. There was a tenor in this opera, a German, M. Adamont, whose voice and manner of singing were very pleasing; and a Baritono, Signor Guglielmini, a man whose action and humour make some amends for a total want of voice. After the opera, I supped with the same company which I had dined with, and was again delighted with trios, sung in such a way, as one never can hope to hear in public, and the chances are many against it in private.

The library of the Elector is more rich in old musical authors, and in old compositions, than any one that I have yet seen in Europe. M. de Visme, the day after my arrival, not only sent his secretary with me to the librarian, in the morning, but did me the honour of going to the
library

library with me himself after dinner.

The books I wanted were not claffed under one head, in the general catalogue, but mixt with mathematics and other arts; it was neceffary, therefore, before I began to feek, and examine thefe books, to draw them out of the mifcellaneous catalogue: the reader will form fome judgment of the number of mufical authors, when he is informed that the lift of their works only, when extracted from the reft, filled near twenty large folio fheets of paper; and thefe are chiefly confined to the fixteenth century. There were few books of any kind printed in the fifteenth, and fince the fixteenth this library has received but a fmall augmentation; in the chapel, however, there is an immenfe quantity of manufcript mufic, from the earlieft time of counterpoint to the prefent.

NYMPHENBERG.

During summer the court usually resides here; it is a magnificent *Chateau*, belonging to the Elector, three miles from Munich, where the principal musicians attend, and where his serene highness has a concert every evening.

On my arrival at Munich I had the pleasure of meeting with M. Naumann, the celebrated *maestro di capella* of the Elector of Saxony, who was brought up in Italy, and who was now on his way thither, to compose an opera for Venice, and another for Naples. He did me the favour to call on me, and to carry me, on Wednesday morning, to Nymphenberg, where I was engaged to dine with Signor Guadagni. During our ride I obtained from M. Naumann an account of the present state of music in Saxony, from which court he was just come. At Nymphenberg he attended the rehearsals of the

Electress

Electress dowager of Saxony's opera of *Taleſtri*, which was on the point of being performed at court, and in which Signor Guadagni was to ſing. Here I found M. Kröner, the Elector's firſt violin, Rauzzini, and Panzachi, who, as well as M. Naumann and myſelf, dined with Guadagni.

The gardens of this *Chateau* are reckoned the fineſt in Germany, and are really as beautiful as they can be made, with innumerable fountains, canals, *jets d'eau*, caſcades, alleys, boſquets, ſtrait rows of trees, and woods, where, " Grove nods at grove," in the true French ſtyle.

There is a beautiful porcelain manufacture at Nymphenberg, which the Bavarians ſay rivals that of Dreſden.

Upon my arrival here, I was informed by Signor Guadagni that he had mentioned me, and the buſineſs I was upon, to the Electreſs dowager of Saxony, and to the Elector, and had arranged every thing for my being preſented to that princeſs before dinner, and to his

Electoral highnefs, and the reft of the family, afterwards. Accordingly, about half an hour paft one, a page came to acquaint us that the Electrefs dowager was ready to receive us; and I was conducted through a great number of moft magnificent apartments, by Signor Guadagni, to an anti-chamber, where we waited but a very fhort time, before the Electrefs entered the *Sale d'Audience,* into which we were called, and I was very gracioufly received.

I had enquired into the *Etiquette* of this ceremonial: I was to bend the left knee upon being admitted to the honour of kiffing her hand; after this was over, her highnefs entered into converfation with me in the moft condefcending and eafy manner imaginable; fhe was pleafed to fpeak very favourably of my undertaking, and to add, " that it was not only
" doing honour to mufic, but to myfelf,
" as fhe believed I was the only modern
" hiftorian who thought it neceffary to
" travel, in order to gain information at
" the

" the fource, without contenting myfelf
" with fecond-hand, and hear-fay ac-
" counts." This ftrong compliment,
joined to her gracious and pleafing manner, took off all reftraint; fhe was juft
returned from Italy, where, fhe faid, that
" By the great hurry and fatigue of tra-
" velling and talking lo*r*d, as is cufto-
" mary at the *Converfazioni* there, fhe
" had almoft totally loft her voice, which
" had been much debilitated before, by
" having had a numerous family, and
" feveral very fevere fits of ficknefs."

Guadagni had told me that her highnefs
fpoke Englifh pretty well, and underftood
it perfectly. I ventured, after fome time,
to entreat her to converfe in the language
of my country, which, I had been informed, fhe had honoured fo far as to
ftudy. She complied with my requeft,
for a fhort time, and fpoke very intelligibly; but faid that fhe had learned it
of an Irifhman, who had given her a vicious pronunciation; which, with the

few opportunities she had for practice, made it impossible for her to speak well; but added, that she both read and wrote English constantly every day, and had great pleasure in the perusal of our authors.

I then said that I had seen a great work, both in poetry and music, by her highness, in England, meaning her opera of *Talestri*, in which she had united those arts which had been so long separated. This produced a musical conversation, which I wanted, and in the course of it she said that she could not possibly sit idle; hers was an active mind, and since she had ceased to have matters of more importance upon her hands, she had attached herself seriously to the arts. She then asked my opinion of the comparative merit of Guadagni, and several great singers of Italy: he was out of hearing. She said that Guadagni sung with much art, as well as feeling; and had the great secret of hiding defects.

She

She told me that she would try to prevail on her brother, the Elector, to play on the *viol da gamba* at night; adding, that he was a good performer, for one who was not a professor; but that we had a very great player upon that instrument in England, M. Abel, with whom I must not compare him; and added, *nous autres*, "We, "who are only *Dilettanti*, can never ex- "pect to equal masters; for, with the "same genius, we want application and "experience." After this, and some farther conversation, I had again the honour, when I retired, of kissing her hand.

After dining at Guadagni's, I was carried into the *grande sale*, where the Elector, his family, and his court dined, and were still at table. It is one of the finest rooms I ever saw. I was glad to find M. de Vifme of the company; he had been so kind as to speak of me to the Elector, and to the Electrefs dowager of Saxony, which, with what Guadagni had already done, prepared every thing for my reception;

ception; so that when his highness got up from table, his sister of Saxony treated me as one descended from the *Saxon Race*. For as soon as she had discovered that I was in the room, she mentioned me to the Elector, and brought him towards me. Here I had the honour to kiss his hand, and had a short conversation with him. I was then presented to the Electress, and the Margravine of Baden; after which I returned to the Elector and his sister, the Electress dowager, and had a long conversation with them.

The Elector is a very handsome and gracious prince, has an elegant appearance, and a figure which is neither too fat, too lean, too tall, nor too short, if I was not too much dazzled by his condescension, to see any of his defects. He told his sister that he supposed I could not speak German, and that she, therefore, who spoke English, must serve as my interpreter; but she said that as I spoke French and Italian, there was no occasion for that slow method

thod of converſation. Upon which his highneſs began to talk to me in French. He told me that mine was a very uncommon journey, and aſked, if I was ſatisfied with what materials I had hitherto found. This afforded me an opportunity of telling him, what was moſt true, that in point of books on my ſubject, and ancient muſic, I had as yet met with nothing equal to his electoral highneſs's library; and I had reaſon, from the reputation of the performers, and eminent muſicians in his ſervice, to expect great ſatisfaction, as to modern practical muſic. You will hear ſome of them to-night, ſaid the Electreſs dowager, and I hope my brother will play, who, for one that is not a profeſſor, ſometimes plays very well. The Elector, in revenge, told me, that his ſiſter was both a compoſer and a ſinger.

At this time ſome wild beaſts were brought to the palace gates, which all the company running to ſee, put an end, for the preſent, to our converſation.

This

This was wholly a mufical day; for after dinner, even in feeing the gardens and buildings, Guadagni and Rauzzini fung a great part of the time, particularly in the bath, where there was an excellent room for mufic; here they went fuccefsfully through all Tartini's experiments, in order to produce the *third found*.

At eight o'clock the Elector's band affembled, for his private concert. The Electrefs of Bavaria, and the ladies of the court were at cards, in the mufic room: the concert was begun by two fymphonies of Schwindl; M. Kröner, who played the firft violin, is rather a bold ftrong leader of an orcheftra than a folo player. The firft fong was fung by Signor Panzachi, who has a good tenor voice, a pleafing expreffion, and a facility of execution: he is likewife faid to be an admirable actor.

After this fong, the Electrefs dowager of Saxony fung a whole fcene in her own opera of *Taleftri*; M. Naumann accompanied her on the harpfichord,

chord, and the Elector played the violin with Kröner. She sung in a truly fine style; her voice is very weak, but she never forces it, or sings out of tune. She spoke the recitative, which was an accompanied one, very well, in the way of great old singers of better times. She had been a long while a scholar of Porpora, who lived many years at Dresden, in the service of her father-in-law, Augustus, king of Poland. This recitative was as well written as it was well expressed; the air was an *Andante*, rich in harmony, somewhat in the way of Handel's best opera songs in that time. Though there were but few violins, in this concert they were too powerful for the voice, which is a fault that all the singers of this place complain of.

After this the Elector played one of Schwindl's trios on his *Viol da gamba*, charmingly: except Mr. Abel, I never heard so fine a player on that instrument; his hand is firm and brilliant, his taste and expression are admirable, and his steadiness

ness in time, such as a *Dilettanti* is seldom possessed of.

Rauzzini had, in an obliging manner, thrown himself in the Elector's way, on purpose to be asked to sing, that I might hear him, which I had expressed a great desire to do, with a band: for though he is first singer, at the serious opera, in winter, yet he never performs at the summer concerts, unless particularly desired. He sung an air of his own composition admirably well; then Guadagni sung a pathetic air by Traetta, with his usual grace and expression, but with more voice than he had when in England.

The concert concluded with another piece, performed by the Elector, with still more taste and expression than the first, especially the *Adagio*. I could not praise it sufficiently; it would really have been thought excellently well performed, if, instead of a great prince, he had been a musician by profession. I could only tell his highness, that I was astonished as much as if I had never before heard how great a performer he was.

After

After this, his highness and the court supped in the same great hall and public manner, in which they had dined. I went with Guadagni, and the rest of the principal performers, to make my court during the supper. The Elector was pleased to speak a considerable time to Guadagni, concerning my future History of Music; which encouraged me to desire him to entreat his highness, to honour me with a piece of his composition, as I had been informed by all the musicians of this place, that he had composed several excellent things for the church, particularly, a *Stabat Mater:* he agreed to give me a *Litany,* provided I would not print it; but Guadagni quite teazed him to let me have the *Stabat Mater,* as he said, it was the best of all his musical productions; and even a promise of this was granted before my departure *.

* Both these compositions were transcribed for me, after I left Munich, and delivered to M. de Vismes, by whose care and kindness they have been since transmitted to me in London.

The lords in waiting offered us refreshments; and the Elector condescended to ask Guadagni, if he gave a supper to the Englishman, and his other company? meaning Panzachi, Rauzzini, and Naumann; he answered, that he should give us bread and cheese, and a glass of wine. "Here," cried the Elector, emptying two dishes of game on a plate, "send that "to your apartments." His highness was implicitly obeyed. We supped together, after which I returned to Munich, abundantly flattered and satisfied with the events of the day.

MUNICH.

The next morning was spent in the library. I had afterwards the pleasure of dining with Signora Mingotti, who invited to meet me, father Kenedy, a worthy Scotsman, of real parts and learning. After dinner, a long and spirited conversation took place; for the lady is animated, eloquent, and well informed:

she

she related her adventures in Spain, and other parts of the world, and interspersed them with reflections concerning music, upon which it is impossible to hear her speak unimproved, as she treats the subject with uncommon depth, precision, and perspicuity.

From hence I went to see the Elector's theatre, where his serious operas are performed in winter. It is not large, having but four rows of boxes, fifteen in each; but it is more richly fitted up, than any that I had ever seen.

On Thursday, father Kenedy was so obliging, as to carry me to the academy, where he shewed me all that was worthy of notice, in machines, mathematical instruments, models, minerals, fossils, and other curiosities; but what most attracted my attention, as coming nearest to my *business*, if not my *bosom*, was a collection of thirty-six thousand tracts and dissertations on different subjects, bound up in near nine hundred volumes;

they

they were bought for the prefent Elector, at Leipfic. There is an index of authors, but as yet, none completed of things; there is one begun, but it goes no farther than the letter M, and this father Kenedy, who is at the head of the academy, was fo obliging as to lend me. This inftitution has not been founded above eleven years; however, feveral volumes of its Tranfactions are already printed, and it feems, at prefent, to be carried on with fpirit.

To-day I had the honour of dining with M. de Vifme, who after dinner, was fo kind as to go with me to the Jefuit's college, where I had a very particular enquiry to make, which not only concerned the Hiftory of Mufic, but its prefent ftate. In my progrefs through Germany, I had frequently heard mufic performed in the churches, and ftreets by *poor fcholars,* as they were always called, but never could make out how, or by whom they were taught, till on

my

my arrival here. M. de Vifme, who neglected to inform me of nothing, which in the leaft related to my defign, told me, that there was a *mufic fchool* at the Jefuits college. This awakened my curiofity, and made me fufpect, that it was a kind of *Confervatorio*; and, upon a more minute enquiry, I found, that the *poor fcholars* whom I had heard fing, in fo many different parts of Germany, had been taught, in each place, where the Roman catholic religion prevailed, at the Jefuits college; and, further, I was informed, that in all the towns throughout the empire, where the Jefuits have a church or college, young perfons are taught to play upon mufical inftruments, and to fing. Many muficians have been brought up here, who afterwards have rendered themfelves eminent. This will, in fome meafure account for the great number of muficians, with which Germany abounds, as

L well

well as for the national taste and passion for music.

The music school in Munich takes in eighty children, at about eleven or twelve years old; they are taught music, reading, and writing, and are boarded, but not cloathed. A Jesuit, to whom we applied for information, promised to write down, in Latin, an account of this foundation, as far as it might be necessary to the History of Music in Germany, and send it to M. de Vismes next day; and he kept his word. The boys that are admitted here, in order to be taught music, must play upon some instrument, or know something of the art, to qualify them for admittance. They are kept in the college till twenty years of age; and, during the time of their residence there, they are taught by masters of the town, not by the Jesuits themselves.

There are others, under the denomination of *poor scholars*, who are intended for

for the church, and who are taught the learned languages, mathematics, and theology.

From hence I went to the burletta of *Le Finte Gemelli, Farza per musica, à quattro voci*, set by Matteo Rauzzini, brother to the singer of that name, a young man of only eighteen years of age. The music was most of it common, but pretty, and in good taste. The Lodi sung charmingly; her voice and figure would make her a capital singer in a serious opera, if she were well taught. Her voice wants only a little more room in its passage through the throat; in every thing else, she is admirable; having a pretty figure, a good expression, and an exquisite manner of taking *appogiature*.

The second singer of this company, Signora Manservisi, deserves to be mentioned; her figure is agreeable, her voice, though not strong, is well-toned, she has nothing vulgar in her manner, sings in tune, and never gives offence.

There was a tenor, Signor Fiorini, who sung to-night, whom I had not heard before; he has perhaps been a better singer than he is at present; but now, neither his voice, nor manner, had any thing interesting in it, though both were free from any common defects; for he sung in tune, had a shake, and was far from vulgar.

In going home from the opera, I heard a very good concert in the street; it was performed at the door of M. de Visme, by torch-light, and attended by a great crowd: after I returned to my lodgings, I heard the same performers at the inn door; upon enquiring who they were, I was told, that they were *poor scholars*; but I did not discover till the next day, that this concert was intended, as a regale, for M. de Visme and me, on account of our having been at their college to inform ourselves concerning their institution.

Friday. I spent the greatest part of this morning with Signor Rauzzini; he
was

was so obliging as to sing to me a great number of excellent songs, in different styles, among which there were many of his own composition. As to his abilities in singing, I think his shake is not quite open enough, nor did I then think his voice sufficiently powerful for a great theatre; but in all other respects he is a charming performer; his taste is quite modern and delicate; the tone of his voice sweet and clear; his execution of passages of the most difficult intonation amazingly neat, rapid, and free: and his knowledge of harmony is far beyond that of any great stage-singer I ever knew: he has likewise a very good person, and, I am told, is an excellent actor.

The rest of this day was employed in the Elector's, and in other libraries. At night I heard the *poor scholars* again in the streets, where they performed some full pieces very well: there were violins, hautboys, French horns, a violoncello, and bassoon. I was informed, that they were obliged frequently to perform thus in the streets, to convince the public, at whose expence they are maintained, of the proficiency they make.

Saturday 22d. I was this whole morning at Signora Mingotti's, from whom I obtained, in conversation, a sketch of her musical life. I am doubtful as to the propriety of publishing these anecdotes; however, as no secrecy was enjoined, and as they contain nothing disgraceful to the person who furnished them, I shall venture to do it, supposing a curiosity concerning the most trivial circumstances, relative to eminent persons, to be as strong in others as in myself.

Her parents were Germans; her father was an officer in the Austrian service, who being called to Naples, upon duty, his wife travelled with him thither during her pregnancy, and was there brought to bed of this daughter; who, however, was carried to Gratz, in Silesia, before she

she was a year old; and her father dying while she was young, her uncle placed her in a convent of Ursulines, where she was educated, and where she received her first lessons of music.

She told me, that during her childhood, she remembers being so pleased with the music performed in the chapel of her convent, particularly with a Litany sung there one festival, that she went to the abbess, with tears in her eyes, and trembling, both with fear of anger, and of a refusal, to intreat her to teach her to sing, as *she* did in the chapel. The abbess put her off, with saying, that she was very busy that day, but would think of it. The next day she sent one of the elder nuns to ask her who bid her make that request, when the little Regina (as she was then called) replied, that nobody had bid her, but that it was merely her own love for music, which inspired the thought. After this the abbess sent for her, and told her, that she had very little time to spare; but, if she would promise to be diligent, she would teach her herself; adding, that she could only afford her half an hour à day; but with that, she would soon find what her genius and industry were likely to produce, and she should go on with, or discontinue, her instructions, accordingly.

Regina was in rapture with this compliance of the abbess, who began to instruct her the next day, *à table sec*, as she expressed it, without a harpsichord, or any other instrument *.

In this manner she was taught the elements of music, and *solfeggi*, with the principles of harmony, and was obliged to sing the treble, while the abbess sung the base. She shewed me a very small

---

* She applied herself to the harpsichord several years after, and still accompanies upon it very well. But it was perhaps owing to her manner of learning to sing *without* an instrument, that she acquired the firmness in her performance, for which she has always been remarkable.

book,

book, in which all her firſt leſſons were written; the explanations were in the German language.

She remained in this convent till ſhe had attained her fourteenth year, at which time, upon the death of her uncle, ſhe went home to her mother. During the life of her uncle, ſhe had been intended for the veil. When ſhe quitted the convent, ſhe appeared, in the eyes of her mother and ſiſters, to be one of the moſt uſeleſs and helpleſs of beings; they looked upon her as a fine lady, brought up in a boarding ſchool, without knowing any thing of houſhold concerns; and her mother neither knew what to do with her, or her fine voice, which both ſhe and her ſiſters deſpiſed, not foreſeeing that it would one day be productive of ſo much honour and profit to the poſſeſſor.

Not many years after ſhe quitted the convent, Signor Mingotti, an old Venetian, and manager of the opera at Dreſden, was propoſed as a huſband for her.

She

She detested him, but was at length worried into a compliance, which was the sooner extorted from her, perhaps, as she, like other young women, imagined that by losing, she should gain her liberty.

People talked very much of her fine voice, and manner of singing. Porpora was at this time in the late king of Poland's service, at Dresden: he had heard her sing, and spoke of her at court as a young person of great expectations; which occasioned a proposal to her husband for her entering into the service of the Elector: he had before marriage promised never to suffer her to sing on the stage; however, he came home one day, and asked her, if she should like to engage in the service of the court. She thought this was done in derision, and gave him a short and peevish answer; but he continuing to teize her on the subject, at length convinced her that he was in earnest, and had a commission to treat with her. She liked the thoughts of sing-

singing, and turning her voice to some account, and therefore gladly entered into articles for a small stipend, not above three or four hundred crowns a year.

When her voice had been heard at court, it was supposed to raise a jealousy in Faustina, who was then in that service, but upon the point of retiring; and consequently in Hasse, her husband, particularly when he heard that Porpora, his old and constant rival, was to have a hundred crowns a month for teaching her. He said it was Porpora's last stake; the only twig he had to catch at; *un clou pour s'accrocher*. However, her talents made such a noise at Dresden, that the fame of them reached Naples, to which place she was invited, to sing at the great theatre. At this time she knew but little Italian; however, she now went seriously to work in studying it.

The first character she appeared in was *Aristæa*, in the opera of the *Olimpiade*, set by Galuppi. Montecelli performed the part of *Megacles*. On this occasion her talents, as an actress, gained her as much applause as her singing: she was bold and enterprising; and, seeing the character in a different light from what others had done before her, would, in spite of the advice of old actors, who durst not deviate from custom, play it in a way quite different from any one of her predecessors. It was in this original and courageous manner that Mr. Garrick first surprised and charmed an English audience; and, in defiance of contracted rules, which had been established by ignorance, prejudice, and want of genius, struck out a style of speaking and acting, which the whole nation has ever since continued to approve with acclamation, rather than applause.

After this success at Naples, Signora Mingotti received letters from all parts of Europe, to offer her terms for engaging at different operas; but she was not then at liberty to accept of any of them,

being

being obliged to return to the court of Dresden, in which service she was still a pensioner; however, her salary was considerably augmented, and she frequently expresses her gratitude to that court, and says she owes to it all her fame and fortune. Here she repeated, with great applause, her part in the *Olimpiade*; every one agreed, that in point of voice, execution, and acting, her powers were very great; but many thought that she was wholly unfit for any thing pathetic or tender.

Hasse was now employed to set *Demofoonte**; and she imagined that he kindly gave her an *Adagio*, accompanied by the violins, *Pizzicati*, merely to expose and shew her defects. But suspecting the snare, she studied hard to escape it; and in the song, *Se tutti i Mali Miei*, which she afterwards sung in England, with great applause, she succeeded so

* This happened in 1748.

well,

well, as to silence even Faustina herself. Sir Ch. H. Williams was English minister here at this time, and being intimate with Hasse and his wife, had joined their party, publicly declaring that Mingotti was utterly unable to sing a slow and pathetic song; but when he had heard her, he made a public recantation, asked her pardon for doubting of her abilities, and ever after remained her firm friend and adherent.

From hence she went into Spain, where she sung with Gizziello, in the operas under the direction of Signor Farinelli; who, she told me, was so severe a disciplinarian, that he would not allow her to sing any where but in the opera at court, or even to practise, in a room next the street. She was requested to sing at private concerts, by many of the first nobility and grandees of Spain, but could not obtain permission from the director; who carried his prohibition so far, as to deny a pregnant lady, of great rank,

rank, the satisfaction of hearing her, though she was unable to go to the theatre, and declared that she *longed* for a song from Mingotti. The Spaniards have a religious respect for these involuntary and unruly affections in females thus circumstanced, however they may be treated as problematical in other countries*. The husband, therefore, of the lady, complained to the king of the cruelty of the opera director, who, he said, would kill both his wife and child, if his majesty did not interfere. The king lent a favourable ear to the complaint, and ordered Mingotti to receive the lady at her house, in which his majesty was implicitly obeyed, the lady's desire was satisfied, and the child prevented, perhaps, from being marked, in some part of its body, with a music paper, or from having an Italian song written with indelible characters on its face.

* See *l'Histoire Naturelle*, de M. de Buffon, tom. ii.

Signora Mingotti remained two years in Spain, from whence she came to England, for the first time. How much she was then admired, at our opera, is too recent to need being mentioned here. She afterwards sung in every great city of Italy; but she always regarded Dresden as her home, during the life-time of the Elector Augustus, late king of Poland. She is now settled at Munich, more, it is thought, from cheapness than attachment. She has no pension from this court, as was reported, but, with œconomy, she has just sufficient, from her savings, to bring her through the year. She seems to live very comfortably, to be well received at court, and to be esteemed by all such as are able to judge of her understanding, and to enjoy her conversation.

It gave me great pleasure to hear her speak concerning practical music, which she does with as much intelligence as any *maestro di capella* with whom I ever conversed.

Her knowledge in singing, and powers of expression, in different styles, are still amazing, and must delight all such as can receive pleasure from song, unconnected with the blandishments of youth and beauty. She speaks three languages, German, French and Italian, so well, that it is difficult to say which of them is her own. English she likewise speaks, and Spanish, well enough to converse in them, and understands Latin; but, in the three languages first mentioned, she is truly eloquent.

In the afternoon father Kenedy was so obliging as to attend me again at the academy, in order to assist in finding such tracts, among the great number which are bound up together, as I had marked in the catalogue.

From hence I returned, by appointment, to Signora Mingotti. She had got her harpsichord tuned, and I prevailed on her to sing, to no other accompaniment, for near four hours. It was now that

that I difcovered her fuperior knowledge in finging. She is wholly out of practice, and hates mufic here, fhe fays, as fhe can feldom be well accompanied, or well heard; her voice is, however, much better than when fhe was laft in England.

Prince Sapieha, a Polifh nobleman, and his princefs, lodged at the fame inn as myfelf, the Golden Hart. The prince is very mufical, and plays well on the violin. I had the honour of being known to him a little by living in the fame houfe; but M. de Vifme was fo kind as to explain to him the nature of my mufical enquiries, and to tell him how curious I was after national mufic of all kinds: upon which his highnefs was pleafed to fend me word, that if I would call upon him about nine o'clock, any morning, he would gladly give me a fpecimen of the mufic of his country, as it depended fo much on the *coup d'archet*, that feeing it on paper, without hearing it performed, would afford but a very imperfect idea of it.

The day before my departure from Munich, when I had the honour of paying my respects to this prince, he condescended to receive me in a most obliging manner, and to play to me a great number of very pretty Polish pieces, which he executed very well, and to which he gave an expression that was at the same time delicate and singular. He had two German musicians to accompany him in these pieces; the one on the violin, and the other on the violoncello; every movement was in triple time, or $\frac{3}{4}$, with the close constantly on the second note in the bar, instead of the first; but upon my asking if there was no such thing as Polish music, in common time, the prince told me that there were some Cossack tunes in $\frac{4}{2}$, used chiefly in dancing, and he played me some of them. The accompaniment was constantly the $\frac{3}{8}$ and $\frac{4}{8}$, of the key, played a bar full, or four quavers of each, alternately.

His highness told me that they have no church music in Poland, which is not Italian; and the kind of music which we call Polonoise, is played quicker for dancing than at other times. The military music of Poland is like that of other countries, consisting only of marches in the usual time. I enquired after the Polish instruments, in order to know if there were any of a different construction from ours, but found that they had only guittars and lutes, somewhat differing in form, and in tuning, from those in other parts of Europe. The Poles have no plays, with songs intermixt, or operas, but such as are either French or Italian.

After answering these questions, the prince played a very pretty minuet, and two or three Polonoises of his own composition; and, upon my expressing approbation, he was pleased to make me a present of them: he likewise ordered some of the best pieces which he had played

played before, to be transcribed for me, which he sent to me at night, together with a specimen of Cossack melody; and, when I retired, he condescended to say that he should be very glad to meet me again, in the course of my journey, and to render me every service in his power.

Prince Sapieha told me, that he had long had in his service an Englishman, who was an excellent musician, and of so good a character, that he had not only made him his *maestro di capella*, but also his *homme de confiance*. He had been brought into Poland very young.

This prince is young and handsome in person. He is a diffident, and retired hither, from the troubles and desolation of his country, with his princess, a sensible and accomplished lady, as I was informed by a person who had several times conversed with her *.

* Since my departure from Munich, his estates in Poland have been confiscated, by order of the Empress of Russia, on account of his having refused to do homage for them to that princess, and
confess

I went again to court at Nymphenberg, before my departure, and was again honoured by the notice of the Elector and his sister, and obtained a reiterated promise from both of a piece of music of their composition. The Elector at first made some difficulty, lest I should publish it; as his *Stabat Mater* had been stolen, and printed at Verona, without his permission, and would have been published, had not his highness purchased the plates, and the whole impression; but upon my assuring him that without licence I should never make any other use of the piece, with which he should honour me, than to enrich my collection of scarce and curious compositions, he was pleased to give orders for its being transcribed.

The Electress dowager told me that her disposition, in this particular, was different from her brother's; for, instead

confess her legal sovereignty to the Polish territories, of which, by force of arms, she has possessed herself.

of concealing what she was able to produce, she took as much care to have it known, as the birth of a legitimate child; and had, accordingly, printed and published her two operas in score: so that she feared she had nothing left among her papers, worth bestowing; however, she gave Guadagni permission to look them over, and to let me have whatever he thought best worth my acceptance.

After this I had the honour of being presented, by M. de Visme, to the Dutchess of Bavaria, the widow of the Elector's brother, and sister to the Electress Palatine of the Rhine; she is of a very pleasing figure and character. It was at the desire of this princess that M. de Visme called me to her: they had previously been talking of my having been at Manheim and Schwetzingen; and, upon her being told that I had not been presented to her brother, the Elector Palatine, for want of a minister, or proper person at that court, to do me that ho-

nour, she expressed great surprize, and indeed concern. She was pleased to say that it would have given her brother great pleasure to have conversed with a person whose pursuits were such as mine, as he was particularly fond of music; and added, that he not only read and spoke English, but had a natural partiality to all who were of my country. I told her highness how I was circumstanced; that I had been favoured with a letter from Mr. Cressener, our minister at Bonn, which had not operated so soon as I could have wished; and that I was too much pressed in time to be able to wait long enough for it to take effect; and added, that all I aspired at in this journey, was to obtain an opportunity of hearing the best performers, and seeing the works of the best composers of Germany, in order to be enabled, in the course of my History of Music, to do justice to their talents and genius. The Dutchess was pleased to say, that she was certain her
bro-

brother, the Elector Palatine, would be sorry to find, that I had been at his capital, and at Schwetzingen, without his having been apprized of it.

After this M. de Visme was so kind, as to carry me back to Munich as fast as possible, in order to attend at a concert, which Signora Mingotti obligingly made for me, of the best musicians which she could get together upon short notice, whom I had not heard before. M. Kröner, whose performance I had only heard at Nymphenburg in full pieces, was first violin. There was M. Sechi, a very good hautboy, who, if I had not lately heard Fischer, would have charmed me; M. Rheiner, the bassoon, who, when in England, was so ill, that he was unable to play more than once in public, and whom I had not yet heard, was here tonight, and had quite recovered his health. His tone is sweet, and execution neat, and he must be allowed by every competent and impartial judge, to be a very able and pleasing performer.

Madame la Presidente, a lady of fashion, a friend and neighbour of Signora Mingotti, opened the concert, by a lesson on the harpsichord, which she executed with uncommon rapidity and precision. A *quintetto* was played next, that was composed by M. Michel, a young man that had been brought up at the Jesuit's music school. He has a genius, that wants only the pruning knife of time and experience to lop off luxuriance; every performer in this piece had an opportunity of shewing the genius of his instrument, and his own powers of execution. There was, in the solo parts, the brilliant, pathetic, and graceful, by turns; and the *tutti* parts had no other imperfection, than being too learned, and *recherchées* in modulation. I hardly ever heard a composition, that discovered more genius and invention, one that required

quired more abilities in the execution, or that was better performed; it was made for a violin, a hautboy, tenor, baſſoon, and violoncello.

Signor Guadagni and Signor Rauzzini were both at this concert, and the latter, whom I had only heard before, in one ſong, with full accompaniments, was ſo obliging, as to ſing a very pretty air of his own compoſition, and another admirable one, by Signor Sacchini, in the *Eroe Cineſe*. In the execution of theſe airs, he manifeſted great and captivating powers: a ſweet and extenſive voice, a rapid brilliancy of execution, great expreſſion, and an exquiſite and judicious taſte. I was to-day even ſurpriſed by the ſtrength of his voice, which had before appeared rather too feeble for a great theatre; but it was want of exertion, for now it made its way through all the inſtruments, when playing *fortiſſimo*.

A duet by Sechi and Rheiner, which finiſhed the concert, put me in mind of the

the two Bezozzis, at Turin; as their inſtruments, ſo their genius and abilities ſeem made for each other, there being a like correſpondence in both.

After theſe charming performances were over, I haſtened to the comic opera, at which were the Elector, and all the electoral family. Count Seeau, intendant of the Elector's muſic, had moſt obligingly changed the opera, in order to afford me an opportunity of hearing Signora Lodi in her beſt character. The burletta of to-night was the *Moglie Fedele*, compoſed by Signor Guglielmi; her voice is brilliant, and ſtyle of ſinging charming; but as I had, in London, ſeen Signora Guadagni in the ſame character, her acting did not ſtrike me ſo much as it would otherwiſe have done. After the opera, there was a long dance, which was an ingenious and entertaining pantomime, and of which, the ſcenes and decorations were well contrived, and ſplendid.

The

The next day, which was that of my departure from Munich, at nine o'clock in the morning, Signora Mingotti, who was indefatigable in rendering me every service in her power, had prepared another small, but select band, for me at her house, in order to afford me an opportunity of hearing two scholars of Tartini on the violin; M. Holtzbogn, and Lobst, which political reasons had prevented her from inviting the day before. They are both good performers; had been in the service of the late duke of Bavaria, and have still a pension, though but few opportunities of being heard.

Holtzbogn has a great hand, a clear tone, and more fire than is usual, in one of the Tartini school, which is rather remarkable for delicacy, expression, and high finishing, than for spirit and variety. This performer writes well for his instrument, and played a very masterly concerto of his own composition. Lobst played a concerto of Tartini with great delicacy;

delicacy; he is naturally timid, and want of practice added nothing to his courage; however, through these disadvantages, he discovered himself to be a worthy disciple of the great Tartini.

After these pieces Signora Rosa Capranica, in the service of this court, and scholar of Signora Mingotti, brought hither from Rome by the Electress dowager of Saxony, sung a very difficult song by Traetta, with great neatness, and in a pleasing and agreeable manner. This performer is young, and has natural powers capable of great things, at which if she does not arrive, under such a mistress as Signora Mingotti, it must be totally attributed to want of diligence.

The city of Munich is one of the best built, and most beautiful in Germany; I am ashamed to mention all the honours and favours, which were undeservedly conferred upon me, during my short residence there. All that I can add to this article is, that I quitted it with great regret;

gret; as I had so numerous an acquaintance, and so many protectors, that I lamented the not being able to spare more time, to avail myself of their kindness and good offices.

* * * *

I went from Munich to Vienna, down the two rivers Iser and Danube; and as the musical incidents during this voyage are but few, and no itinerary or book of travels, that I remember to have seen, has described the course of these rivers, or the method by which persons are conveyed upon them, from one place to another, I shall not scruple to add to my few musical memorandums, such other remarks and observations as I find set down in my miscellaneous journal.

The Iser, upon which the city of Munich is situated, and which empties itself into the Danube, about a hundred miles below, though very rapid, is too much spread and scattered into different channels, to be sufficiently deep for a bark, or any kind of passage-boat, that has a bottom to float upon it. The current of this river is even too rapid for any thing to be brought back against it; but Bavaria being a country abounding with wood, particularly fir, rafts, or floats made of those trees, lashed together, are carried down the stream, at the rate of seventy or eighty miles a day. Upon these rafts, a booth is built for passengers in common; but if any one chuses to have a cabin to himself, he may have it built for about four florins. I preferred this, not only to avoid bad company and heat, but to get an opportunity of writing and digesting my thoughts and memorandums, being at this time very much in arrears with my musical journal.

I quitted Munich at two o'clock in the afternoon. The weather was intensely hot, and I was furnished with no means of tempering it; a clear sky and burning sun, reflected from the water, having rendered my fir cabin as insupportable as the open air. It was constructed

constructed of green boards, which exuded as much turpentine as would have vanquished all the aromatics of Arabia.

As I was utterly ignorant of the country, through which I was to pass, and the accommodations it would afford, all that my foresight had suggested to me, in the way of furniture and provisions, were a mattress, blanket, and sheets; some cold meat, with bread, and a bottle of wine; there was water in plenty always at hand. But I soon found myself in want of many other things; and, if I were ever to perform this voyage again, which I hope will never happen, experience would enable me to render the cabin a tolerable residence, for a week or ten days.

In quitting Munich by water, the city is a beautiful object; but the country we passed through is a wretched one, to all appearance; there being nothing but willows, sedge, sand, and gravel in sight. The water was so shallow in several

veral places, that I thought our float would have ftuck faft. At fix o'clock we arrived at Freifing, the fee and fovereignty of a prince bifhop; his palace is placed on a high hill at a little diftance from the town, which is on another hill, and looks very pretty from the waterfide. I would not go on fhore to pay for a bad bed and fupper, with which I was already furnifhed in my cabin; my fervant however went with the common company, which amounted to upwards of fifty perfons, in order to get fome frefh bread, but which the place did not afford.

There had been no rain in thefe parts of Germany for fix weeks; but, when we arrived at Freifing, I faw a little black cloud to the weftward, which, in lefs than half an hour, produced the moft violent ftorm of thunder, lightning, rain, and wind, that I ever remember to have feen. I really expected every moment, that the lightning would have fet fire to my cabin; it continued all night with prodigious

gious fury, so that my man could not get back, and I was left on the water, sole inhabitant of the float, which was secured by a hawser to a wooden-bridge.

Two square holes were cut in the boards of my cabin, one on each side, by way of window; the pieces were to serve as casements, one of these was lost, so that I was forced to fasten with pins, a handkerchief against the hole, to keep out wind and rain; but it answered the purpose very ill, and moreover, it rained in, at a hundred different places; drop, drip, drop, throughout my little habitation, sometimes on my face, sometimes on my legs, and always somewhere or other. This, with the violent flashes of lightning and bursts of thunder, kept off drowsiness; luckily, perhaps, for I might have caught cold, sleeping in the wet. I had been told, that the people of Bavaria were, at least, three hundred years behind the rest of Europe in philosophy, and useful knowledge. Nothing

thing can cure them of the folly of ringing the bells whenever it thunders, or persuade them to put up conductors to their public buildings; though the lightning here is so mischievous, that last year, no less than thirteen churches were destroyed by it, in the electorate of Bavaria. The recollection of this, had not the effect of an opiate upon me; the bells in the town of Freising were jingling the whole night, to remind me of their fears, and the real danger I was in. I lay on the mattress, as far as I could from my sword, pistols, watch-chain, and every thing that might serve as a conductor. I never was much frightened by lightning before, but now I wished for one of Dr. Franklin's beds, suspended by silk cords in the middle of a large room. I weathered it out till morning, without a wink of sleep; my servant told me, that the inn on shore was miserable; it rained into every room of the house, and no provisions could be found for thefe fifty people, but black bread and beer, boiled up with two or three eggs.

At fix, we got into motion, the rain and wind continuing with great fury, and from violent heat, the air grew fo chill and cold, that I found it impoffible to keep myfelf warm with all the things I could put on. For though I added to my drefs a pair of thick fhoes, woollen ftockings, a flannel waiftcoat, great-coat and night-cap, with all the warm garments in my poffeffion, yet I was benumbed with cold.

We advanced for four hours through a dreary country, as far as I was able to defcry, but the weather was fo bad, that I could not often examine it. At ten o'clock fome fir trees appeared, which enlivened the view, and at eleven, nothing elfe could be feen on either fide. There was a very high and fteep fhore on the right, covered with firs, and on the left, trees fcattered near the water, and groves at a diftance. At eleven, the float ftopped at Landshut, where the passengers dined. I stuck to my cabin and cold meat: if it had not rained in, I should have thought myself very well off; but, in my present circumstances I was so uncomfortable, that I could not, for a long time, write a word in my journal books; the weather had so lowered my spirits, and stiffened my fingers; however, towards the afternoon, I made an effort, and transcribed many things from my tablets, which were full. At six o'clock, the float stopt at Dingelsing; in the evening I got a candle, which was a luxury denied to me the night before in the thunder-storm. Rain, rain, eternal rain, and wind made the water nothing less than pleasant.

The next morning was clear, but cold. The passengers landed at Landau about ten; at one we entered the Danube, which did not appear so vast a river here as I expected. However, it grew larger as we descended; we stopt at two o'clock at a miserable village, with a fine convent in it, however. Here the wind became

came so violent, that I thought every minute it would have carried away both my cabin and myself; at three, it was determined to stay here all night, as it was not safe to stir during this wind; but as this seems, and is called, *Le Païs des vents*, it was an excercise for patience to be stopt at a place, where I had nothing to do. My provisions grew short and stale, and there were none of any kind to be had here!

I had suffered so much the night before, that I now seriously set about contriving how to keep myself warm. The blanket bought at Munich for me, by my knave, or fool of a servant, and which I had not seen soon enough to change, was a second-hand one, and so filthy, ragged, and likely to contain all kinds of vermin, and perhaps diseases, that hitherto I could not find in my heart to touch it; however, cold and hunger will tame the proudest stomachs. I put the blanket

ket over the sheet, and was gladdened by its warmth.

At three in the morning, the passengers were called, and soon after the float was in motion; it was now a huge and unwieldy machine, a quarter of a mile long, and loaded with deals, hogsheads, and lumber of all kinds. The sun rose very bright; but at six there was a strong easterly wind, full in our teeth, and so great a fog, that not a single object could be seen on either side the river.

When I agreed to live night and day, for a week, upon the water, I forgot to bargain for warm weather; and now it was so cold, that I could scarcely hold the pen, though but the 27th of August! I have often observed, that when the body is cold, the mind is chilled likewise; and this was now so much the case with myself, that I had neither spirits nor ideas for working at my musical journal.

At eight o'clock we ſtopt at Vilſchofen, a ſweet ſituation. Here is a wooden bridge, of ſixteen arches, over the Danube. The hills on the oppoſite ſide of the town are covered with wood, and exceedingly beautiful. The fog was diſſipated, and the ſun now ſhone on them in great glory. There is a gentle viſit here from the cuſtom-houſe officers; the ſeals were cut off my trunk, being the laſt town in Bavaria. They threatened hard as to the ſevere examination I was to undergo upon entering Auſtria; however, I had little to loſe, except time; and that was now too precious to be patiently parted with to theſe inquiſitorial robbers.

At half an hour paſt nine we ſet off for Paſſau, in very fine weather, which revived my ſpirits, and enabled me to hold my pen. The Danube abounds in rocks, ſome above water, and ſome below, which occaſion a great noiſe by the rapidity of the current, running over, or againſt them.

We

We met this morning a gang of boats, laden with salt, from Saltzburg and Paſſau, dragged up the river by more than forty horſes, a man on each, which expence is ſo great, as to enhance the price of that commodity above four hundred per cent. We did not ſeem to move ſo faſt now as upon the Iſer, which had frequent caſcades; and ſometimes the float dipped ſo deep, as to have three or four feet of water ruſh ſuddenly into my cabin.

PASSAU.

This is the boldeſt, and at the ſame time the pleaſanteſt ſituation, that I ever ſaw. The town is built on the ſide and ſummit of a ſteep hill, on the right of the Danube. There is a hill on the other ſide, anſwering to that on which the town is built; however, there are but few houſes upon it.

Paſſau is a large imperial city. In the cathedral, which is a very beautiful modern

dern building, of the Corinthian order, there is a very magnificent organ, to look at. The cafe is finely carved and gilt, and the pipes are highly polifhed: it is divided into two columns of large pipes, one on each fide, and has a complete little organ in the middle, which joins them together, and faves the weft window: it is what builders call a thirty-two foot organ. M. Snetzler, when it was laft repaired, made fome of the front pipes, but there is little variety in the infide: he likewife made the *vox humana*, and octave *dulciana*, in the little organ, which are the two beft folo ftops that the inftrument contains.

On each fide of the choir, in this church, there is likewife a fmall organ, with the pipes fo highly burnifhed, that I cannot help fuppofing them to be of filver: indeed the perfon who fhewed me the great one, affured me that they were filver pipes; but as he likewife would have perfuaded me that the front of the great organ was of that metal, in which

I was

I was certain he was mistaken, I cannot depend on his word.

At the end of this town is the confluence of three rivers; the *Inn*, on the right hand; the *Iltz*, on the left; and the *Danube* in the middle. After this junction, the Danube becomes more and more rapid: the shore on each side, for a considerable way below Passau, has hills and rocks as high as those at Bristol; but these are covered with spruce fir trees and box, and look much less terrible, though quite as high. These rocks deprived us of the sun at three in the afternoon. About four miles below Passau, Austria is on the left, and Bavaria on the right, as far as Ingelhartzeil, when we were fairly entered into Austria. Here is the custom-house with which I had been threatened, and which I approached with trepidation; but my trunk was not opened, and nothing was examined except my writing box, which the officers would have unlocked. A seal was, however, set on my trunk, which

which I hoped would have enabled me to pafs on to Vienna, without further plague, and then I expected to pay for all.

Thus far the Danube runs between two high mountains, and fometimes it is fo compreffed and fhut up, as to be narrower than the Thames at Mortlake. The defcent is often fo confiderable, that the water cannot be feen at the diftance of a quarter of a mile, and fometimes the noife againft rocks is as violent, and as loud as a cataract.

At the entrance into Auftria the value of money is lowered; fo that a filver piece, worth twelve *creuzers*, in Bavaria, is inftantly lowered to ten; a florin, of fixty creuzers, becomes only worth fifty; a ducat of five florins, is lowered to four florins, twelve creuzers; and a fovereign of fifteen florins, to twelve florins thirty creuzers; a louis d'or, from eleven to nine florins, twelve creuzers; and a great crown to two florins.

We went upwards of eight leagues,

between two mountains, and ſtopt for the night, at a wretched place, which afforded no kind of refreſhment; though I had indulged the hope of ſupplying myſelf here for two days to come, which being Friday and Saturday, among Auſtrian catholics, I knew would be kept ſtrictly *maigre*.

I had now filled up the chinks of my cabin with ſplinters, and with hay; got a new button to the door, reconciled myſelf to my filthy blanket, and made a pair of ſnuffers out of a chip of deal; but alas! the eſſential failed: this was all external, and I wanted internal comfort! the laſt bit of my cold meat was flyblown, to ſuch a degree, that, ravenous as I was, I threw it into the Danube; bread too, that ſtaff was broken! and nothing but Pompernichl was to be had here; which is ſo black and ſour, as to diſguſt two ſenſes at a time.

Friday morning, Auguſt 28th. This river continues running through the ſame woody,

woody, wild, and romantic country; which, to pafs through, is pleafant and entertaining, to a ftranger, but produces nothing, except firing, to the poor inhabitants. For fifty miles not a corn field or pafture is to be feen. Sheep, oxen, calves, and pigs, are all utter ftrangers in this land. I afked what was behind thefe mountains, and was anfwered, huge forefts. At Afha the country opens a little.

What an aggregate of waters is here! river after river, comes tumbling into the Danube, and yet it grows rather more deep than wide, by thefe acceffions; but many fmall rivers detach themfelves from it, and iflands are frequently formed in the middle and fides of this world of waters: before we arrived at Lintz, however, a flat fenny country appeared, with high mountains, covered with trees, at a diftance.

LINTZ.

L I N T Z.

The approach to this town, by water, is very beautiful. There is a road on each fide the Danube, at the foot of high mountains and rocks, covered with trees, by which the river is again bounded. The caftle is feen at a diftance, and houfes and convents, upon the fummit of fome of the higheft hills, have a fine appearance. There is a bridge over the Danube of twenty very wide arches. The town is built on the fummit and fides of high hills, and in fituation much refembles Paffau. The churches were fhut up, as it was twelve o'clock when we arrived; however, I obtained permiffion to enter the collegiate church, where I found a large organ.

There is fuch an appearance of piety here, as I never faw before in the moft bigoted catholic countries. All along the Danube, near any town, there are little

little chapels erected, at only twenty or thirty yards distance from each other, sometimes on the sides of these mountains, and in places too narrow for a foot-path*; and I saw not a house in Lintz that had not a Virgin or a saint, painted or carved, upon it.

I walked about the town for near two hours. It was market day, though but for poor stuff; as nothing eatable appeared, perhaps, because it was Friday, but 𝔅𝔯𝔬𝔡, vile cheese, bad apples, pears, and plums; and of other wares, only tape, toys, ordinary Missals, and wretched prints of virgins and saints. I saw not a good shop in the town, though there are many showy and fine houses. Gable ends and pear-topt steeples, in the Bavarian style, are still in fashion here.

At SPIEBURG, which is only the shell of an old castle, upon a little island, is the first of the two water-falls in the Da-

---

* These chapels are not sufficiently spacious to contain either persons or priest, they are only intended as receptacles for a crucifix or a Virgin.

O nube,

nube, said to be so dangerous; however, now, there was nothing formidable in it but the noise.

Ens, a large city, is here in sight, upon the right hand; we went through an ugly country till it was dark; the river is sometimes like a sea, so wide that there is scarce any land in sight; at other times it is broken, and divided into small streams, by islands. The raft stopt at a hovel, on the left bank of the river, where the passengers landed, and spent the night. I remained in my cabin, where, I believe, I was much better off, as to bed, than any of them; but, for provisions, we were all on a footing. Pierre, with great difficulty, clambered up the rocks, to a village, and procured me half a dozen eggs, with which he returned in triumph. But, alas! two of them were addled, and a third had a chicken in it; which, being fast day, I could not in conscience eat.

Saturday,

Saturday, we set off at five o'clock, but were stopt, after having gone three or four miles, by a violent fog, which rendered the navigation dangerous, among so many rocks, shoals, and islands. When this was dispelled, we soon reached STRUDEL, which is situated in a wilder country than ever I saw in passing the Alps. Here is the famous water-fall and whirlpool, which the Germans so much dread, that they say it is the habitation of *Der Teufel*; however, they had talked so much about it, that it appeared to me less formidable than I expected. The shooting London bridge is worse, though not attended with more noise. The company prayed and crossed themselves most devoutly; but though it may, especially in winter, be a very dangerous pass in a boat, this raft may dip into the water, but it covers such a surface, that it cannot possibly either sink or be overset.

At IPS, a pretty town, with a new, handsome, and large *caserne*, or barrack, just

just by it, the country opens, and is very beautiful. Hereabouts they begin to make Austrian wine: the white wine is a pretty, pleasant sort, but small.

At MELK, on the right of the Danube, is a most magnificent convent of Benedictines; it seems to cover two thirds of the town; the architecture is beautiful, and it has the appearance of being but lately built: here are vines all along the shore, on the left hand. Harvest was quite got in hereabouts; indeed there is but little appearance of agriculture in this wild country. I believe I remarked before, that the quantity of useless woods and forests, in several parts of Germany, indicate a barbarous and savage people; and, to say the truth, except in the great trading towns, or those where sovereign princes reside, the Germans seem very rude and uncultivated.

The country becomes more and more wild, as far as STEIN. The rocks were often so high, on each side, as to prevent us us from seeing the sun at two or three o'clock in the afternoon. At Stein there is a wooden bridge of twenty-five or twenty-six very wide arches, which leads to KREMS, where the Jesuits have a most sumptuous college, beautifully situated on a hill; it has more the appearance of a royal palace, than any thing that we can boast of in England. Stein is on the left, and Krems on the right hand of the Danube, going down. Here our float anchored for the night, though it was but five o'clock: indeed it had not stopt, except early in the morning, for the fog, the whole day. We had now near fifty miles to Vienna; and the scoundrel Floßmeister, or waterman, assured me, and every body at Munich, that we should certainly be there on Saturday night.

At Krems there is an immense organ, in the Jesuits' church. Here, and all the way to Vienna, the common people, in the public houses, and the labourers, at their work, divert themselves with singing in two, and sometimes more parts. Near Ips there was a great number of Bohemian women, whom we should call gypsies, on a pilgrimage to St. Mary *Tafel*, a church placed on the summit of a very high mountain, facing the town of Ips, on the other side the Danube. No one could inform me why it was called St. Mary *Tafel*; but, in all probability, it had this appellation from the form of the mountain on which it is placed, which resembles a *table*. These women, however, did not sing in parts, like the Austrians, but in *canto fermo*, like the pilgrims that I heard in Italy, who were going to Assisi; the sound was carried several miles, by the stream and wind, down the river, upon whose smooth surface it passed, without interruption.

The musical events of this week are so trivial, as scarce to deserve recording. I must, however, add, to what I have already said, concerning the turn for music which I found among the Austrians, that

at

at Stein, opposite Krems, I heard several songs and hymns, sung very well, in four parts; who were the singers I could not learn, as I was on the water; but it was a fortunate circumstance for me to be placed, by accident, where I heard as good a performance as could have been procured by premeditation and design; it was a woman who sung the upper part, and the melody was not only expressed with simplicity, but the harmony had all the advantages of being swelled and diminished, which, to me, had the effect of advancing and retreating; and the performers seemed to understand each other, and what they were about, so well, that each chord had that kind of equality, in all its parts, which is given to the same number of notes, when played upon the swell of an organ. At this place the soldiers, and almost all the young people that were walking by the water side, were frequently singing, and never in less than two parts.

It is not easy to account for this facility of singing in different parts, in the people of one country, more than in those of another: whether it arises in Roman catholic countries, from the frequency of hearing music sung in parts, in their churches, I cannot say; but of this I am certain, that in England it costs infinite trouble, both to the master and scholar, before a young practitioner in singing is able to perform, with firmness, an under part to the most simple melody imaginable; and I never remember hearing the ballad singers, in the streets of London, or in our country towns, attempt singing in two different parts.

Sunday, August 30. This day was trifled away without getting to Vienna with the float, as I had been fully made to expect: an officer on board, tried with me to procure a land carriage for that purpose, but in vain. As we approached Vienna, the country became less savage. There are vineyards on the sides of
all

all the hills, and large islands innumerable which divide the Danube.

TULN is a little fortified town, with a *fine* church, and a *fine* convent, which, with a *fine* custom-house, usually constitute all the *finery* of Austria.

At KOR NEUBURG, there is a very strong citadel, on the summit of an extreme high hill, which commands the river and city.

At NUSDORF, a village within three miles of Vienna, with nothing in it but a church and a custom-house, I was quite out of patience, at being told, that the float could not, as it was Sunday, on any account, enter Vienna. It was now but five o'clock, and the seventh day of my being immured in a sty, where, indeed I might have grown fat if I had had any thing to eat; but that not being the case, hunger as well as loss of time, made me very impatient to be released; and after an hour lost in trying to procure a chaise, I at

I at laſt got a miſerable boat to carry me and my ſervant to Vienna.

This voyage added but little to my knowledge of German muſic, but a great deal to that of the people, and country through which I paſſed: indeed I had an opportunity of landing at every conſiderable town in the paſſage, where I viſited the churches, though I had not time to make acquaintance with muſical people, or to collect hiſtorical materials; but as to *national muſic*, perhaps the rude ſongs which I heard ſung by the boors and watermen, gave me a more genuine idea of it, than is to be acquired from the corrupted, motley, and Italianiſed melody, to be heard in the capitals of this extenſive country.

VIENNA.

This city, the capital of the empire, and reſidence of the imperial family, is ſo remote from England, has been ſo imperfectly described, by writers of travels, and is so seldom visited by Englishmen, that I should have presented my readers with a minute account of its public buildings and curiosities, if it had not furnished me with ample materials for a long article, relative to my principal subject, MUSIC, to which every other must give place. I shall, however, bestow a few words on its peculiarities, and then proceed to my musical journal.

The approach to Vienna from the river, is not very unlike that of Venice, though there is much less water, for the Danube divides itself into three streams, about a mile and a half above the town; forty or fifty towers and spires may be seen from the water.

The custom-house did not disappoint my expectation of its being remarkably troublesome, particularly, in the article of *books*; all are stopt there, and read more scrupulously than at the inquisition of Bologna, in Italy; and mine,
which,

which, except mufic, were merely geographical and defcriptive, were detained near a fortnight before I could recover them; and his excellency lord vifcount Stormont, his majefty's ambaffador at this court, afterwards told me, that this was the only thing in which it was not in his power to affift me. On entering the town, I was informed, that if a fingle book had been found in my *fac de nuit*, or travelling fatchel, its whole contents would have been forfeited.

The ftreets are rendered doubly dark and dirty by their narrownefs, and by the extreme height of the houfes; but, as thefe are chiefly of white ftone, and in a uniform, elegant ftyle of architecture, in which the Italian tafte prevails, as well as in mufic, there is fomething grand and magnificent in their appearance, which is very ftriking; and even many of thofe houfes which have fhops on the ground-floor, feem like palaces above. Indeed the whole town and its fuburbs,

appear,

appear, at the firſt glance, to be compoſed of palaces, rather than of common habitations. The churches and convents are chiefly of Gothic architecture; however, the Jeſuits' college is an extenſive and elegant modern building; and the church of St. Sophia, built on the model of St. Peter's at Rome, but upon a much ſmaller ſcale, is a beautiful copy of that ſtructure in miniature; as is the Auſtin Friars, of the chapel of Loretto.

The emperor's prerogative of having the firſt floor of almoſt every houſe in Vienna for the uſe of the officers of his court and army, is as ſingular in itſelf, as it is inconvenient to the inhabitants. The houſes are ſo large, that a ſingle floor ſuffices for moſt of the firſt and largeſt families in the city.

The inhabitants do not, as elſewhere, go to the ſhops to make purchaſes; but the ſhops are *brought to them*; there was literally a fair, at the inn where I lodged, every day. The trades-people

ſeem

seem to sell nothing at home, but, like hawkers and pedlars, carry their goods from house to house. A stranger is teased to death by these chapmen, who offer to sale wretched goods, ill manufactured, and ill-fashioned. In old England, it is is true, things are very dear, but if their goodness be compared with these, they are cheap as dirt.

I must observe, that I have never yet found, in any country on the continent, that the trades-people, like many in England, could be trusted, without beating them down, and fixing the price of what is purchased of them, previous to possession. In London there is little danger of being charged unreasonably for any thing that is had from a reputable shop, though the price is not asked, when the goods are sent for, nor paid, till the bill is brought in, perhaps a year after.

A little way out of the town, there is a famous walk, or rather ride, called the

Prat;

Prat; it is an extensive wood, or open grove, with a coach-road cut through it. There is verdure on the ground, and shade from some of the largest trees that I ever saw, with frequent views of the Danube. It is the Hyde-park of Vienna, but more flat and gloomy than that of London.

The first time I went to a theatre, I was, by mistake, carried to a German tragedy, though there was a burletta performed in Italian, the same night, at another theatre, at which were the emperor and his sisters, the arch-duchesses of Austria; but my ignorance of this, at the time, contributed to fortify, in me, that accommodating principle, which seeks profit and enjoyment from the present situation, by whatever accidents thrown into it, without repining at the loss of remote pleasures, that are unattainable.

I hoped, however, that there would be singing in this piece, but was wholly
dis-

disappointed; it was ein Trauerspiel, von Gotthold Ephraim Lessing, called Emilia Galotti.

I should suppose this play to have been well acted; there were energy and passion, and many speeches were much applauded; but I was so young at German declamation, that I could only catch a sentence now and then. However, I made out the drift of the piece, which very much resembles, in the catastrophe, that of Virginia.

A prince of Guastallo, formerly in love with a countess, named Orsina, becomes inconstant upon seeing *Emilia Galotti*, the daughter of a country gentleman, who was engaged to a worthy Graf, or count. He meets with this lady, at mass, on the morning, which was fixed on for her marriage with the *Graf*.

Princes et rois vont très vite en amour, says M. de Voltaire. This prince has among his courtiers, a friend and confident, named Marinelli, who is a more

hateful

hateful character, than Jago, in Shakespeare's Othello.

This personage readily undertakes to pander for his master; and having, in vain, endeavoured to persuade the betrothed *Graf*, to accept of a foreign appointment, he hires a banditti to attack the carriage, in which *Emilia*, her mother, and the *Graf*, were proceeding to a country-house, in order to celebrate their marriage. The *Graf* is killed by the assassins, and *Emilia* is conveyed, in a seeming friendly and hospitable manner, to a *Chateau*, or country seat, of the prince, near the road.

Orsina, the deserted mistress of the prince, meeting with *Emilia*'s father, insinuates, that the unhappy young lady had consented to the plan, of her being carried off, and to the murder of her lover; which induces the irritated father, to receive from her a dagger, with the barbarous design of plunging it into his daughter's bosom.

Marinelli assumes the character of the friend and avenger of the deceased *Graf*, and acquaints the father, that, as it had been rumoured, that a lover of *Emilia* had been the murderer, it would be expedient to have her separated from her family, till the affair was cleared up.

The alarmed old man, desires permission to see his daughter, alone; as soon as she is made acquainted with her danger, from the artful plan of Marinelli, she seizes the dagger which her father had shewn her, with a resolution to destroy herself. He, however, prevents her; but is at length prevailed upon, to give the fatal stroke himself, stimulated by her entreaties, and exaggerations of the danger to which she was exposed, from the lawless passion of the prince, who enters at this instant, with Marinelli.

The father confesses the fact to the prince, and, with savage ferocity, asks him, whether he likes her now? Emilia has but

but juſt ſtrength ſufficient left, to vindicate the act of her father before ſhe expires. The old man delivers himſelf into the hands of juſtice; the mother runs diſtracted; while Marinelli, the chief cauſe of all the miſchief, receives no other puniſhment, with which the audience is made acquainted, than to be ordered by the prince, to get out of his ſight.

Lady Mary Wortley Montague, gives a curious deſcription of the ſtate of this theatre, when ſhe ſaw the comedy of Amphitrion repreſented here, in the year 1716. " I could not eaſily pardon, ſays " her ladyſhip, the liberty the poet has " taken of larding his play with not only " indecent expreſſions, but ſuch groſs " words, as I don't think our mob would " ſuffer from a mountebank; beſides the " two Socias very fairly let down their " breeches, in the direct view of the " boxes, which were full of people of " the firſt rank, who ſeemed very well
" pleaſed

" pleased with their entertainment, and af-
" sured me, this was a celebrated piece *."

This ribald taste has taken another turn, and in tragedy seems now to exhale itself in impious oaths and execrations; for, in the piece of to-night, the interlocutors curse, swear, and call names, in a gross and outrageous manner. I know not, perhaps, the exact ideas annexed by the Germans to the following expressions, of Bey Gott; Gott verdamm' ihn, &c. but they shocked my ears very frequently.

However, there is an original wildness in the conduct and sentiments of this piece, which renders it very interesting. It is concluded by the prince himself, with the following bold and admirable exclamation; " Gods! is it
" not a sufficient curse to mankind, that
" princes should be men, but must

* Letters of the right honourable lady Mary Wortley Montague, vol. I.

" devils

" devils take the semblance of their
" friends * !"

This theatre is lofty, having five or six rows of boxes, twenty-four in each row. The height makes it seem short, yet, at the first glance, it is very striking; it does not appear to have been very lately painted, and looks dark; but the scenes and decorations are splendid. The stage had the appearance of being oval, which, whether is was produced by deception or reality, had a pleasing effect, as it corresponded with the other end of the theatre, which was rounded off at the corners, and gave an elegant look to the whole.

The orchestra has a numerous band, and the pieces which were played for the overture and act-tunes, were very well performed, and had an admirable

* Gott! Gott! — Ist es, zum Unglücke so mancher, nicht genug, daß Fürsten Menschen sind: müssen sich auch noch Teufel in ihren Freund verstellen?

effect; they were composed by Haydn, Hoffman, and Vanhall.

The first time I went to the cathedral of St. Stephen, I heard an excellent mass, in the true church style, very well performed; there were violins and violoncellos though it was not a festival. The great organ at the west end of this church has not been fit for use these forty years; there are three or four more organs of a smaller size in different parts of the church, which are used occasionally. That which I heard in the choir this morning is but a poor one, and as usual, was much out of tune; it was played, however, in a very masterly, though not a modern style. All the responses in this service, are chanted in four parts, which is much more pleasing, especially where there is so little melody, than the mere naked *canto fermo* used in most other catholic churches; the treble part was sung by boys, and very well; particularly, by two of them, whose

whose voices, though not powerful, had been well cultivated.

I cannot proceed farther in the journal of my musical transactions at Vienna, without mentioning the flattering manner in which I was received, protected, and even assisted in my enquiries there, by his excellency lord viscount Stormont, his majesty's ambassador extraordinary at that court; as it was to his lordship's influence and activity, that I owed the greatest part of my entertainment, and the information I acquired during my residence at Vienna.

His lordship had been prepared for my arrival by a letter, which Mr. de Visme had been so kind as to write in my behalf, before I left Munich, in which he had explained the nature of my journey and pursuits; so that I very soon obtained an audience, and he condescended to enter heartily into my views, and to interest himself about them immediately on my arrival. This was a most fortunate circumstance for me, as his long residence here, had furnished opportunities for his being perfectly acquainted with all such persons and things as I wished to know; and that universal esteem and respect, which a steady, judicious, and amiable conduct had acquired him, joined to his high rank and station, rendered him all powerful in whatever cause he espoused.

One of the first signal favours which his lordship conferred on me, was doing me the honour of presenting me to the countess Thun, a most agreeable and accomplished lady of very high rank, who, among many other talents, possesses as great skill in music as any person of distinction I ever knew; she plays the harpsichord with that grace, ease, and delicacy, which nothing but female fingers can arrive at.

Her favourite author for the instrument, is a *dilettante*, M. le Comte de Becke. His pieces are very original, and

in

in a good taſte: they ſhew the inſtrument much, but his own delicacy and feelings more. He was, unluckily for me, in Bohemia at this time, ſo that I could not have the honour and advantage of his converſation.

The ſecond evening after my arrival, I went to the French theatre, where I ſaw a German comedy, or rather a farce of five acts: however, I ſhould not ſuppoſe the piece to be without merit, as the natives ſeemed much pleaſed with it. This theatre is not ſo high as that at which I had been the night before, but it is ſtill better fitted up; here the beſt places ſeem to be in the pit, which is divided in two parts, and all the ſeats are ſtuffed, and covered with red baize; the ſcenes were ſeldom changed during the piece; but the principal, that is, the ſcene of longeſt continuance, was flat in front, where there were two large folding doors, as in the French theatres, for the entrance and exit of the principal characters. At each side there was an elegant projection, in the middle of which there was likewise a door, used chiefly by the servants, and inferior characters. The comedy was often too grosly farcical; but there were scenes, as well as characters, of real humour, and one or two of the *Comedie larmoyante* kind, that were truly pathetic.

Premiums are now no longer given, as heretofore, in this theatre, to actors who voluntarily submit to be kicked and cuffed, for the diversion of the spectators. It is but a few years since, that bills were regularly brought in, at the end of each week; " So much for a slap on the " face;" " So much for a broken head; " and so much for a kick on the breech," by the comic actors. But, in process of time, the effect of these wearing out, it became necessary to augment their number, and force, in order to render the

plea-

pleasure of the spectators more exquisite; 'till the managers, unable any longer to support so intolerable an expence, totally abolished the rewards for these heroic sufferings.

And now, since this *active wit* has ceased to be practised, it is observed that the theatre is not only more seldom crowded than formerly, but the audience is become more difficult to please. Indeed the consequences seem to have been so fatal, that many attribute the frequent bankruptcies of the managers to the *insufferable* dullness and inactivity of the performers *.

The orchestra here was full as striking as that of the other theatre, and the pieces played were admirable. They were so full of invention, that it seemed to be music of some other world, info-

* In consideration of their great utility, it is hoped that the worthy managers of our theatres do not let " the spurns and patient sufferings" of our pantomime clowns, go unrewarded at the end of the week.

much.

much, that hardly a passage in this was to be traced; and yet all was natural, and equally free from the stiffness of labour, and the pedantry of hard study. Whose music it was I could not learn; but both the composition and performance, gave me exquisite pleasure *.

At the end of the play, there was a very spirited and entertaining dance, planned by the celebrated ballet-master, M. Noverre, in which the four principal performers displayed great abilities, in point of grace, activity, and precision.

Three large boxes are taken out of the front of the first row, for the imperial family, which goes frequently to this theatre; it was built by Charles the sixth. The empress queen continues in weeds, and

* The symphonies of *Manheim*, excellent as they are, have been observed, by persons of refined taste, to be *Manierées*, and tiresome to such as continue there any time, being almost all of one cast, from the writers of them giving too much into imitation.

has appeared in no public theatre since the death of the late emperor.

At night two of the poor scholars of this city sung, in the court of the inn where I lodged, duets in *falset*, *soprano*, and *contralto*, very well in tune, and with feeling and taste. I sent to enquire whether they were taught music at the Jesuits' college, and was answered in the affirmative. Though the number of poor scholars, at different colleges, amounts to a hundred and twenty, yet there are at present but seventeen that are taught music.

After this there was a band of these singers, who performed through the streets a kind of glees, in three and four parts: this whole country is certainly very musical. I frequently heard the soldiers upon guard, and centinels, as well as common people, sing in parts. The music school at the Jesuits' college, in every Roman catholic town, accounts in some measure for this faculty; yet other

other caufes may be affigned, and, among thefe, it fhould be remembered, that there is fcarce a church or convent in Vienna, which has not every morning its *mafs in mufic:* that is, a great portion of the church fervice of the day, fet in parts, and performed with voices, accompanied by at leaft three or four violins, a tenor and bafe, befides the organ; and as the churches here are daily crowded, this mufic, though not of the moft exquifite kind, muft, in fome degree, form the ear of the inhabitants. Phyfical caufes operate but little, I believe, as to mufic. Nature diftributes her favours pretty equally to the inhabitants of Europe; but moral caufes are frequently very powerful in their effects. And it feems as if *the national mufic of a country was good or bad, in proportion to that of its church fervice;* which may account for the tafte of the common people of Italy, where indeed the language is more mufical than in any other country of Europe,

Europe, which certainly has an effect upon their vocal mufic; but the excellent performances that are every day heard for nothing in the churches, by the common people, more contribute to refine and fix the national tafte for good mufic, than any other thing that I can at prefent fuggeft.

I had the good fortune to meet with the admirable poet Metaftafio here, and the no lefs admirable mufician Haffe, as well as with the chevalier Gluck, one of the moft extraordinary geniufes of this, or, perhaps, of any age or nation; and as I was fo happy as to enjoy the converfation of thefe illuftrious perfonages very frequently, during my refidence in this city, it will incline me to be very circumftantial concerning them, which I hope my readers will pardon in behalf of their extraordinary merit, and the enthufiaftic admiration of it, with which I confefs my mind to be impreffed.

Before I had the honour of being introduced to Signor Metastasio, I obtained, from undoubted authority, the following particulars relative to this great poet, whose writings have perhaps more contributed to the refinement of vocal melody, and, consequently, of music in general, than the joint efforts of all the great composers in Europe; this supposition I shall hereafter endeavour to explain and confirm, in speaking of him only as a lyric poet.

The *Abate Pietro Metastasio*, was adopted at Rome, while very young, by the celebrated civilian, Gravina, who discovering in him an extraordinary talent for poetry, undertook the care of his education; and, after he had been instructed under his eye, in all the parts of polite literature, he sent him to Calabria, in the kingdom of Naples, to learn Greek, as a living language, it being still spoken in that province, by the natives. He had

had such a faculty of speaking verses extempore, so early as at five years old, that Gravina used to set him on a table, to perform the part of an *Improvvisatore*; but this exercise was found to exhaust him so much, that a physician assured his patron, if he continued the practice, it would destroy him; for at such times he was so truly *afflatus numine*, that his head and stomach swelled, and became inflamed, while his extremities grew cold. Gravina seeing this, thought it necessary to take the physician's advice, and would never suffer him more to *improvvisare*. Metastasio now speaks of the practice as equally repugnant to grammar, and to common sense; for whoever accustoms himself in this rapid manner, to distort every thought into rhyme, destroys all taste, and totally precludes selection: till, by degrees, the mind and genius accommodating themselves to inaccuracies and absurdities, not only lose a relish for labour, but for every thing that is chaste and correct.

Gravina made Metastasio translate all Homer into Italian verse, before he was fourteen years of age; and this, perhaps, destroyed some of that veneration for the ancients, with which most men of true genius are possessed [*]. Fielding said of himself, that he bore *marks* of the difficulty of Homer about him all his life. Gravina idolized the ancients, and, perhaps, Metastasio, taking the *contrepied*, respects them too little.

He has opinions fixed and unalterable, peculiar to himself, concerning many things, particularly rhyme: he still thinks that the Hebrew Psalms are in rhyme, and that this consonance of verses is infinitely more ancient than is generally imagined. He thinks that Milton's Paradise Lost cannot be a perfect poem because it is written in *blank verse*, though all

[*] Gravina died in the year 1718, and made Metastasio his heir.

the narrative parts of his own dramatic pieces are in meafured profe; indeed, before each fong, he has a couplet, or clofe, ufually in rhyme, which prepares for the change.

The whole tenor of his life is equally innoxious with his writings. He lives with the moſt mechanical regularity, which he fuffers none to difturb; he has not dined from home thefe thirty years; he is very difficult of accefs, and equally averfe to new perfons, and new things; he fees, in a familiar way, but three or four people, and them, conſtantly every night, from eight o'clock till ten; he abhors writing, and never fets pen to paper but by compulfion: as it was neceffary to bind Silenus, before he would fing; and Proteus, to oblige him to give oracles.

He has long been invefted with the title and appointments of imperial laureate; and when the emperor, emprefs, or any one of the imperial family orders it, he fits down and writes, two hours at a time only, just as he would transcribe a poem written by any one else; never waiting for a call, invoking the Muse, or even receiving her favours at any other than his own stated periods.

He was applied to by the editors of the *Encyclopedie,* to write the article *Opera* for that work; but he politely declined the task, supposing it impossible that his sentiments on the subject should be pleasing to the French nation.

Tasso is his favourite of all poets; he likes not Fingal, on account of its wildness and obscurity*; he reads with his select friends ancient and modern authors every evening; he is extremely fond of the writings of count Medini, a Bohemian, whose poetical compositions, he says, are superior to those of all other living writers. This count is translating

---

* The poems of Ossian are translated into Italian, by the Abate Melchior Cesarotti, and were published at Padua in 1763.

the

the *Henriade*, of Voltaire, into Italian *Ottave Rime*.

A person of very high rank assured me, that he had been five years in Vienna before he could get acquainted with Metastasio, or even into conversation with him; and, after that time, but three visits had been exchanged between them in several years; indeed, in my applications for letters of recommendation to this exquisite poet, before I left England, I had been mortified by an assurance, " that " it would be in vain for me to attempt " even a sight of Metastasio, as he was " totally worn out, incommunicative, " and averse to society on all occasions."

However, this account had been expressed in too strong terms; for, upon my arrival at Vienna, I found that besides the constant society of his particular friends every evening, he had a kind of levee each morning, at which he was visited by a great number of persons of high rank and distinguished merit.

If he is attended to with complaisance, he converses very freely and agreeably; but if contradicted, he becomes immediately silent; he is too well-bred, as well as too indolent, to dispute; if what he thinks erroneous be advanced, in opposition to any thing that he has said, he passes it over in silence. He likes not animated discussions, such as generally subsist among men of talents and learning; but rather chuses the ease and moderation of a private individual, than to lay down the law in the decisive manner of a public and exalted character. Indeed there seems to be that soft calmness in his life, which subsists in his writings, where he reasons, even in passion, more than he raves; and that even tenor of propriety and correctness which runs through all his works, is, in some degree, constitutional. He is as seldom, perhaps, violently agitated in his writings as in his life, and he may be called the poet of the golden age; in which simplicity

plicity and decorum are said to have reigned, more than the wild and furious passions. The effusions of patriotism, love, and friendship, which he pours out with exquisite sweetness, are affections of a soft and gentle kind, which his heart felt, and his soul has coloured.

He has not, perhaps, the fire of a Corneille, or the wit and variety of a Voltaire; but he has all the pathos, all the correctness of a Racine, with more originality. I need only mention his well-known poem, *Grazie a gl'Inganni tuoi*, which has been so many times imitated and translated in all languages: this contains a species of wit, peculiar to Metastasio, in which he turns trivial circumstances to account. Shakespeare has said, in derision, of one of his characters, that " he has a *reasonable* good wit," and this is seriously true with respect to Metastasio, whose wit is not composed of epigrammatic points, or whimsical conceits; neither is it biting nor sarcastical; but

but confifts of familiar and natural things, highly polifhed, and fet in diamonds.

> ———'Tis nature to advantage drefs'd,
> What oft was thought, but ne'er fo well exprefs'd.

The fweetnefs of his language and verfification, give a grace to all that he writes, and the natural tendency of his genius, is to point out rectitude, propriety, and decorum; and though he difcovers in every ftanza of his Nifa, that he is not cured of his paffion for a jilt, yet he plainly proves that he ought to be fo.

Party runs as high among poets, muficians, and their adherents, at Vienna as elfewhere. Metaftafio and Haffe, may be faid, to be at the head of one of the principal fects; and Calfabigi and Gluck of another. The firft, regarding all innovations as quackery, adhere to the ancient form of the mufical drama, in which the poet and mufician claim equal attention from an audience; the bard

bard in the recitatives and narrative parts; and the compofer in the airs, duos, and choruffes. The fecond party depend more on theatrical effects, propriety of character, fimplicity of diction, and of mufical execution, than on, what *they* ftyle, flowery defcriptions, fuperfluous fimiles, fententious and cold morality, on one fide, with tirefome fymphonies, and long divifions, on the other *. It is lefs my bufinefs and intention here, to take fides, or to determine which of thefe parties are right, than to point out the different merit of both. For I fhould not only be an enemy to my own pleafure, but unworthy of the title I have affumed, of a faithful hiftorian, if I encouraged exclufive approbation. I fhall therefore proceed in characterifing the

* *L'Autore a foftuito alle fiorite defcrizioni, ai Paragoni fuperflui, e alle fentenziofe e fredde moralità, il linguaggio del cuore, le paffioni forti, le fituazioni intereffanti, e uno fpettacolo fempre variato.* Dedicaz. d' Alefte, dal cav. Gluck.

genius

genius of the two great composers above-mentioned, to the best of my judgment and feelings, unbiassed by the decisions of others.

The merit of Signor Hasse has so long, and so universally been established on the continent, that I have never yet conversed with a single professor on the subject, who has not allowed him to be the most natural, elegant, and judicious composer of vocal music, as well as the most voluminous now alive [*]; equally a friend to poetry and to the voice, he discovers as much judgment as genius, in expressing words, as well as in accompanying those sweet and tender melodies, which he gives to the singer. Always regarding the voice, as the first object of attention in a theatre, he never suffocates it, by the learned jargon of a multiplicity of instruments and subjects; but is

[*] He was born at Bergendorf, in Lower Saxony, within eight miles of Hamburg, and is best known in Italy, by the name of *Il Sassone*.

as careful of preserving it's importance, as a painter, of throwing the strongest light upon the capital figure of his piece.

In 1769, he produced at Vienna the music of a little opera, or *Intermezzo tragico*, *Piramo e Tisbe*, *à tre voci*; and in 1771, he set *Ruggiero*, at Milan, for the marriage of the arch-duke Ferdinand, brother of the emperor, with the princess of Modena, both written by Metastasio*.

Dr. Brown pretended to prove, the separation of music and poetry; if he was right, it must, however, be allowed that this poet and musician are the *two halves* of what, like Plato's *Androgyne*, once constituted a *whole*; for as they are equally possessed of the same characteristic marks of

---

* These pieces are the last productions of the great poet and musician, who, with more propriety than Pope and Jarvis, might say,
Smit with the love of sister arts we came,
And met congenial, mingling flame with flame.

true

true genius, taste, and judgment; so propriety, consistency, clearness, and precision, are alike the inseparable companions of both. When the voice was more respected than the servile herd of imitative instruments, and at a time when a different degree, and better judged kind of study rendered it, perhaps, more worthy of attention than at present, the airs of Signor Hasse, particularly those of the pathetic kind, were such as charmed every hearer, and fixed the reputation of the first singers in Europe*.

His abilities are but little known in England, as but few of his compositions are printed, and those of the most trivial kind; but, as his works are more numerous than those of any vocal composer now living, he may, without injury to his brethren, be allowed to be as superior to all other lyric composers, as Metastasio is to all other lyric poets.

* Such as Farinelli, Faustina, Mingotti, &c.

The chevalier Gluck is simplifying muſic; and with unbounded invention and powers for creating capricious difficulties, and decking his melodies with meretricious ornaments, he tries all he can to keep his muſe chaſte and ſober, his three operas of *Orfeo*, *Alceſte*, and *Paride*, are proofs of this, as they contain few difficulties of execution, though many of expreſſion.

He has lately ſuggeſted to an able writer, a plan for a new ode on St. Cecilia's day, which diſcovers both genius and diſcernment. Lord Cowper had, ſome time ſince, Dryden's Ode performed to Handel's muſic at Florence; but ſet to a literal Italian tranſlation given *totidem ſyllabis*, in order to preſerve the muſic as entire as poſſible. But this tenderneſs for the muſician, was ſo much at the expence of the poet, that Dryden's divine Ode, became not only unpoetical, but unintelligible in this wretched verſion. The muſic has ſince been performed at

Vienna to the same words, and many parts of it were very much liked, in despite of the nonsense through which it was conveyed to the ears of the audience.

Gluck was exceedingly struck with the thoughts of our great poet, and wished to have an ode on the same subject, but written on a different plan, which would preserve as many of them as possible. His idea was this; a poem of so great a length, could never be sung to modern music by *one person*. Now, as Dryden's Ode is all *narrative*; there seems no propriety in distributing it among different persons, in the performance. He wished therefore, to have it thrown into a dramatic form, in which the interlocutors might speak what passion suggests; and this has been done in the following manner: it begins with a feast of Bacchus, at which Alexander and Thais preside. They agree to call in Timotheus to sing to them; but before his arrival, the hero and his mistress differ in opinion

con-

concerning his merit; the one supposes him to be inferior to what has been reported of him; and the other, superior. This contention enlivens the dialogue, and interests the audience till the arrival of the bard, who begins to sing of the Trojan war, which animates Alexander so much, that he breaks out into the complaints attributed to him by the old story of having no Homer, like Achilles, to record his actions.

Tuesday, September 1st. At vespers, this afternoon, I heard, in the cathedral, some admirable old music composed by Fux, not very well performed, indeed, as to singing or accompaniments; the former was feeble, and the latter, I mean the violins, were despicable: however, the organ was very well played, by the organist, M. Mittermeir. M. Hoffman, an excellent composer of instrumental music, particularly of symphonies, is *maestro di capella*. The church is a dark, dirty, and dismal old Gothic building, though richly ornamented; in

it

it are hung all the trophies of war, taken from the Turks and other enemies of the house of Austria, for more than a century past, which gives it very much the appearance of an old wardrobe.

At half an hour past six this evening, I went to the comic opera of *Il Barone.* The music, composed by Signor Salieri, a scholar of M. Gasman. I did not receive much pleasure from the overture, or the two first airs; the music was languid, and the singing but indifferent. There were only four characters in the piece, and the principal woman did not appear till the third scene; but then she gave a glow to every thing around her; it was one of the Baglioni, of Bologna *, whom I had heard both at Milan and Florence, during my tour through Italy. She is very much improved since that time, and her voice is now one of the clearest,

* Costanza.

sweetest,

sweetest, truest, most powerful, and extensive I ever heard. In compass, it is from Bb, on the fifth space in the base, to D in alt; full, steady, and equal; her shake is good; and her *Portamento* admirably free from the nose, mouth, or throat. There was such a roundness and dignity in all the tones, that every thing she did became interesting; a few plain flow notes from her, were more acceptable to the audience, than a whole elaborate air from any one else.

This singer is young, has good features, the *embonpoint charmant,* and is upon the whole a fine figure; but I cannot attribute all the improvement I now found in her voice to time; something must be given to the difference of theatres; those of Florence and Milan, are are at least twice as big as this at Vienna, which is about the size of our great opera-house; in the Hay-market. The opera of to-night was performed in the German theatre, where I had before seen

seen a tragedy. The two theatres of Vienna are never both open together, except on a Sunday or festival, at other times they are opened alternately.

The emperor, the arch-duke Maximilian, his brother, and his two sisters, the arch-duchesses Marianne, and Mary Elizabeth, were all at this burletta. The box, in which they sate, was very little distinguished from the rest; they came in and went out with few attendants, and without parade. The emperor is of a manly fine figure, and has a spirited and pleasing countenance; he often changes his place at the opera, to converse with different persons, and frequently walks about the streets without guards, seeming to shun, as much as possible, all kinds of unnecessary pomp. His imperial majesty was extremely attentive during the performance of the opera, and applauded the Baglione several times very much.

The

The admission into this theatre is at a very easy rate; twenty-four *Creuzers* only are paid for going into the pit; in which, however, there are seats with backs to them. A *Creuzer* here, is hardly equal to an English halfpenny; indeed, part of the front of the pit is railed off, and is called the amphitheatre; for places there, the price is doubled, none are to be had for money, except in the pit and the slips, which run all along the top of the house, and in which only sixteen *Creuzers* are paid. The boxes are all let by the season to the principal families, as is the custom in Italy.

The size of this theatre may be nearly imagined, by comparing with any one of our own, the number of boxes and seats in each. There are in this five ranks of boxes, twenty-four in each; in the pit there are twenty-seven rows of seats, which severally contain twenty-four persons.

Wednesday, September 2. This morning was dedicated to the delivering of letters, with which I was furnished to different persons in Vienna. Among whom, I must distinguish two, from whose acquaintance I derived great pleasure, as well as assistance in my musical researches; these were the *abáte Taruffi, uditore e segretario di legazione* to the pope's nuncio, to whom I was favoured with a letter from Mr. Baretti; and M. L'Augier, one of the principal physicians to the inperial court, to the knowledge of whom I was indebted to Col. St. Pol, and M. de Visme, who were both so kind as to write to him in my behalf.

It afforded me singular satisfaction to converse with the *abate Taruffi*, as I found him to have not only a general knowledge of every subject that was started, but possessed of a superior taste in literature and the arts; he speaks English, and is so perfectly acquainted with the writings
of

of our best authors, both in verse and prose, that he quotes them as readily and happily as a native of Great Britain.

During my first visit I made him acquainted with the particular object of my journey into Germany, and furnished him with the printed account of my tour through France and Italy. I was happy to find that he was a particular acquaintance of Metastasio and of Hasse, and the more so as he voluntarily offered to introduce me to both. He likewise promised to present me to the legate, and to the Duca di Bresciano, not only as to persons whose influence might be of use to me, from their high rank, but whose conversation, from their knowledge and love of music, might furnish both anecdotes and reflections well worth my attention. He favoured me with several interesting particulars relative to Metastasio, one of which was, that a young lady, the daughter of a deceased friend, who was born, educated, and who still lived in the fame houfe with him, had the greateft genius for mufic, in all its branches of playing, finging, and compofing, of any one living. Metaftafio, at firft, inftructed her, how to fet his fongs; but now fhe delights and even aftonifhes the great poet himfelf.

I was extremely curious to know what kind of mufic would beft fulfil the ideas of Metaftafio, when applied to his own poetry; and imagined that this young lady, with all the advantages of his inftructions, counfel, and approbation, combined with her own genius, muft be an *alter idem*, and that her productions would include every mufical embellifhment which could be fuperadded to his poetry, without deftroying or diminifhing its native beauty. Lord Stormont had kindly undertaken to bring about an interview, between Metaftafio and me; fo that till this had taken place, I was not at liberty to vifit him with Signor Taruffi; however, he promifed immediately

ately to read my book, and to apprize him of its contents, in order to prepare him for my acquaintance.

M. L'Augier, in defpight of uncommon corpulency, poffeffes a moſt active and cultivated mind. His houfe is the rendezvous of the firſt people of Vienna, both for rank and genius; and his converfation is as entertaining, as his knowledge is extenfive and profound. Among his other acquirements he has arrived at great ſkill in mufic, has a moſt refined and diſtiguiſhing taſte, and has heard *national melody* in all parts of the world with philofophical ears.

He has been in France, Spain, Portugal, Italy, and Conſtantinople, and is, in ſhort, a living hiſtory of modern mufic. In Spain he was intimately acquainted with Domenico Scarlatti, who, at seventy-three, compofed for him a great number of harpfichord leffons which he now poffeffes, and of which he favoured me with copies. The book in which they are transcribed, contains forty-two pieces, among which are several flow movements, and of all these, I, who have been a collector of Scarlatti's compositions all my life, had never seen more than three or four. They were composed in 1756, when Scarlatti was too fat to cross his hands as he used to do, so that these are not so difficult, as his more juvenile works, which were made for his scholar and patroness, the late queen of Spain, when princess of Asturias.

Scarlatti frequently told M. L'Augier, that he was sensible he had broke through all the rules of composition in his lessons; but asked if his deviations from these rules offended the ear? and, upon being answered in the negative, he said, that he thought there was scarce any other rule, worth the attention of a man of genius, than that of not displeasing the only sense of which music is the object*.

* Scarlatti was the first who dared to give way to fancy in his compositions, by breaking through

There

There are many passages in Scarlatti's pieces, in which he imitated the melody of tunes sung by carriers, muleteers, and common people. He used to say, that the music of Alberti, and of several other modern composers, did not, in the execution, want a harpsichord, as it might be equally well, or perhaps, better expressed by any other instrument; but, as nature had given him ten fingers, and, as his instrument had employment for them all, he saw no reason why he should not use them.

M. L'Augier sung to me several fragments of Bohemian, Spanish, Portuguese, and Turkish music, in which the peculiar expression depended on the *contre tems*, or breach of strict time; beat the mea-

---

the contracted prohibitions of rules drawn from dull compositions produced in the infancy of the art, and which seemed calculated merely to keep it still in that state. Before his time, the *eye* was made the sovereign judge of music, but Scarlatti swore allegiance only to the *ear*.

sure, and keep it as exactly as is necessary, in more refined and modern music, and it wholly loses its effect*.

He furnished me with an anecdote concerning Caffarelli and Gizziello, similar to that which I have given in my former journal, relative to Senesino and Farinelli.

When Gizziello first sung at Rome, his performance so far enchanted every hearer, that it became the general subject of conversation, which not only contributed to spread his fame through that city, but to extend it to the most remote parts of Italy; it is natural to suppose that the account of this new musical phenomenon soon reached Naples, and equally natural to imagine that it

* It has been supposed, that the ancient Greeks had scales of sounds, in which the *intervals* were divided into more minute parts, than any that are to be found in modern music; and it seems, as if our present divisions of *time*, were far from including every variety of measure possible.

was not heard with indifference in a place where so powerful a propensity to musical pleasure prevails. Caffarelli, at this time in the zenith of his reputation, was so far piqued by curiosity, perhaps by jealousy, that he took an opportunity, the first time he could be spared from the opera at Naples, to ride post all night, in order to hear that at Rome. He entered the pit, muffled up in a *pellice*, or fur-gown, unknown by any one there; and, after he had heard Gizziello sing a song, he cried out, as loud as he possibly could, *bravo! bravissimo! Gizziello, è Caffarelli che ti lo dice,* 'tis Caffarelli who applauds—and, immediately quitting the theatre, he set out on his return to Naples the same night.

M. L'Augier told me that the empress queen had been a notable musician. Some years ago he had heard her sing very well; and in the year 1739, when she was only twenty-two years of age, and very handsome, she sung a *duo* with Senesino, at Florence, so well, that, by

her

her voice, which was then a very fine one, and graceful and steady manner, she so captivated the old man, Senesino, that he could not proceed without shedding tears of satisfaction. Her imperial majesty has so long been a performer, that, the other day, in pleasantry, she told the old Faustina, the wife of Hasse, who is still living, and upwards of seventy years of age, that she thought herself the first, meaning the oldest, *virtuosa* in Europe; for her father brought her on the court stage, at Vienna, when she was only five years old, and made her sing a song.

The whole imperial family is musical; the emperor perhaps just enough for a sovereign prince, that is, with sufficient hand, both on the violoncello and harpsichord, to amuse himself, and sufficient taste and judgment to hear, understand, and receive delight from others. A person of great distinction told me, that he saw, some years ago, four arch-duchesses
of

of Auſtria, the emperor's ſiſters, appear at court in the opera of *Egeria*, written by Metaſtaſio, and ſet by Haſſe, expreſsly for their uſe. They were then extremely beautiful, ſung and acted very well, for princeſſes, and the grand duke of Tuſcany, who was likewiſe very handſome, danced, in the character of Cupid.

I found that M. L'Augier had himſelf been a good harpſichord player: he now reads and judges of muſic very accurately. During my firſt viſit, he was ſo obliging as to promiſe to make me acquainted with Haſſe, Gluck, Wagenſeil, Haydn, and all the muſicians that were worth my attention, in Vienna; and fixed on the next evening for giving me an opportunity of hearing ſome of Haydn's *quartettos*, performed with the utmoſt preciſion and perfection, as well as a little girl, of eight or nine years old, who is regarded here as a prodigy, on the harpſichord.

I had

I had the honour of dining to-day with his excellency lord Stormont, who had been so kindly attentive, as to invite a musical party to meet me; among whom were prince Poniatowski, brother to the king of Poland, a great lover of music, and the count and countess Thun. The countess, who interests herself very much in every thing that concerns music, and who reads and speaks English, honoured my Account of the Present State of Italian Music with an attentive perusal, as lord Stormont had done before: this enabled them to judge of my musical wants better than I could have done in conversation, without bearing too large a share in it.

Countess Thun has nothing about her that reminds one of the pride or heaviness attributed by travellers to the Germans: on the contrary, she is naturally and innocently chearful and humorous: has sallies of wit, and excites mirth by a
pleasant

pleasant irony, peculiar to herself. She had been so kind as to write a note to Gluck on my account, and he had returned, for *him*, a very civil answer; for he is as formidable a character as Handel used to be: a very dragon, of whom all are in fear. However, he had agreed to be visited in the afternoon; and lord Stormont and countess Thun had extended their condescension so far as to promise to carry me to him.

But before we set out, the duke of Braganza, and much other company, came in; lord Stormont did me the honour to present me to his highness, who is an excellent judge of music, and who condescended to converse with me a considerable time on the subject. This prince is a great traveller, having visited England, France, and Italy, before his arrival in Germany. He is very lively, and occasioned much mirth by his pleasantries, which were all seasoned with *good humour*.

His

His royal highness gave me an account of a Portuguese Abbé, whom lord Stormont and M. Laugier had before mentioned as a person of a very singular character; a kind of Rousseau, but still more original. He is of the most difficult access; refuses every offer of service in the way of money and presents, though he has nothing but his mass to subsist on, which produces him just fifteen pence a day. He is determined to be independent, and hates to be talked of by the world, and almost to talk to any one in it. The duke of Braganza, however, thought he had just interest sufficient to make him and me acquainted; and as another select musical party was forming on my account, for Friday, to dine with lord Stormont, the duke promised to do all in his power to bring this extraordinary Abate with him. His musical opinions are as singular as his character. He plays very well on the large Spanish guittar, though in a very peculiar style:

with

with little melody, but, with respect to harmony and modulation, in the most pleasing and original manner.

He is a professed enemy to the system of Rameau, and thinks the *Basse Fondamentale* the most absurd of all inventions; as it destroys all fancy, connection, and continuity, by perpetually tending to a *final close* and termination of whatever is begun: falling a fifth, or rising a fourth, cuts every thing off short, or makes the ear, which is accustomed to a fundamental base, uneasy till a passage is finished.

At five o'clock lord Stormont's coach carried madame Thun, his lordship, and myself, to the house of the chevalier Gluck, in the Fauxbourg St. Mark. He is very well housed there; has a pretty garden, and a great number of neat, and elegantly furnished rooms. He has no children; madame Gluck, and his niece, who lives with him, came to receive us at the door, as well as the veteran

teran composer himself. He is much pitted with the small-pox, and very coarse in figure and look, but was soon got into good humour; and he talked, sung, and played, madame Thun observed, more than ever she knew him at any one time.

He began, upon a very bad harpsichord, by accompanying his niece, who is but thirteen years old, in two of the capital scenes of his own famous opera of *Alceste*. She has a powerful and well-toned voice, and sung with infinite taste, feeling, expression, and even execution. After these two scenes from *Alceste*, she sung several others, by different composers, and in different styles, particularly by Traetta.

I was assured that mademoiselle Gluck had learned to sing but two years, which, considering the perfection of her performance, really astonished me. She began singing under her uncle, but he, in a precipitate fit of despair, had given her up;

up; when Signor Millico, arriving at Vienna about the same time, and discovering that she had an improvable voice, and a docile disposition, begged he might be allowed to teach her for a few months only, in order to try whether it would not be worth her while still to persevere in her musical studies, notwithstanding the late decision against her; which he suspected had its rise from the impatience and impetuosity of the uncle, more than the want of genius in the niece. Her performance now is an equal proof of the sagacity and penetration of Signor Millico, in making this discovery, and of the excellent method with which he conveys his instructions; for this young lady has so well caught his taste and expression, and made them so much her own, that they have none of the coldness of imitation, but seem wholly derived from her own feelings; and it is a style of singing, perhaps, still more irresistibly grateful and enchanting in a female,

male, than even in Signor Millico himself.

Mademoiselle Gluck is thin, seems of a delicate constitution, and, as she sings so much in earnest, I should fear for her health if she were to make singing a profession; but she is not intended for a public performer.

When she had done, her uncle was prevailed upon to sing himself; and, with as little voice as possible, he contrived to entertain, and even delight the company, in a very high degree; for, with the richness of accompaniment, the energy and vehemence of his manner in the *Allegros*, and his judicious expression in the slow movements, he so well compensated for the want of voice, that it was a defect which was soon entirely forgotten.

He was so good-humoured as to perform almost his whole opera of *Alceste*; many admirable things in a still later opera of his, called *Paride ed Elena*; and in a French a French opera, from Racine's *Iphigenie*, which he has juſt compoſed. This laſt, though he had not as yet committed a note of it to paper, was ſo well digeſted in his head, and his retention is ſo wonderful, that he ſung it nearly from the beginning to the end, with as much readineſs as if he had had a fair ſcore before him.

His invention is, I believe, unequalled by any other compoſer who now lives, or has ever exiſted, particularly in dramatic painting, and theatrical effects. He ſtudies a poem a long time before he thinks of ſetting it. He conſiders well the relation which each part bears to the whole; the general caſt of each character, and aſpires more at ſatisfying the mind, than flattering the ear. This is not only being a friend to poetry, but a poet himſelf; and if he had language ſufficient, of any other kind than that of ſound, in which to expreſs his ideas, I am certain he would be a great poet; as it is, music, in his hands, is a most copious, nervous, elegant, and expressive language. It seldom happens that a single air of his operas can be taken out of its niche, and sung singly, with much effect; the whole is a chain, of which a detached single link is but of small importance.

If it be possible for the partizans of *old French music* to hear any other than that of Lulli and Rameau, with pleasure, it must be M. Gluck's *Iphigenie*, in which he has so far accommodated himself to the national taste, style, and language, as frequently to imitate and adopt them. The chief obstacles to his fame, perhaps, among his contracted judges, but which will be most acceptable to others, is that there is frequently *melody*, and always *measure*, in his music, though set to *French words*, and for a *serious French opera*.

I reminded M. Gluck of his air, *Rasserena il Mesto Ciglio*, which was in such great

great favour in England, so long ago as the year 1745; and prevailed upon him, not only to sing that, but several others of his first and most favourite airs. He told me that he owed entirely to England the study of nature in his dramatic compositions: he went thither at a very disadvantageous period; Handel was then so high in fame, that no one would willingly listen to any other than to his compositions. The rebellion broke out; all foreigners were regarded as dangerous to the state; the opera-house was shut up, by order of the Lord Chamberlain, and it was with great difficulty and address that lord Middlesex obtained permission to open it again, with a temporary and political performance, *La Caduta de Giganti*. This *Gluck* worked upon with fear and trembling, not only on account of the few friends he had in England, but from an apprehension of riot and popular fury, at the opening of the theatre, in which none but foreigners and papists were employed.

He then studied the English taste; remarked particularly what the audience seemed most to feel; and finding that plainness and simplicity had the greatest effect upon them, he has, ever since that time, endeavoured to write for the voice, more in the natural tones of the human affections and passions, than to flatter the lovers of deep science or difficult execution; and it may be remarked, that most of his airs in *Orfeo* are as plain and simple as English ballads; and the additions that were made to it when first performed in England, by Messrs. Bach and Guglielmi, were of so different a texture, though excellent in another way, that they destroyed the *unity* of style and characteristic simplicity, for which, when performed at Vienna, this production was so much admired.

M. Gluck has developed his ideas of the necessary requisites of dramatic music so fully, in his dedication of *Alceste*, to the grand duke of Tuscany; and has given his reasons for deviating from the beaten

beaten track, with so much force and freedom, that I shall make no apology for presenting my readers, with an extract from it.

"When I undertook to set this poem, it was my design to divest the music entirely of all those abuses with which the vanity of singers, or the too great complacency of composers, has so long disfigured the Italian opera, and rendered the most beautiful and magnificent of all public exhibitions, the most tiresome and ridiculous. It was my intention to confine music to its true dramatic province, of assisting poetical expression, and of augmenting the interest of the fable; without interrupting the action, or chilling it with useless and superfluous ornaments; for the office of music, when joined to poetry, seemed to me, to resemble that of colouring in a correct and well disposed design, where the lights and shades only seem to

" to animate the figures, without altering
" the out-line.

" I determined therefore not to stop
" an actor, in the heat of a spirited dia-
" logue, for a tedious *ritornel*; nor to
" impede the progress of passion, by
" lengthening a single syllable of a fa-
" vourite word, merely to display agility
" of throat; and I was equally inflexible
" in my resolution, not to employ the
" orchestra to so poor a purpose, as that
" of giving time for the recovery of
" breath, sufficient for a long and un-
" meaning cadence.

" I never thought it necessary to hurry
" through the second part of a song,
" though the most impassioned and im-
" portant, in order to repeat the words
" of the first part, regularly four times,
" merely to finish the air, where the
" sense is unfinished, and to give an op-
" portunity to the singer, of shewing
" that he has the impertinent power
" of varying passages, and disguising
" them,

" them, till they shall be no longer
" known to the composer himself; in
" short, I tried to banish all those vices
" of the musical drama, against which,
" good sense and reason have in vain so
" long exclaimed.

" I imagined, that the overture ought
" to prepare the audience for the action
" of the piece, and serve as a kind of
" argument to it; that the instrumental
" accompaniment should be regulated by
" the interest of the drama, and not
" leave a void in the dialogue between
" the air and recitative; that they should
" neither break into the sense and con-
" nexion of a period, nor wantonly in-
" terrupt the energy or heat of the
" action.

" And lastly, it was my opinion, that
" my first and chief care, as a dramatic
" composer, was to aim at a noble sim-
" plicity; and I have accordingly shun-
" ed all parade of unnatural difficulty,
" in favour of clearness; nor have I
" fought

" fought or ftudied novelty, if it did not
" arife naturally from the fituation of
" the character, and poetical expreffion;
" and there is no rule of compofition,
" which I have not thought it my duty
" to facrifice, in order to favour paffion,
" and produce effects."

From this extract, the reader will infer, that the fymphonies to the fongs in his opera of *Alcefte*, are few and fhort; that there are no divifions in the voice-parts; no formal clofes at the end; fcarce any but accompanied recitatives, and that not one *da capo* is to be found throughout the piece; which, fay thofe who have feen it reprefented, was fo truly theatrical and interefting, that they could not keep their eyes a moment off the ftage, during the whole performance, having their attention fo irritated, and their confternation fo raifed, that they were kept in perpetual anxiety, between hope and fear for the event, till the laft fcene of the drama; fo that the mufic only gave energy or foftnefs to the
decla-

declamation, as the different situations of the several characters required. The syllables were indeed lengthened, and the tones of speech ascertained, but speech it still was, even in the airs, which are almost all of what the Italians call the *Parlante* or speaking kind.

But though M. Gluck studies simple nature so much in his *cantilena*, or voice-part; yet, in his accompaniments, he is not only often learned, but elaborate; and in this particular, he is even more than a *poet* and *musician*, he is an excellent *painter*; his instruments frequently dilineated the situation of the actor, and give a high colouring to passion.

While the chevalier Gluck was singing, count Brühl, a great *dilettante*, joined the company; he is a son of the famous Saxon minister, and plays in a very masterly manner upon several instruments.

From hence I was carried by lord Stormont to general Valmoden's, the Danish minister, quite on the opposite side

side of the city. There was an assembly of foreign ministers, and his lordship did me the honour to present me to the whole *Corps diplomatique*.

Thus ended this busy and important day, in which so much was said and done, that it seemed to contain the events of a much longer period, and I could hardly persuade myself, at night, upon recollecting the several incidents, that they had all happened in the space of about twelve hours.

Thursday 3d. At eleven o' clock this morning, by appointment, I waited upon lord Stormont, who was so kind as to go with me to the public library; and there, after being presented by his lordship to the librarians, and known to have the honour of being countenanced by him, I was not only at liberty to enter the library every day at the usual hours, but had admission even on holidays, and in vacation time, when it was denied to others; and was likewise favoured with

the

the attendance and assistance of the keepers of the books, at all times, with unlimited politeness and courtesy.

This library, which has not long been open to the public, is in possession of a very considerable number of manuscripts, as well as of ancient and modern printed books. The building has been lately enlarged, and the number of books greatly augmented by a purchase of the library of the late prince Eugene. The celebrated physician, baron Van Swieten, lately deceased, had been many years pricipal librarian, an office which was vacant during my residence at Vienna.

The principal room of the library is of an immense size, extremely lofty and much ornamented. There are marble statues in it of the emperors Charles the Vth, and Leopold. The books have lately undergone a new arrangement, and a new catalogue has been likewise made of them, by one of the *custodi*, or keepers. There is a large room set apart

for

for readers and transcribers; and another for the librarians and their assistants.

In my way to lord Stormont's, I stepped into St. Michael's church, in order to examine the organ, as it is one that was recommended to my attention, by Mr. Snetzler, on account of the singular disposition of its keys. This instrument has no front, the great pipes are placed, in an elegant manner, on each side of the gallery, and there is a box only in the middle, of about four feet square, for the keys and stops; so that the west window is left quite open. The compass of the organ, in the manuals, extends only from double E in the base, to C in alt; but the pedals of most German organs have an octave lower than the lowest note of the keys that are played by the hands, which is the case with this instrument. It has forty stops, and three sets of keys, which, by a spring of communication, can be played all together. The pipes

pipes are well-toned; and Mr. Wegerer, the prefent organift, though neither remarkable for tafte or fancy, plays in a full and mafterly manner.

St. Croix was another church which I entered this morning, and here I heard a band play during a *meſſa baſſa*; but the muſic was bad, and performance worſe; however, I was hemmed in by the crowd, and forced to ſtay and hear it, for near an hour, before I could get out decently.

This morning, the *Abate Taruffi* was ſo obliging as to return my viſit. He had already run over my book, and was ſufficiently apprized of my purſuits; after a long converſation at my lodging, he carried me to Signor Adolfo Haſſe, who lives in a handſome houſe in the ſuburbs, called the *Landſtraſs*. Signora Fauſtina was at the window, and ſeeing us ſtop at the door, came to meet us; I was preſented to her by my conductor. She is a ſhort, brown, ſenſible, and lively old woman; ſaid ſhe was much pleased to see a *Cavaliere Inglese*, as she had formerly been honoured with great marks of favour in England.

Signor Hasse soon entered the room; he is tall, and rather large in size, but it is easy to imagine, that in his younger days, he must have been a robust and fine figure; great gentleness and goodness appear in his countenance and manners. He seems to have been more ill-treated by time than Faustina, though he is younger than her by ten years. I presented him a letter, which Sir James Gray had done me the honour to write to him, and which he kept a good while in his hand unread, through politeness; but during this time the *Abate Taruffi* was giving an account of the views, with which I had already travelled through France and Italy, and which had now brought me to the capital of the German empire.

I had but a short time to stay, being engaged at M. L'Augier's concert, at which, as it was made on my account, I should have been extremely ashamed to arrive late; and yet, I was so impatient to see two persons of such distinguished merit, as Hasse and Faustina, that I could not resist my desire of going with Signor Taruffi, only for a quarter of an hour. At length Signor Hasse begged leave to retire to the light, in order to peruse the letter which I had delivered to him; during which time his two daughters came in; they are about twenty-eight or thirty years of age, not handsome, but so perfectly well-bred and agreeable in their manners, that it is easy to discover immediately, great care has been taken of their education; they read English, and speak it a little.

When Miss Davis, who played the Armonica, and her sister, who sung the first woman's part last year, in the great opera at Naples, resided at Vienna, they lodged in the same house with the Hasse family, and it was during this period, that the daughters of Signor Haſſe learned Engliſh of the two Miſs Davis's; and that this great maſter, by his inſtructions, enabled the youngeſt of them to ſing the principal part in the firſt opera of Europe.

Signor Haſſe ſoon returned, and was ſo eaſy and ſoft in his behaviour, that I felt myſelf as well acquainted with him in this quarter of an hour, as if I had known him twenty years. I ſaid all the civil things to him and the Fauſtina, that ſo ſhort a time would allow; indeed, nothing more than I felt; for from his works I had received a great part of my moſt early muſical pleaſure, and the delight they afforded me in youth, has not been diminiſhed ſince, by a more general acquaintance with the writings of other great compoſers; and therefore ſaying, that to ſee and converſe with him were among the moſt intereſting concerns which had brought me to Vienna, that his name was well known in England, and that he had long been my *magnus Apollo*, was moſt true. He received all this very humbly, and ſaid, that he had often been invited, and had often wiſhed to go to England, as he had known many perſons of that kingdom, from whom he had received great civilities.

I aſked him, if it would be poſſible to obtain a liſt of his works; but he ſaid he did not know it himſelf. However, he promiſed to try to recollect the principal of them, and the Fauſtina offered to help him. It was with infinite reluctance that I put an end to my viſit, juſt as we had made an acquaintance, and the worſt and formal part of the buſineſs was over; however, he invited me to come again as often as I could, enquired my lodgings, hoped I ſhould reſide ſome time at Vienna, and other ſuch common civilities as are little attended to, when beſtowed by perſons that are indifferent to us; but which, when uttered by thoſe

we

we love and reverence, make a deep impression.

From hence I went to Mr. L'Augier's concert, which was begun by the child of eight or nine years old, whom he had mentioned to me before, and who played two difficult lessons of Scarlatti, with three or four by M. Becke, upon a small, and not good Piano forte. The neatness of this child's execution did not so much surprise me, though uncommon, as her expression. All the *pianos* and *fortes* were so judiciously attended to; and there was such shading off some passages, and force given to others, as nothing but the best teaching, or greatest natural feeling and sensibility could produce. I enquired of Signor Giorgio, an Italian, who attended her, upon what instrument she usually practised at home, and was answered, " on the Clavichord." This accounts for her expression, and convinces me, that children should learn upon that, or a Piano Forte, very early, and be obliged to give an expreffion to lady Coventry's Minuet, or whatever is their firft tune; otherwife, after long practice on a monotonous harpfichord, however useful for ftrengthening the hand, the cafe is hopelefs.

The company was very numerous, and compofed of perfons of great rank; there was the princefs Piccolomini, to whom I had been honoured with a letter; the duke of Braganza, prince Poniatowfky, lord Stormont, general Valmoden and his lady, count Brühl, the duke of Brefciano, &c. &c. It was one of the fineft affemblies I ever faw. When the child had done playing, M. Mut, a good performer, played a piece on the fingle harp, without pedals, which renders it a very difficult inftrument, as the performer is obliged to make the femitones by brafs rings with the left hand, which being placed at the top of the harp, are not only hard to get at, but difagreeable to hear, from the noife, which, by a fudden motion of the hand they occasion. The secret of producing the semitones by pedals, is not yet arrived at Vienna; and the double harp is utterly unknown there. This player, though highly esteemed, did not fulfil all my ideas of the power of that instrument.

The room was too much crowded for full pieces: some trios only were played by Signor Giorgi, a scholar of Tartini, Conforte, a scholar of Pugnani, and by count Brühl, who is an excellent performer on many instruments, particularly the violin, violoncello, and mandoline. The pieces they executed were composed by Huber, a poor man, who plays the tenor at the playhouse; but it was excellent music, simple, clear, good harmony, and frequently fancy and contrivance.

Friday 4. This morning Signor Taruffi did me the honour of presenting me to the bishop of Ephesus, Monsignore Visconti, the pope's nuncio at the imperial court,

court, and descended from the famous family of Visconti, which once possessed the sovereignty of Milan*. His excellency is a notable musician, and sings in a very pleasing manner; he condescended to honour me with a long conversation, on the subject of music, and of my voyage into Italy, and even to shew and sing with me, some manuscript canons, of which he was pleased to permit me to take copies; he likewise gave me an Italian sonnet, transcribed with his own hand, which Metastasio had written at the desire of the present king of Poland, to a favourite Polish minuet, sent by that prince from Warsaw to Vienna for that purpose; and he finished by inviting me to dine with him on Sunday.

The Emperor went this day, for a month, to Laxemberg, where his mother, the

* Matthew Visconti, surnamed the Great, was acknowledged sovereign of Milan, in 1313; and John Galeas Visconti his grandson, who died in 1402, was the most celebrated of all the dukes of Milan.

Empress Queen then was; on this occasion, almoſt all the firſt people of Vienna were preparing to follow him. The night before his departure, at a kind of riding-houſe in the ſuburbs, there was a ſpecies of tilts and tournaments, which the Germans call 𝕮𝖆𝖗𝖗𝖔𝖚𝖘𝖊𝖑, 𝖊𝖎𝖓 𝕿𝖍𝖚𝖗𝖓𝖎𝖊𝖗 𝖟𝖚 𝕻𝖋𝖊𝖗𝖉, 𝖔𝖉𝖊𝖗 𝕽𝖎𝖓𝖌𝖊𝖑𝖗𝖊𝖓𝖓𝖊𝖓. The Emperor himſelf was one of the combatants on this occaſion; after which his imperial majeſty gave fire-works on the Danube, at which he was likewiſe preſent; but by viſiting Signor Haſſe, and by being at M. L'Augier's concert, I was prevented from going thither myſelf.

The muſical party, which dined to-day at lord Stormont's, was ſelect, and in the higheſt degree entertaining and pleaſing. It conſiſted of the prince of Poniatowſki, the duke of Braganza, the Portugueſe miniſter, count and counteſs Thun, M. L'Augier, the chevalier, madame and mademoiſelle Gluck, the Abate Coſta, &c. This Abate is the extraordinary muſician

musician that I mentioned before, who, disdaining to follow the steps of others, has struck out a new road, both as composer and performer, which it is wholly impossible to describe: all I can say of his productions is, that in them melody is less attended to than harmony and uncommon modulation; and that the time is always difficult to make out, from the great number of ligatures and fractions; however, his music, when well executed, which happens but seldom, has a very singular and pleasing effect: but it is certainly too much the work of art to afford great delight to any ears but those of the learned.

This Abate is possessed of as great a love for independence as M. Rousseau; he refuses every kind of assistance from the rich, though poor, with such inflexibility, that the duke of Braganza and he had a contention, which lasted a fortnight or three weeks, upon the following

occa-

occasion, in which, however, the Abate remained victorious.

He wanted very much to correct the imperfections of the finger-board of his guittar, which being strung with catgut, and having three strings to each tone, he found it frequently happen, that these strings, though perfectly in unison, when open, were out of tune when stopped, and this at some of the frets more than others; in order to obviate this, an ingenious mechanic was found, who, with great study and pains, invented moveable frets for each string; but as these were made of brass, and had taken up much of the workman's time to accommodate them, they amounted to four or five florins, a sum the Abate could not afford to pay, and yet he would by no means allow the duke of Braganza to do it. At length the dispute was ended by the duke taking the instrument at prime cost, and the Abate inventing a more cheap and

and simple method of correcting the finger-board of another, and this he effected in the following manner: he placed longitudinally, under the upper covering, or veneer, as many rows of catgut strings as there were strings upon his instrument; then cutting through the ebony at each fret, and laying these under strings open, he placed under them little moveable bits of ebony, which rendered the chords upon his instrument equally perfect in all keys. He can, at pleasure, take off this finger-board laterally; and as his modulation is very learned and extraneous, this expedient was the more necessary. But his compositions are not more original in this particular than in the measure; which, from its singularity, is very difficult to feel, and, consequently, to keep with any degree of exactness.

He played two movements on his guittar, before dinner, the subjects of which,

which, as nearly as I can remember, were thefe:

I fate between this Abate and the chevalier Gluck, during dinner, and we all three talked more than we eat. Gluck recounted to me the difficulties he had met with in difciplining the band, both of vocal and inftrumental performers, at the rehearfals of *Orfeo*, which was the firft of his operas that was truly dramatic; and even after it had fucceeded with the public, at the coronation of the prefent sent Emperor, as king of the Romans, upon which occasion it was first performed, the Empress Queen did not like it; however, hearing every one speak favourably of it at court, and finding it the general topic of conversation, she determined to give it a second hearing, after which her imperial majesty expressed her approbation of this opera, by sending the poet Calsabigi a diamond ring, and Gluck a rich purse, lined with a hundred ducats.

A few years since, a comic opera of Gluck's was performed at the Elector Palatine's theatre, at Schwetzingen: his Electoral highness was much struck with the music, and enquired who had composed it; and, upon being informed that it was the production of an honest German, who loved old hock; "I think, "says the Elector, he deserves to be "made drink for his trouble;" and ordered him a tun, not indeed quite so big
as

as that at Heidelberg, but a very large one, and full of excellent wine.

After dinner, a duet, for two violins, by the Abate, was tried by himself and M. Startzel, an excellent player, and as good a musician. This performer is remarkably happy in the composition of ballet and pantomime music, for the theatre; but the Abate Costa's duo was so difficult, both in time and style, that it was never well performed after twenty or thirty trials.

At length the company, which was now much encreased, became impatient to hear mademoiselle Gluck sing, which she did, sometimes with her uncle's accompaniment, on the harpsichord only, and sometimes with more instruments, in so exquisite a manner, that I could not conceive it possible for any vocal performance to be more perfect.

She executed, admirably, several entire scenes in her uncle's operas, of which the

the music was so truly dramatic, picturesque, and well expressed, that, if my conjecture be admissible, of the first vocal music being the voice of passion and cry of nature, the chevalier Gluck's compositions, and his niece's performance, entirely fulfill that idea.

In some scenes of great distress, in which the human heart is torn by complicated misery, by " horrors accumulate," it is then that M. Gluck, transported beyond the bounds of ordinary genius, gives such energy and colouring to passion, as to become at once poet, painter, and musician. He seems to be the Michael Angelo of music, and is as happy in painting difficult attitudes, and situations of the mind, as that painter was of the body; indeed, his expression of passion may sometimes be too strong for common hearers: but,

Il échappe souvent des sons à la douleur,
Qui sont faux pour l'oreille, & sont vrais pour le cœur.
DORAT.

Between the vocal parts of this delightful concert, we had some exquisite quartets, by Haydn, executed in the utmost perfection; the first violin by M. Startzler, who played the *Adagios* with uncommon feeling and expression; the second violin by M. Ordonetz; count Brühl played the tenor, and M. Weigel, an excellent performer on the violoncello, the base. All who had any share in this concert, finding the company attentive, and in a disposition to be pleased, were animated to that true pitch of enthusiasm, which, from the ardor of the fire within them, is communicated to others, and sets all around in a blaze; so that the contention between the performers and hearers, was only who should please, and who should applaud the most!

When this musical repast was over, I went home with M. L'Augier, to hear a Florentine poet, the Abate Casti, repeat his own verses, which he did from memory, for several hours, without the

least

least stop or hesitation. Lord Stormont and most of the company came after us, and stayed till twelve o'clock. This poet has energy, humour, fire, and invention; he has versified some of Boccaccio's and Voltaire's loosest tales, and written other very free ones himself.

Saturday 5th. This morning was spent in the imperial library, and at the countess Thun's, who was on the point of going to Laxemberg for a longer time than I was likely to stay at Vienna. This was an afflicting circumstance, as her house was always open to me, and she did every thing in her power to procure me entertainment and services.

She was now surrounded by her friends, who, though they were not in my situation, but were sure of seeing her again very soon, either here, or at Laxemberg; yet they had almost tears in their eyes, at the thoughts of losing her, only for a few days. During this visit she was so kind as to produce all
her

her musical curiosities, for me to hear and see, before we parted. Her taste is admirable, and her execution light, neat, and feminine; however, she told me that she *had* played much better than at present, and humourously added, that she had had six children, and that "every "one of them had taken something from "her." She is a chearful, lively, and beneficent being, whom every one here seems to love as a favourite sister. She is niece to the once handsome prince Lobkowitz, who was in England in 1745 and 46, and much connected with the famous count St. Germain, who made so much noise at that time, not only with his fiddle, but his mysterious conduct and equivocal character. This prince is now retired from the world, and will not see even his relations and best friends for many months together. He had cultivated music so far, as not only to play and to judge well, but even to compose in a superior manner; and

his

his niece gave me several of his pieces, which had great merit and novelty, particularly a song for two orchestras, which no master in Europe need be ashamed of.

In consequence of the application which lord Stormont had kindly made for my being introduced to Metastasio, his lordship had received a very polite message from him, with an assurance that he would be glad to see him and me, any evening his excellency would be pleased to appoint. This was a most desirable circumstance, as Metastasio is usually inaccessible of an afternoon, to all but his three or four select friends, and in a morning nothing but a general conversation could be obtained. Lord Stormont being engaged every day till Saturday, fixed on that afternoon for gratifying my desire of seeing and conversing with the favourite poet of every musician, who has the least knowledge of the Italian language. Saturday

turday was now come, and I was big with expectation for the event.

At six o'clock in the evening lord Stormont carried me to him. We found only one of his particular friends with him, who is likewise one of the imperial librarians, and the person to whom I had been introduced at the library, and who had arranged the visit.

This great poet is lodged, as many other great poets have been before him, in a very exalted situation, up no less than four pair of stairs. Whether modern bards prefer the sublimity of this abode, on account of its being somewhat on a level with Mount Parnassus, nearer their fire Apollo, or in the neighbourhood of gods in general, I shall not determine; but a more plain and humble reason can be assigned for Metastasio's habitation being " twice two stories high," if we consider the peculiar prerogative which the emperor enjoys at Vienna,

Vienna, of appropriating, to the use of the officers of his court and army, the *first floor* of every house and palace in that city, six or eight privileged places only excepted. On this account, princes, ambassadors, and nobles, usually inhabit the second stories; and the third, fourth, and even fifth floors, the houses being very large and high, are well fitted up, for the reception of opulent and noble families; and our poet, though he occupies that part of a house, which, in England, is thought only fit for domestics to sleep in, has, nevertheless, an exceeding good and elegant apartment, in which an imperial laureate may, with all due dignity, hold dalliance with the Muses.

He received us with the utmost chearfulness and good-breeding; and I was no less astonished than pleased at finding him look so well: he does not seem more than fifty years of age, though he is at least seventy-two*; and, for that time of life, he is the handsomest man I ever beheld There are painted on his countenance all the genius, goodness, propriety, benevolence, and rectitude, which constantly characterise his writings. I could not keep my eyes off his face, it was so pleasing and worthy of contemplation. His conversation was of a piece with his appearance: polite, easy, and lively. We got him to open upon music much more than we expected; for, in general, he avoids entering deep into any particular subject. He set off, however, by saying, that he could furnish me with very few new lights upon my subject, as he had never considered it with sufficient attention; however, in the course of our conversation, he discovered him-

---

* There is an edition of his opera of Giustino extant, which was printed in 1713; and as he was said to have been fourteen when he wrote that poem, it throws his birth into the last century.

self

self to have a very good general knowledge both of the history and theory of music; and I was very much flattered to find his sentiments correspond with my own in many doubtful particulars.

We discussed the following subjects: the musical scales of the ancient Greeks; their melody, chorus, modes, and declamation; the origin of modern harmony and operas; the fondness for fugues in the last century, and for noise in this, &c. &c.

He seems rather pleased with Mr. Hoole's translation of the two first volumes of his works; but thinks, with me, that if he has failed, it is more in the songs than recitatives: however, in excuse for Mr. Hoole, he says, that the case is hopeless in translating Italian poetry, for the language itself is so soft and musical, that no other can furnish words equivalent in sweetness. He likes no one of the many thousand translations and imitations of his *Grazi e agl' Inganni tuoi.*

tuoi. I asked him, if he was author of a duo to these words, which I had procured many years ago, and sung him the two or three first bars; and he said, " something like it."

We talked of the different editions of his works; he thinks those of Paris and Turin, in ten volumes, are the most complete and correct. These contain all that he intended to publish, except the opera of *Ruggiero*, performed at Milan last year; lord Stormont lamented that the pieces were not arranged in an exact chronological order; but Metastasio said, that it was of little moment to the public whether he wrote *Artaserse*, or *Didone* first; however, he confessed, that there were some particulars which gave birth to several of these pieces, which perhaps should be known.

Here he told us, that when his mistress, the Empress Queen was going to be married to the duke of Lorrain, he was applied to for an opera on the occasion,

and

and he had only eighteen days allowed him to write it in. He immediately cried out, that it was impossible; but, when he got home, he sketched out the story of *Achilles in Sciros*; he delineated a kind of argument upon a large sheet of paper; here he was to begin; thus far the first act; these the incidents of the second, and this, the catastrophe of the third. Then he distributed business to his several characters; here a song, here a duo, and here a soliloquy. He then proceeded to write the dialogue, and to divide it into scenes, which were severally given to the composer the moment they were finished, and by him to the performer to be got by heart. For the eighteen days included the whole arrangement of poetry, music, dancing, scenes, and decorations.

He said, that necessity frequently augmented our powers, and forced us to perform, not only what we thought ourselves incapable of, but in a much more expeditious,

tious, and often in a better manner, than the operations of our choice and leisure; he added, that *Hypermnestra* was produced in nine days, and it is remarkable, that *Achilles* and *Hypermnestra* are two of Metastasio's best dramas.

Lord Stormont asked if he had ever set any of his operas to music himself, and he answered, that he was not musician sufficient; he had, indeed, now and then given a composer the *motivo*, or subject of an air, to shew how he wished it should express his words; but no more. His lordship told him, that old Fontenelle had said, in his hearing, that no musical drama would be perfect, or interesting, till the poet and musician were one, as in ancient times; and that when Rousseau's *Devin du Village* came out, and so delighted every hearer, the literary patriarch Fontenelle, attributed its success to that union of poet and musician.

But Metastasio said, that musical composition, was now an affair of so much skill

skill and science, in regard to counterpoint, the knowledge of instruments, the powers of a singer, and other particulars, that it required too much time and application for a modern poet, or man of letters, to acquire them.

He said, he did not think there that was now one singer left, who could sustain the voice in the manner the old singers were used to do. I endeavoured to account for this, and he agreed with me, that theatrical music was become too instrumental; and that the cantatas of the beginning of this century, which were sung with no other accompaniment than a harpsichord or violoncello, required better singing than the present songs, in which the noisy accompaniments can hide defects as well as beauties, and give relief to a singer.

He seemed to think, that the music of the last age was in general too full of *fugues*, of parts, and contrivances, to be felt or understood, except by artists. All the

the different movements of the several parts, their inversions and divisions, he said, were unnatural, and, by covering and deforming the melody, only occasioned confusion.

He confirmed to me the story of his having been forced, by Gravina, to translate the whole Iliad of Homer into Italian *Ottave Rime*, at twelve years old. He likewise mentioned his having made verses *all' improvvisa* when young; but that he had discontinued the practice before he was seventeen.

Several jokes escaped him in the course of our conversation, and he was equally chearful, polite, and attentive, the whole time. We stayed with him just two hours; and, at my going away, he shook me by the hand, enquired where I lodged, and said he would wait on me; but I begged he would not give himself that trouble, saying that I should be perfectly happy in a permission to pay my respects to him again: he then desired me to come

come whenever I pleaſed, and aſſured me that he ſhould be always glad to ſee me.

He called for candles, and ſaid it was ſo dark that our words could not find the way to their deſtination. He ſpoke to his ſervant in German, ein Licht: upon which I aſked him if he had had patience to learn that language? he replied, "A few words only, to ſave my life:" meaning to aſk for neceſſaries, or he ſhould have been ſtarved to death.

Lord Stormont ſaid that news of a revolution in Sweden had arrived that morning. This occaſioned a political converſation for ſome time, which I wiſhed very much to have changed——— *Ecco,* ſays Metaſtaſio, turning to me, *un' altra ſcena per la drama!* Here's a new ſcene for the drama! He obſerved, that the intereſts of mankind were ſo various and ſo oppoſite, and even a man's own conceptions were ſo frequently at ſtrife

with

with themselves, that it was not possible for the world to go on without these sudden events, which should surprise no one who considers how full the head of man is of contradictions and caprice.

Sunday morning, 6th. In my way to the nuncio's, whence I was to set off with the Abate Taruffi, to make Metastasio another visit, I was stopt by a procession of, literally, two or three miles long, singing a hymn to the Virgin, in three parts, and repeating each stanza after the priests, in the van, at equal distances; so that the instant one company had done, it was taken up by another behind, till it came to the women in the rear, who, likewise, at equal distances, repeated, in three parts, the few simple notes of this hymn; and even after them it was repeated by girls, who were the last persons in the procession. When these had done, it was begun again by the priests. The melody was something like this:

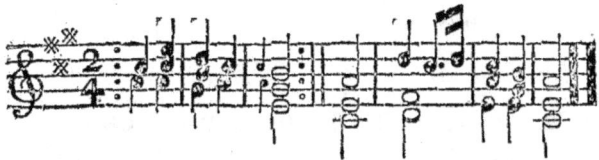

I was told by an Italian at Vienna, that the Auſtrians are extremely addicted to proceſſions, *portatiſſimi alle proceſſioni.* There were five or ſix of theſe proceſſions this morning; and yet it is obſerved, that they are much leſs frequent than formerly: however, not a day paſſed, while I remained in this city, without one or more to ſome church or convent: but all this helps to teach the people to ſing in different parts.

When Signor Taruffi and I arrived at Metaſtaſio's levee, we found about ſix or eight perſons with him, chiefly Italians; his excellency the governor of the city, came in after us. The great poet received me very courteouſly, and placed me on a ſopha, juſt by him. I now delivered him a letter from Mingotti, and Signor Taruffi read Mr. Baretti's ti's letter concerning me; so that here were many claims upon him: however lord Stormont had done the business completely, without any other help.

After the perusal of these letters, the conversation turned upon the poet Migliavacca, of Milan, who has long been laureate to the court of Dresden. Metastasio mentioned him with great praise: he said that he was a man of infinite knowledge, and of great genius; yet he wrote but little, for he had ideas of perfection which neither himself, nor perhaps any one else, could satisfy; besides, added Metastasio, " he has had but little " practice. And all is *habit* in mankind, " even *virtue itself*."

The discourse then became general and miscellaneous, till the arrival of a young lady, who was received by the whole company with great respect. She was well dressed, and had a very elegant appearance: this was Signora Martinetz, sister to Signor Martinetz, deputy
librarian

librarian at the imperial library, whose father was an old friend of Metastasio. She was born in the house in which he now lives, and educated under his eye: her parents were Neapolitans, but the name is Spanish, as the family originally was.

After the high encomiums bestowed by the Abate Taruffi on the talents of this young lady, I was very desirous of hearing and conversing with her; and Metastasio was soon so obliging as to propose her sitting down to the harpsichord, which she immediately did, in a graceful manner, without the parade of diffidence, or the trouble of importunity. Her performance indeed surpassed all that I had been made to expect. She sung two airs of her own composition, to words of Metastasio, which she accompanied on the harpsichord, in a very judicious and masterly manner; and, in playing the ritornels, I could discover a very brilliant finger.

The airs were very well written, in a modern style; but neither common, nor unnaturally new. The words were well set, the melody was simple, and great room was left for expression and embellishment; but her voice and manner of singing, both delighted and astonished me! I can readily subscribe to what Metastasio says, that it is a style of singing which no longer subsists elsewhere, as it requires too much pains and patience for modern professors: *è perduta la scuola; non si trova questa maniera di cantar; domanda troppa pena per i professori d'oggi dì.* I should suppose that Pistocco, Bernacchi, and the old school of singing, in the time of cantatas, sustained, divided the voice by minute intervals, and expressed words in this manner, which is not to be described: common language cannot express uncommon effects. To say that her voice was naturally well-toned and sweet, that she had an excellent shake, a perfect intonation, a facility of executing

cuting the moſt rapid and difficult paſſages, and a touching expreſſion, would be to ſay no more than I have already ſaid, and with truth, of others; but here I want words that would ſtill encreaſe the ſignificance and energy of theſe expreſſions. The Italian augmentatives would, perhaps, gratify my wiſh, if I were writing in that language; but as that is not the caſe, let me only add, that in the *portamento,* and diviſions of tones and ſemi-tones into infinitely minute parts, and yet always ſtopping upon the exact fundamental, Signora Martinetz was more perfect than any ſinger I had ever heard: her cadences too, of this kind, were very learned, and truly pathetic and pleaſing.

After theſe two ſongs, ſhe played a very difficult leſſon, of her own compoſition, on the harpſichord, with great rapidity and preciſion. She has compoſed a *Miſerere,* in four parts, with ſeveral

veral Pſalms, in eight parts, and is a moſt excellent contrapuntiſt.

The company broke up ſooner than I wiſhed, as it was Metaſtaſio's time for going to maſs. During this viſit, I diſcovered that Signora Martinetz, among her other accompliſhments, both reads and ſpeaks Engliſh. She invited me to come again, as did the divine poet; ſo that I now regarded myſelf as *amico della caſa*.

The imperial laureate was carried to church in a very elegant carriage, which I rejoiced to ſee: his talents and his virtues merit all that can be done for him. His penſion is about five hundred pounds ſterling a year, which, with his regular life and œconomy, enables him to live in a very reputable, though not ſplendid manner.

After dining with his excellency Monſignore Viſconti, his ſecretary carried me a ſecond time to the houſe of Signor Haſſe,

Hasse, in the 𝔏𝔞𝔫𝔡𝔰𝔱𝔯𝔞𝔰, the prettiest of all the Fauxbourgs of Vienna. It is a delightful drive of about a mile and half beyond the gates, and is within the lines, though without the walls; chiefly through one street, with frequent openings, that let palaces, churches, and fine houses, into the prospect.

We found all the family at home, and were very chearful and social. Signora Faustina is very conversable, and is still possessed of much curiosity concerning what is transacting in the world. She has likewise good remains, for seventy-two, of that beauty for which she was so much celebrated in her youth, but none of her fine voice! I asked her to sing—*Ah non posso!—hò perduto tutte le mie facoltà.* Alas! I am no longer able, said she, I have lost all my faculties.

I was extremely captivated with the conversation of Signor Hasse. He was easy, communicative, and rational; equally free from pedantry, pride, and prejudice.

dice. He spoke ill of no one; but, on the contrary, did justice to the talents of several composers that were occasionally named, even to those of Porpora; who, though his first master, was ever after his greatest rival. He thinks, with Metastasio, that the good school for singing is lost; and says, that since the time of Pistocco, Bernacchi, and Porpora, no great scholars have been made.

I asked him again for a list of his works, and he told me that he had set all the operas of Metastasio, except *Temistocle*; some of them three or four times over, and almost all of them twice: besides these, he had set many operas, written by Apostolo Zeno; for, in his youth, Metastasio did not write fast enough for him. To these compositions for the theatre, must be added fourteen or fifteen *Oratorios*, with *Masses, Misereres, Stabat Maters*, and *Salve Reginas*, for the church. Besides all which, he added, that his *Cantatas, Serenatas, Inter-*

mez-

mezzos, and *Duets* for voices; his trios, quartets, and concertos, for inſtruments, were ſo numerous, that he ſhould not know many of them again, if he was either to ſee or hear them. He modeſtly compared himſelf to animals of the greateſt fecundity, whoſe progeny were either deſtroyed during infancy, or abandoned to chance; and added, that he, like other bad fathers, had more pleaſure in producing, than in preſerving his offſpring. However, this cenſure muſt be confined to the offspring of his brain, for, as I before obſerved, he has taken great care of the education of his daughters.

During this viſit, theſe young ladies were ſo obliging as to ſing to me a *Salve Regina*, lately ſet by their father, in *duo*. It is an exquiſite compoſition, full of grace, taſte, and propriety.

One of his daughters has a ſweet *ſoprano voce di camera*, of which the tone is delicate and intereſting: the other has
a rich

a rich and powerful *contralto* voice, fit for any church or theatre in Europe: both have good shakes, and such an expression, taste, and steadiness, as it is natural to expect in the daughters and scholars of Signor Hasse and Signora Faustina.

After the *Salve Regina*, these excellent performers sung several airs, in different styles, of their father's composition, in a truly noble and elegant manner.

Signor Hasse is so much afflicted with the gout, that his fingers are stiff, and distorted with it; and yet there are remains of a great player, in his manner of touching the harpsichord, and of accompanying; nor is it for want of knowing learned, extraneous, and equivocal modulation, that he is so sparing of it in his works. He played me an extempore *Toccato* or *Capriccio*, in which he introduced some that was truly wonderful; but he has too sound a judgment, to lavish upon common and trivial occasions,

what

what should be reserved for extraordinary purposes. His modulation is, in general, simple, his melody natural, his accompaniments free from confusion; and, leaving to fops and pedants all that frights, astonishes, and perplexes, he lets no other arts be discoverable in his compositions, than those of pleasing the ear, and of satisfying the understanding.

His daughters complain of want of practice, and say they hardly ever sing; for their father is always either ill or busy.

He is going, next spring, to Venice, the birth-place of Signora Faustina; and it seems as if they both had determined to spend the rest of their days there.

It does not appear that Signor Hasse has at present either pension or employment at Vienna. He had great losses during the last war; all his books, manuscripts, and effects were burned at the bombardment of Dresden, by the King of of Pruſſia, to a very confiderable amount. He was going to print a complete edition of all his works; the late king of Poland promifed to be at the expence of paper and prefs; but after M. Breitkopf, of Leipzig, had made a beginning, and got together materials for the whole impreſſion, the war broke out, and put an end to all his hopes from this enterprize, and to thofe of the public. He, however, does great juftice to the muſical talents of the King of Pruſſia; and is even fo candid, as to fay, that he believes, if his majefty had known that contingencies would have obliged him to bombard Drefden, he would previoufly have apprized him of it, that he might have faved his effects.

Fauftina, who is a living volume of muſical hiftory, furnifhed me with many anecdotes of her cotemporary performers, She fpoke much of Handel's great ftyle of playing the harpfichord and organ when fhe was in England, and faid, fhe remem-

remembered Farinelli's coming to Venice, in the year 1728, and the rapture and aſtoniſhment with which he was then heard.

Monday 7th. This whole morning was ſpent in the public library, in ſearch of old Miſſals, muſical treatiſes, and compoſitions. M. Martinetz, brother to the young lady whom I had heard ſing and play her own compoſitions ſo well at Metaſtaſio's, attended and aſſiſted me the whole time. I aſked him, of whom his ſiſter learned muſic, and where ſhe had acquired her expreſſive manner of ſinging; he ſaid, ſhe had had ſeveral maſters to teach her the grammar and mechaniſm of muſic; but that it was Metaſtaſio who had done the reſt.

I obtained the following particulars from a perſon of high rank, who has reſided at Vienna ſo long, that he is perfectly acquainted with the hiſtory of muſical people.

The

The great singer signora Tesi, who was a celebrated performer, upwards of fifty years ago, lives here; she is now more than eighty, but has long quitted the stage. She has been very sprightly in her day, and yet is at present in high favour with the Empress Queen. Her story is somewhat singular. She was connected with a certain count, a man of great quality and distinction, whose fondness, encreased by enjoyment, to such a degree as to determine him to marry her: a much more uncommon resolution in a person of high birth on the continent than in England. She tried to dissuade him; enumerated all the bad consequences of such an alliance; but he would listen to no reasoning, nor take any denial. Finding all remonstrances vain, she left him one morning, went into a neighbouring street, and addressing herself to a poor labouring man, a journeyman baker, said she would give him fifty ducats if he would marry her; not
with

with a view to their cohabiting together, but to serve a present purpose. The poor man readily consented to become her nominal husband: accordingly they were formally married; and when the count renewed his solicitations, she told him it was now utterly impossible to grant his request, for she was already the wife of another; a sacrifice she had made to his fame and family.

Since this time she has lived, many years, with a man of great rank at Vienna, of near her own age; probably in a very chaste and innocent manner.

The Teuberinn, another celebrated opera singer, likewise resides here; but, she is peremptorily ordered by her physician never to sing again. Her health was so impaired in Russia, that it is pronounced by the faculty, that the exercise of her former profession would certainly be fatal to her.

It was the Tesi who taught both the Teuberinn and De Amici to sing as well as to act. She had in her youth been very superior to all her cotemporaries in both capacities of singer and actress, and was afterwards remarkably happy in conveying instructions to her pupils.

Sept. 8. I expected that this would be a fruitless day, with regard to my musical researches; it was a great festival; the library was shut up, and all the world was in *gala*, and at their devotions; it is pleasant enough to walk the streets on these days, and see the people, freed from toil and care, appear all clean and chearful.

The Portuguese abate called on me early in the morning, and after a long musical discourse, he invited me to his room, to hear some of his compositions on the guittar, in peace and quiet, which it had been impossible to do at lord Stormont's; he hates mortally more than two or three hearers at a time. I followed him to his garret, more than twice two stories high; here he played the same pieces

pieces as at lord Stormont's, but with more effect, in ſtill ſilence. He is quite original in his ideas and modulation, but repeats his paſſages too often.

From hence, I went to St. Stephen's cathedral, where high maſs was juſt begun, on account of its being the Nativity of the Virgin. The band was reinforced; there were more than the uſual number of inſtruments, as well as voices; but the organ was inſufferably out of tune, which contaminated the whole performance. In other reſpects, the muſic, which was chiefly by Colonna, was excellent in its kind, conſiſting of fugues well worked, much in Handel's way, with a bold and active baſe. Some fine effects were produced with the *fortes* and *pianos*, by ſtriking the firſt note of a bar loud, the reſt ſoft,

and by introducing a piece of pathetic

for voices only, in the middle of a noisy, full, instrumental chorus.

There was a girl, who sung a solo verse, in the *Credo*, extremely well, in a *mezzo soprano* voice; her shake and style of singing were good. There were likewise several symphonies for instruments only, composed by M. Hofman, *maestro di capella* of this church, which were well written and well executed, except that the hateful sour organ, poisoned all whenever it played. In the music composed by M. Hofman, though there was great art and contrivance, yet the modulation was natural, and the melody smooth and elegant. "As much art as "you please in your music, gentlemen", said I, frequently, to the Germans, "provided it be united with nature; and "even in a marriage between art and "nature, I should always wish the lady "to wear the breeches."

In the afternoon, I called on M. L'Augier, and there, among other company

pany met again with the Florentine poet, Abate Casti, who repeated several of his poems, particularly, a tale from Voltaire, called *L'Art d'élever une Fille*; which was extremely arch and comic.

M. L'Augier being in the service of the court, was obliged to attend the emperor the next day at Laxemberg; I was sorry to lose him, as his house was an excellent retreat, when I could spare time to enjoy it; and his conversation concerning music and musicians was in a particular manner entertaining and profitable.

He blamed me much for not continuing the whole winter at Vienna, but if I had stayed a full year in every great city of Europe, the inhabitants would have thought its curiosities and importance merited still more attention; and what a longevity must I be possessed of, to gratify such patriotism? and when would my enquiries, and my history end? When M. L'Augier said, that Vienna deserved a much longer visit, I asked him, after Hasse, Gluck, and Wagenseil, what more great muficians were to be found in this city? Haydn, Ditters, and Scarlatti, the nephew to Dominico Scarlatti, were out of town; I knew there were Gafman, Vanhall, Hofmann, Mancini; and he added Kohaut, a great lutanift, La Motte, a violinift, and Venturini, a hautboy; but moft of thefe I could fee and hear, before my departure. To get admiffion into the archives of the imperial chapel, was now the moft important bufinefs I had to tranfact; and my Portuguefe Abate had promifed to introduce me to M. Gafman, the Emperor's *maeftro di capella*, for that purpofe.

After quitting M. L'Augier, I vifited M. Wagenfeil, where I found my good friend the Abate Cofta, who had played the precurfor, and prepared him for my arrival.

Wagenfeil is rather in years, thin, and infirm; he was confined to his couch, but received me very politely, and converfed freely on the fubject of mufic for

for a confiderable time; he has a great refpect for Handel, and fpeaks of fome of his works with rapture; he could not ftir from his feat, and his left hand had been fo ill treated by the gout, that he was hardly able to move two of his fingers. However, at my urgent requeft, he had a harpfichord wheeled to him, and he played me feveral *capriccios*, and pieces of his own compofition, in a very fpirited and mafterly manner; and though I can eafily believe, that he once played better; yet, he had fufficient fire and fancy left to pleafe and entertain, though not to furprife me very much; he was fo obliging as to promife me copies of feveral of his manufcript compofitions for the harpfichord, and to make a fmall mufical party for me, at his houfe, in order to give me an opportunity of hearing fome of his fcholars.

He has been confined to his room thefe feven years by a lamenefs, which came on by degrees in a very uncommon manner. The finews of his right thigh are contracted, and the circulation ſtopt; ſo that it is become incurably withered, and uſeleſs. He is fifty-eight years of age, was a ſcholar of Fux, and many years maſter to the Empreſs Queen, on which account he ſtill enjoys a penſion of fifteen hundred florins a-year. He is now nominal maſter to the arch-ducheſſes, for which he has, likewiſe, a ſmall penſion.

Theſe are fortunate circumſtances for a perſon totally incapable of quitting his room, in order to exerciſe his profeſſion. However, he teaches at home, and compoſes, by which he ſomewhat augments his income; and, as he is luckily a ſingle man, and Vienna not a dear place for the natives to live in, he may be ſuppoſed in eaſy circumſtances.

The diverſions for the common people of this place, are ſuch as ſeem hardly fit for a civilized and poliſhed nation to allow. Particularly the *combats*, as they are

are called, or baiting of wild beasts, in a manner much more savage and ferocious than our bull-baiting, throwing at cocks, and prize-fighting of old, to which the legislature has so wisely and humanely put a stop*.

These

---

* The most exact and least suspicious description I can give of these diversions will be literally to translate a hand-bill, such as is distributed through the streets every Sunday and festival.

"This day, by imperial licence, in the great "amphitheatre, at five o'clock will begin the fol- "lowing diversions.

"1st. A wild Hungarian ox, in full fire, "(that is, with fire under his tail, and crackers "fastened to his ears and horns, and to other "parts of his body), will be set upon by dogs.

"2d. A wild boar will, in the same manner, "be baited by dogs.

"3d. "A great bear will, immediately after, "be torn by dogs.

"4th. A wolf will be hunted by dogs of the "fleetest kind.

5th. "A very furious and enraged wild bull "from Hungary, will be attacked by fierce and "hungry dogs.

6th. "A fresh bear will be attacked by hounds.

7th. "Will

These barbarous spectacles, are usually attended by two or three thousand people, among whom are a great number of ladies!

Wednesday 9th. This morning, I went, with the Abate Costa, to M. Gassman, *maestro di capella del corte imperiale*. He was very obliging, and did me the favour to shew me all his curious books and manuscript compositions.

He surprised me much by the number of fugues, and chorusses, which he shewed me of a very learned and singular construction, which he had made as exercises and

7th. "Will appear a fierce wild boar, just
" caught, which will now be baited for the first
" time, by dogs defended with iron armour.
8th. " A beautiful African tyger.
9th. " This will be changed for a bear.
10th. " A fresh and fierce Hungarian ox.
11th. " And lastly, a furious and hungry bear,
" which has had no food for eight days, will at-
" tack a young wild bull, and eat him alive up-
" on the spot; and if he is unable to complete
" the business, a wolf will be ready to help him."

and ſtudies. Some of them were compoſed in two or three different *times,* as well as upon two or three different *ſubjects*; and ſeveral of theſe, he ſaid, the emperor had practiſed.

M. Gaſman is accuſed by ſome of want of fire in his theatrical compoſitions; but the gravity of his ſtyle is eaſily accounted for, by the time and pains he muſt have beſtowed on church muſic. To aim at equal perfection in both, is trying to ſerve God and Mammon; and thoſe excellent compoſers for the church, whoſe works have ſurvived them, ſuch as Paleſtrina, Tallis, Birde, Allegri, Benevoli, Colonna, Caldara, Lotti, Perti, and Fux, have confined themſelves wholly to the church ſtyle. Aleſſandro Scarlatti, Handel, Pergoleſi, and Jomelli, are exceptions. But, in general, thoſe ſucceed beſt in writing for the church, ſtage, or chamber, who accuſtom themſelves to that particular ſpecies of compoſition only.

I do not call every modern oratorio, maſs, or motet, *church muſic*; as the ſame compoſitions

compositions to different words would do equally well, indeed often better, for the stage. But by *Musica di Chiesa*, properly so called, I mean grave and scientific compositions for voices only, of which the excellence consists more in good harmony, learned modulation, and fugues upon ingenious and sober subjects, than in light airs and turbulent accompaniments.

There are two musical archives or libraries belonging to the Imperial theatre and chapel. Of one, the emperor had taken away the key; but it contained only the works of composers, who had flourished in the present century, such as Fux, Telemann, Handel, and Porpora. Of the other, M. Gasman had the key, and promised to go with me thither the next day: the public library occupied the rest of this.

There was music every day, during dinner, and in the evening at the inn, where I lodged, which was the Golden Ox;

Ox; but it was ufually bad, particularly that of a band of wind inftruments, which conftantly attended the ordinary. This confifted of French horns, clarinets, hautboys, and baffoons; all fo miferably out of tune, that I wifhed them a hundred miles off.

In general I did not find that delicacy of ear among the German ftreet-muficians, which I had met with in people of the fame rank and profeffion in Italy. The church organs being almoft always out of tune here, may be occafioned by the parfimony or negligence of the clergy, bifhop, or fuperior of a church or convent; but the being, or ftopping, in or out of tune, among ftreet muficians, muft depend on themfelves, and on their organs being *acute* or *obtufe*.

It is perhaps not eafy to determine what kind of air is moft fit for the propagation of mufical found; whether thick or thin, moift or dry; and if this were determined, it might ftill be doubted in
what

what kind of air mufic would be heard to the greateſt advantage, becauſe, poſſibly, that air which is moſt favourable to the tranſmiſſion of ſound, abſtractedly conſidered, may render the organs, by which it is perceived, leſs acutely ſenſible.

Thurſday 10th. This morning Signor Mancini, of Bologna, ſinging maſter to the Imperial court and family, was ſo obliging, at the requeſt of the auditor Taruffi, as to call on me at my lodgings. He was a ſcholar of Bernacchi, and has been fifteen years in the ſervice of this court. He has taught eight of the archdutcheſſes to ſing, moſt of whom, he ſays, had good voices, and had made a conſiderable progreſs, particularly the princeſs of Parma, and the arch-dutcheſs Elizabeth, who have good ſhakes, a good *portamento*, and great facility of executing ſwift diviſions.

Signor Mancini ſpeaks with much intelligence of his art, and I was greatly pleaſed

pleased with his conversation. He has for some time been writing a book upon the art of singing, which is in great forwardness; and it is hoped that a person of such consummate knowledge, and long experience, will not keep from the world a work so much wanted, as a well-written, profound, and, at the same time, practical treatise on the art of singing.

I obtained from this able professor, a list of the Pistocco and Bernacchi school. Bernacchi was the scholar of Pistocco, but his voice was never naturally good; and when he sung, for the first time, at a church in Bologna, he was so very much disliked, that some of his acquaintance peremptorily told him, he should leave off singing, unless he could perform better. This stimulated and piqued him to take uncommon pains, well knowing that there was then no possibility of changing his profession: a castrato has seldom strength or spirit sufficient for any other employment than that of music; he therefore went seriously

riously to work, and, by a severe study, acquired a style and manner of singing, which was afterwards the standard of perfection in that art.

His principal scholars were Antonio Pasi, Geo. Battista Minelli, Bartolomeo di Faenza, Mancini, and Guarducci.

Signor Mancini thinks it practicable, with time and patience, not only to give a shake where nature has denied it, but even to give voice; that is, to make a bad one tolerable, and an indifferent one good, as well as to extend the compass: always observing the natural tendency of the organ.

He told me of a curious operation performed frequently at Naples, of cutting the glands of the throat, when so inflated, or big, as to obstruct the free passage of the voice.

For the shake, he thinks it ruined ninety-nine times out of a hundred, by too much impatience and precipitation, both
in

in the master and scholar; and many who can execute passages, which require the same motion of the larynx as the shake, have notwithstanding never acquired one. There is no accounting for this, but from the neglect of the master to study nature, and avail himself of these passages, which, by continuity, would become real shakes.

On quitting Signor Mancini, I hastened to M. Gasman, who was waiting to carry me to the Imperial musical library. I found in it an immense collection of musical authors, but in such disorder, that their contents are, at present, almost wholly unknown. However, M. Gasman has begun a catalogue, and is promised, by the Emperor, a large and more commodious room for these books, than the present, in which they are promiscuously piled, one on another, in the most confused manner imaginable. Yet I found a great number of curious

rious things from the beginning of counterpoint to the prefent time. Indeed the quantity of mufic here, of the Emperor Leopold's collecting, which is uniformly bound, in white vellum, with his arms on the back, is almoft incredible; it feems to be all that Italy and Germany had then produced: and for operas, in fcore, and parts, the lift of fuch only as have been performed at this court, would fill a folio volume.

M. Gafman has affured me, that in the courfe of his writing a complete catalogue, he will remark all that is curious in this collection, both as to theory and practice, and will communicate it to me by letter; and for this purpofe he defired me to give him my addrefs in England, which I wrote on parchment, and left in the library.

I went again this afternoon to Wagenfeil's; he had with him a little girl, his fcholar, about eleven or twelve years old,

old, with whom he played duets upon two harpsichords, which had a very good effect. The child's performance was very neat and steady. M. Wagenseil was so kind as to promise, at my request, to get, if possible, some of his duets, and other new pieces, transcribed for me by Sunday, when I was to return to him again, to hear them accompanied by violins, and to take my leave: there was a young count here, another of his scholars, who had a very rapid finger, and who executed some very difficult harpsichord lessons with great precision. My friend, the ingenious and worthy Portuguese abate, was likewise of the party.

From hence I went to the opera, which was *i Rovinati*, composed by Gasman, who was at the harpsichord. Whether his civilities in the morning had operated secretly on my mind and ears, I cannot tell: but this music pleased me much more than any of his compositions which I had heard before. There was a con-

trast,

trast, an opposition and dissimilitude of movements and passages, by which one contributed to the advantage and effect of another, that was charming; and the instrumental parts were judiciously and ingeniously worked.

A song of Clementina Baglioni, and a scolding *duo* between her and the second woman, who was a German, and who, indeed, performed but indifferently, were encored. The men who sung to-night pleased me more than those I had heard before; a tenor, in particular, discovered much taste, and had a pleasing, though not powerful voice. These vague accounts of anonymous singers, will afford the reader but small satisfaction; but it is all I am able to give him of performers of a lower order, as the names of singers are never printed in the *dramatis personæ* of Italian operas in Germany, and memory seldom assists us in retaining the names of either persons, or things, that are indifferent to us.

Friday

Friday 11th. This morning I went to take leave of the chevalier Gluck; and, though it was near eleven o'clock, when I arrived, yet, like a true great genius, he was still in bed; *Madame* told me, that he usually wrote all night, and lay in bed late to recruit. Gluck, when he appeared, did not make so good a defence but frankly confessed his sluggishness, *je suis un peu poltron ce matin.* The niece too was not yet visible, and the aunt in her defence, said, that she encouraged her sleeping in the morning; *pour fortifier la poitrine,* to strengthen the lungs; and, I believe she was right, for this excellent little performer is far from robust.

M. Gluck and I had a long conversation concerning musical and dramatic effects; concerning *those* which had been produced in his *Orfeo* at Vienna ten years ago, when it was first performed; and three or four years since, when it was revived at Parma, upon the marriage of the arch-duchess, Amelia, with the present duke; as well as at Bologna, last year. He is a great disciplinarian, and as formidable as Handel used to be, when at the head of a band; but he assured me, that he never found his troops mutinous, though he, on no account, suffered them to leave any part of their business, till it was well done, and frequently obliged them to repeat some of his manœuvres twenty or thirty times. This was the best proof he could give of the wholesomness of his discipline; for there is a strong presumption, that, when it is endured without murmur, by men not absolute slaves to their commander, they are convinced of its expediency.

Before we parted, which we did on very good terms, he furnished me with copies in score of his two last operas of *Alceste* & *Paride*, and promised to send me a copy of his famous ballet of *Don Juan*

Juan the next morning; and he kept his word.

From hence I went to Metaſtaſio where I was immediately admitted, though he was in diſhabille, and juſt going to dreſs.

Mademoiſelle Martinetz was at her muſical ſtudies, and writing; ſhe directly complied with my requeſt, of ſitting down to the harpſichord. Metaſtaſio deſired her to ſhew me ſome of her beſt ſtudies; and ſhe produced a pſalm for four voices, with inſtruments. It was a moſt agreeable *Meſcolanza,* as Metaſtaſio called it, of *antico e moderno*; a mixture of the harmony, and contrivance of old times, with the melody and taſte of the preſent. It was an admirable compoſition, and ſhe played and ſung it in a very maſterly manner, contriving ſo well to fill up all the parts, that though it was a full piece, nothing ſeemed wanting. The words of this pſalm were Italian, and of Metaſtaſio's tranſlation.

After this she obliged me with a Latin *motet*, for a single voice, which was grave and solemn, without languor or heaviness; and then played me a very pretty harpsichord *sonata* of her own, which was spirited, and full of brilliant passages.

I could not finish this visit till I had petitioned Mademoiselle Martinetz to oblige me with copies of some of her compositions, which she readily granted; and I had my choice of whatever had pleased me most among the pieces which I had heard.

I had the honour of dining with lord Stormont to-day, for the sixth and last time, as he was to set out on a journey at four o'clock the next morning: his lordship was extremely kind to the last, offering me letters to Dresden, Berlin, and Hamburg. The frequent mention of these honours, will, I fear, have the appearance of vanity; but a total silence about

about them, would surely favour of the worse vice of ingratitude.

After this I made a short visit to signor Taruffi, and then a very long one to Signor Hasse, who to-day read the plan of my history, in German, with great attention, and talked over every article of it with the utmost cordiality. It was an infinite satisfaction to me, I must own, to find my ideas similar in almost all points, to those of such a man as this; whose merit has been universally felt, and is now universally allowed.

He said, that his first opera was *Antigono*, which he set, when he was only eighteen years of age, before he went into Italy. On his arrival at Naples, he was thought a very good player on the harpsichord. He studied at first a little while under Porpora, as I had been before told by Barbella; but Hasse denied, that it was Porpora who introduced him to old Scarlatti. He says, that the first time Scarlatti saw him, he luckily conceived

ceived such an affection for him, that he ever after treated him with the kindness of a father.

When he went back into Germany, he was taken into the service of the Elector of Saxony, who made him set *Antigono* again. After this, he set a German opera, which, with one more, was all he ever worked upon in that language.

As he was born near Hamburg, he told me, that he was not only glad I was going thither, as it was his country, but, as I should see the great Emanuel Bach there, whom he very much respected, and hear the best organists and organs, of any part of the world, unless they were much degenerated since he was there. Above all things, he recommended to me the soliciting Bach, to let me hear him upon the clavichord; and likewise desired me to enquire after a symphony of that author in E *la mi*, minor, which he thought the finest he had ever heard.

I asked him about the disposition of the orchestra at Dresden, in 1754, mentioned by Rousseau in his dictionary, as the best possible. He said, this author's account of it was so exact, that he should suppose him to have been there at the time. The king of Poland had then given Hasse unlimited power; and he had every thing of the best kind, both in vocal and instrumental music, which it was possible for him to assemble together.

He frequently attended that prince to Warsaw, in Poland, where he composed several operas. He said the Polish music was truly national, and often very tender and delicate. He mentioned to me a song which he had made in the Polonoise style, which was one of the most singular and the best received of any one of his compositions: of this he promised me a copy, as well as of many other of his most curious and choice pieces.

In speaking of composers, he commended, the most of all, old Scarlatti,

and

and Keiſer *: Keiſer, he aſſured me, was, according to his conceptions, one of the greateſt muſicians the world ever ſaw. His compoſitions are more voluminous than thoſe of old Scarlatti, and his melodies, though more that fifty years old, are ſuch as would now be thought modern and graceful. This he ſaid had been always his opinion; and he was not likely to be biaſſed by prejudice, as this compoſer was neither his relation, his maſter, nor even his acquaintance; but having lately looked at ſome of his works, he was aſtoniſhed to ſee ſo much more elegance, clearneſs, and grace, than are to be found in moſt modern compoſitions, even now. He added, that Keiſer compoſed chiefly for Hamburg, and, in general, to the German language. He was not very well verſed in Italian, and often blundered in ſetting words; but

* He was born at Weiſſenfels, in Saxony, and was *maeſtre di capella* to the duke of Mecklenburg.

had always merit of other kinds to compenfate this defect.

He always fpoke refpectfully of Handel, as a player and writer of fugues, as well as for the ingenuity of his accompaniments, and the natural fimplicity of his melody, in which particulars he regarded him as the greateft genius that ever exifted; but faid, that he thought him too ambitious of difplaying his talent of working parts and fubjects, as well as too fond of noife: and Fauftina added, that his *cantilena* was often rude.

I afked him, if he had ever heard Domenico Scarlatti play? he faid that he had: as he came from Portugal to Naples, on a vifit to his father, while he ftudied under him; and he allowed him to have been poffeffed of a wonderful hand, as well as fecundity of invention.

He could not think Durante, as a contrapuntift, deferved the place which M. Rouffeau has given him in his dictionary; but faid that it was old Scarlatti, whom

he

he should have called *le plus grand harmoniste d'Italie, c'est à dire du monde,* the greatest master of harmony of Italy, that is, of the whole universe; and not Durante, who was not only dry, but *baroque,* that is, coarse and uncouth *.

He spoke of mademoiselle Martinetz, as a young person of uncommon talents for music: said that she sung with great expression, played very neat and masterly, and was a thorough contrapuntist; but, added he, " it is pity that her writing should affect her voice." I had observed, indeed, the same morning, that she took the high notes with difficulty. It is an axiom among all good masters of singing, that stooping to write, and even sitting much at the harpsichord, hurts the chest, and greatly affects the voice.

* M. Hasse's opinion of Alex. Scarlatti, corresponds exactly with that of Jomelli, who told me, at Naples, that his compositions for the church, tho' but little known, were the best of his productions, and perhaps the best of the kind.

Hasse

Hasse said, that after he was fifty he had never been able to sing a note; and, indeed he is now so hoarse, that he can with difficulty be heard when he speaks. This he wholly attributes to his having been so constantly employed in writing. Faustina said, that when she knew him first, he had a very fine tenor voice; and it was then usual for masters to make their scholars in counterpoint, not only sing, but declaim.

I cannot quit Hasse and Gluck, without saying that it is very necessary to use discrimination in comparing them together. Hasse may be regarded as the Raphael, and I have already called Gluck the Michael Angelo of living composers. If the affected French expression of *le grand simple* can ever mean any thing, it must be when applied to the productions of such a composer as Hasse, who succeeds better perhaps in expressing, with clearness and propriety, whatever is graceful, elegant, and tender, than what is

boisterous

boisterous and violent; whereas Gluck's genius seems more calculated for exciting terror in painting difficult situations, occasioned by complicated misery, and the tempestuous fury of unbridled passions.

Saturday 12. This morning, after another long visit to Metastasio, and hearing mademoiselle Martinetz play and sing with new delight and amazement, I determined to find out the habitation of Vanhall, a young composer, several of whose productions, particularly his symphonies, had afforded me such uncommon pleasure, that I should not hesitate to rank them among the most complete and perfect compositions, for many instruments, which the art of music can boast.

The spirit of party, in musical matters, runs high every where; and I every where found that it was wished that I should hear, or at least like, none but the friends of my friends. However, I soon saw, and *heard* through all this, and seldom

dom suffered myself to be the dupe of partial decisions. For I was not contented with hearing music in fine houses, theatres, and palaces, but visited cottages, and garrets, wherever I could get scent of a good performer, or a man of genius.

I had sent my servant, and made several attempts myself, to find M. Vanhall before, but in vain. However, to-day I had been told that he lived without the gates of the city; but, after crossing a branch of the Danube, and walking several miles through a very dusty road, to the place where I expected to find him, I was told that he was removed, no one knew whither: this did not discourage me from enquiring after him all the way back, and, at length, I luckily found him, in an obscure corner of the town, and in a more lofty than splendid situation. I groped my way up a totally dark, winding stone stair-case, at the summit of which was his bower.

He

He is a civil young man; and though he could speak no French, yet he had a little Italian, which is the case with many German musicians. I told him that I was a stranger, and in quest of whatever was most curious in music; that I had heard some of his symphonies performed, which had pleased me very much; and wished to be in possession of a few of them, if he had any ready transcribed, or if he knew of a copyist who had *. We soon came to a right understanding, and finding he played the harpsichord, I got him to sit down to a little clavichord, and play to me six lessons which he had just made for that instrument; but I found them neither so wild nor so new as his compositions for violins.

* As there are no music shops in Vienna, the best method of procuring new compositions, is to apply to copyists; for the authors, regarding every English traveller as a *milord*, expect a present on these occasions, as considerable for each piece, as if it had been composed on purpose for him.

Though there have been many admirable composers of vocal music, who, for want of voice, could not *sing*, yet it seems as if it were absolutely necessary to be a great *player* on an instrument in order to write in such a manner for it, as will best shew its powers. With respect to the organ and harpsichord, the most original and striking pieces for those instruments have been the productions of great performers, such as Handel, Scarlatti, Bach, Schobert, Wagenseil, Müthel, and Alberti: but a rage for universality, or for gain, tempts many composers to quit the road which nature and art have made familiar to them, for another; in which they are either bewildered or so destitute of the necessary requisites for travelling through it, as to be obliged to rob and plunder every one they meet.

A little perturbation of the faculties, is a promising circumstance in a young musician, and M. V. began his career very

very auspiciously, by being somewhat flighty. Enthusiasm seems absolutely necessary in all the arts, but particularly in music, which so much depends upon fancy and imagination. A cold, sedate, and wary disposition, but ill suits the professor of such an art; however, when enthusiasm is ungovernable, and impels to too frequent and violent efforts, the intellects are endangered. But as insanity in an artist is sometimes nothing more than an ebullition of genius, when that is the case, he may cry out to the physicians who cure him,

———Pol me occidistis, amici,
Non servastis.

M. V. is now so far recovered, and possesses a mind so calm and tranquil, that his last pieces appear to me rather insipid and common, and his former agreeable extravagance seems changed into too great œconomy of thought.

In the afternoon I went to the play, it was Romeo and Juliet, new written, by
M. Weitz.

M. Weitz. The first act was almost over when I arrived; but I soon found that it was not a translation of Shakespeare, by the small number of characters in it; there being only eight in this tragedy, and in the English one of the same name, there are upwards of twenty.

The personages introduced by M. Weitz are Montecute, Capulet, lady Capulet, Romeo, Julie, Laura a Confidant, instead of the Nurse, Benvoglio a physician, who supplies the place of Fryar Lawrence, and Peter a servant to Romeo, instead of Balthazar.

Though the speeches and scenes were long, the four first acts were very affecting; but the performance both of poet and actors in the last act was abominable. There was no procession; but Juliet, dead at the end of the fourth act, is found buried at the beginning of the fifth. The tomb scene was bad, ill written and ill acted; and there was so much confusion, at last, that it was impossible to find out whether Romeo lived or died. He fwallowed poifon, indeed, which had racked, tortured and deprived him of his fenfes; but, as the doctor plied him well with drops, and a fmelling bottle, he recovered juſt enough to ſay Juliet!—oh my Juliet! Julie! Oh meine Julie! and the curtain dropped.

Sunday 13th. There was a proceſſion through the principal ſtreets of this city to day, as an anniverſary commemoration of the Turks having been driven from its walls in 1683, by Sobieſki king of Poland, after it had fuſtained a ſiege of two months. The Emperor came from Laxemberg to attend the celebration of this feſtival, and walked in the proceſſion, which ſet off from the Franciſcan's church, and proceeded through the principal ſtreets of the city to the Cathedral of St. Stephen, where *Te Deum* was ſung, under the direction of M. Gaſman, imperial *maeſtro di capella*. The muſic was by Reüter, an old German composer, without taste or invention. As there was a very numerous band, great noise and little meaning characterized the whole performance. I hoped something better would have succeeded this dull, dry stuff; but what followed was equally uninteresting. The whole was finished by a triple discharge of all the artillery of the city, and the military instruments were little less noisy now, than the musical had been before.

From hence I went to Metastasio, for the last time! I found with him much company, and the St. Cecilia Martinetz at the harpsichord, to which she had been singing. At her desire there was a commutation of compositions between us. She had been so kind as to have transcribed for me, among other things, a song of Metastasio, set by herself, with which I had been greatly struck in a former visit.

The good old poet embraced me heartily; said he was sorry to lose me so soon; that he must have my book, when published, and desired to hear from me. Thus we parted at Vienna; but I cannot quit him here, without adding a few lines to this article, long as it is already.

I had been told, and it was likewise the opinion of Signor Hasse, that Metastasio had more of his own manuscript poetry in his possession, than had hitherto been published; but lord Stormont doubts much of the fact; alledging his principle of never working but when he is called upon, against his writing verses merely to lock them up. Metastasio laughs at all poetic inspiration, and makes a poem as mechanically as another would make a shoe, at what time he pleases, and without any other occasion than the want of it.

However, lord Stormont says, that he has seen a translation of Horace's *Ars Poetica*, in Italian verse, by Metastasio, which he thinks far superior to every one that has been made in other languages. He has likewise translated the *Hoc erat in votis*, of the same poet, admirably well. In this, like Horace, he has told the story of the Town and Country Mouse, as a serious fact, and kept more closely, both to the letter and spirit of the original, than any other who has hitherto attempted it.

Metastasio, like most other persons in years, has an aversion to the talking about his own age, about the infirmities of his friends, or the calamities, or death, even of persons that are indifferent to him. He is extremely candid in his judgment of men of genius, and even of poets with whom he has had a difference, which indeed are very few. For, when he has been attacked by them, it has often happened, that, after writing an epigram or couplet, to shew his particular friends how he could defend himself, he has thrown it into the fire; and he has never been known either to print or publish a line, by way of retaliation, against the bitterest enemy to his person or poems.

He has a natural chearfulness and pleasantry, in his manner and conversation, which give a gaiety to all around him; and is possessed of as easy an eloquence in speaking as in writing. He is, indeed, one of the few extraordinary geniuses who lose nothing by approximation or acquaintance: for, it is a melancholy reflection that, very few, like him, are equally intitled to the epithets *good* and *great*.

The following anecdote has been given me by a person of veracity, well informed of every particular, relative to this great poet. Many years ago, when Metastasio's circumstances were far from affluent, and he was only known at Vienna as an assistant writer for the Opera, under Apostolo Zeno; a person with whom

whom he had contracted a great intimacy and friendship, dying, left him his whole fortune, amounting to fifteen thousand pounds sterling. But Metastasio hearing that he had relations at Bologna, went thither in search of them; and having found such as he thought best intitled to these possessions, told them, that though his deceased friend had bequeathed to him his whole fortune, he could suppose it to be no otherwise than in trust, till he should find out the most deserving of his kindred, in order to divide it equitably among them; which he immediately did, without the least reserve in his own favour.

After dinner, I had the pleasure of a long visit from M. Gasman, who not only furnished me with a list of his works, but obliged me with copies of a great number of his manuscript quartets, for various instruments *. M.

* It is but justice to say, that since my return to England, I have had these pieces tried, and have
found

Gasman is of a middle age, and yet his works are very voluminous. For the serious opera, he has composed, in Italy, *Merope, Issipile, Catone in Utica, Ezio,* twice, and *Achille in Sciro.* At Vienna, *Olimpiade, Amore di Psiche,* and *Il Trionfo d'Amore.* For the comic opera, at Venice, *l'Uccilatore,* twice: *il Filosofo inamorato, un Pazzo ne fa Cento,* and *il Mondo nella Luna.* At Vienna, *i Viaggiatori ridicoli, l'Amore Artigiano, la Notte Critica, l'opera Seria, la Contessina, il Filosofo inamorato* a second time, *la Pescatrice,* and *i Rovinati.*

When M. Gasman left me, I went, for the last time, to M. Wagenseil, and heard him and his little female scholar play several brilliant duets upon two harpsichords: here I again met with my

found them excellent: there is pleasing melody, free from caprice and affectation; sound harmony, and the contrivances and imitations are ingenious, without the least confusion. In short, the style is sober and sedate, without dulness; and masterly, without pedantry.

friend

friend, the Portuguese Abbé, and, after a long conversation upon musical matters, we parted; but not till we had mutually exchanged directions, and promises to keep alive our friendship, by a literary intercourse.

After this I flew home, to pack, and to pay; here, among other things, I was plagued with copyists the whole evening; they began to regard me as a greedy and indiscriminate purchaser of whatever trash they should offer; but I was forced to hold my hand, not only from buying bad music, but good. For every thing is very dear at Vienna, and nothing more so than music, of which none is printed.

As it was, I did not quit Vienna till I had expended ten or twelve guineas in the purchase of music; which, with what had been given me, what I had transcribed myself, and the printed books I had collected, rendered my baggage so unwieldy, as to cost me an additional horse

horse to my chaise, all the way to Hamburg.

Indeed, Vienna is so rich in composers, and incloses within its walls such a number of musicians of superior merit, that, it is but just to allow it to be, among German cities, the imperial seat of music, as well as of power.

This might be manifested by a recapitulation of what I heard, and saw, during my short residence there; but I shall leave that to the reader's recollection, and only mention the names of Hasse, Gluck, Gasman, Wagenseil, Salieri, Hofman, Haydn, Ditters, Vanhall, and Huber, who have all greatly distinguished themselves as composers; and the symphonies and quartets of the five last mentioned authors, are perhaps among the first full pieces and compositions, for violins, that have ever been produced.

To these celebrated names, may be added those of Misliwiceck, a Bohemian,

just

just returned from Italy, where he has established a great reputation by his operas, as well as instrumental music; Scarlatti, nephew to the famous Domenico Scarlatti; Kohaut, an excellent lutanist; Venturini, a hautbois player of the first class; Albrechtzberger, and Stefani, two eminent harpsichord players, in the service of the court, and La Motte, a Flamand, the best solo player and sightsman, upon the violin, at Vienna. He was some time scholar to Giardini; and it is related of him, that when he quitted his first master, he travelled through Italy, still in search of another; and being arrived at Leghorn, where Nardini then lived, he would have become his scholar; but after hearing that performer execute one of his own solos, of the most difficult kind, and being, in his turn asked to play, he desired leave to perform the same solo, which he had just heard, and which was new, and in manuscript, so that he never could have practised it;

how-

however, he acquitted himself so well, that Nardini declined taking as a *scholar*, one who was already so able a master of his instrument.

I omit particularizing here, all the able organists of this city, the *dilettanti*, male and female, and the several masters and performers, vocal and instrumental, who constantly reside here, and contribute to the cultivation of music, and the pleasure of its votaries and protectors; and shall only remark that, rich as this city is at present, in musicians of genius and eminence, there is no serious opera either at the court or public theatre.

Lady Mary Wortley Montague mentions an opera that was performed in the open air, when she was at Vienna, the decorations and habits of which cost the emperor thirty thousand pounds sterling; and, during the reigns of the late emperors, from the first years of Leopold, to the middle of the present century, there used to be operas at the expence of the

the court, written, compofed, and performed, by perfons of the greateft abilities that could be affembled from all parts of Europe: but the frequent wars, and other calamities of this country, have fo exhaufted the public treafure, and impoverifhed individuals, that this expenfive cuftom is now,

> "To my mind,
> "More honoured in the breach, than the obfervance,"

For though I love mufic very well, yet I love humanity better.

INDEX.

Abel, 135, 139.
Actors, French, their excellence, 2.
Adamont, singer at Munich, 128.
AIX LA CHAPELLE, 64.
Alberti, 353.
Albrechtzberger, harpsichord player at Vienna, 365.
Allegrante, Signora, a singer at Schwetzingen, 90.
Allegri, 329.
ALOST, 20.
ANTWERP, 28.
Astronomical machine in the public library at Ludwigsburg, 109.
AUGSBURG, 113.

B.

Bach, C. P. E. 344.
———, John Christian, 92.
Baglioni, violin player at Ludwigsburg, 101.
————, Costanza, a singer at Vienna, 240.
————, Clementina, singer at Vienna, 338.
Bartolomeo di Faenza, 334.
Basse fundamentale of Rameau, 257.
Benevoli, 329.
Bernacchi, 308, 333.
Birde, 329.
Blaviere, M. singing master at Antwerp, 45.
Blithe, brother, 32.
BONN, 70.
Brown, Dr. 235.
BRUSSELS, 22, 49.
Bull, harpsichord maker at Antwerp, 48.

C.

Caffarelli, 250.
Caldara, 329.
Calsabigi, 232, 287.
Canabich, leader in the Italian operas at Schwetzingen, 86.
Capranica, Signora Rosa, singer at Munich, 174.
Carilloneur at Ghent, 13.
Carillons, 15. At Courtray 13. At Ghent, ibid.
Casti, Abate, poet at Vienna, 290, 323.
COBLENTZ, 71.

Colista

Colista, 4.
COLOGN, 68.
Colonna, 321, 329.
Comedy at Lisle, 7.
Conforte, violin player at Vienna, 280.
Conversations, with a French Abbé at Antwerp, 38. M. Schubart at Ludwigsburg, 105. Signora Mingotti, 142. Abate Taruffi, 244. M. l'Augier, 247. Cavalier Gluck, 257, 286, 339. Signor Hasse, 273, 311, 343. Signor Abate Metastasio, 293, 305, 341, 358. Wagenseil, 324. Signor Mancini, 332. M. Gasman, 335.
Costa, Abate, 256, 282, 288, 320, 363.
COURTRAY, 11.
Custom-house, at Vilchofen, 185. Ingelhartziel, 188. Vienna, 203.

D.

Danzy, Mademoiselle, singer at Schwetzingen, 37, 90.
DARMSTADT, 77.
Davis, Miss, 275.
De Amici, 319.
Defoix, Mademoiselle, singer at Brussels, 25, 27.
Ditters, composer, 324, 364.
Diversions of the common people at Vienna, 326.
Dulcimer player, 64.
Dulcken, J. D. harpsichord maker, 48.
Duni, a French composer, 52.
Durante, 347.

E.

English pronunciation of *th*, a shibboleth to the Germans, 64.
Ettori, il cavalier, 100.

F.

Farinelli, a severe disciplinarian, 158, 236, 317.
Faustina, Signora, 236, 252, 273, 311.
Ferrari, 103.
Fiorini, singer at Munich, 148.
Fischer, 169.
Fitzthumb, M. *maestro di capella* at the theatre of Brussels, 22.
FRANKFORT, 72.
French music, 54.
——— organ builders much esteemed, 21.

French performers upon keyed inſtruments excellent, 10.
——— plagiariſts in muſic, 54.

G.

Gardens, at Nymphenburg, 131. At Schwetzingen, 96.
Garrick, Mr. 156.
Gaſman, compoſer at Vienna, 324, 328, 337, 362, 364.
German language, better calculated for muſic than the French, 83.
——— manner of ſinging preferable to any except Italian, 115.
Geſquiere, father, 32, 45, 48.
Giorgi, violin player at Vienna, 280.
Giorgietto, ſinger at Schwetzingen, 90.
Girard, M. 56, 58.
Gizziello, 158, 250.
Gluck, chevalier, 223, 232. His plan for a new ode on St. Cecilia's day, 253. Viſited by the author, 257. His opera of Iphegenie, 262. His dedication to Alceſte, 264, 282, 286. The Michael Angelo of muſic, 239, 289, 349, 364.
———, Mademoiſelle, 257, 288.
Gode-Charle, a German compoſer and violin player, 59.
Goſſec, a French compoſer, 52.
Gretry, a French compoſer, his opera of l'Amitié a l'Epreuve, 7. Zemire and Azor, 23, 82. Les deux Miliciens, 55.
Groſſwald, of Hanau, organ builder, 75.
Guadagni, Signor, 123, 130, 138, 140, 171.
———, Signora, 172.
Guarducci, 334.
Guglielmi, Signor, 172.
Guglielmini, ſinger at Munich, 128.
Guicciardini, Lodovico, 19, 24.

H.

Handel, 263, 316, 325, 329, 347, 353.
Harp, 279. With pedals, 59.
Haſſe, M. 223, 232, 253. Viſited by the author, 273, 311, 343. The Raphael of muſic, 349, 364.
———, Meſdemoiſelles, 275, 313.
Haueiſon, organiſt of Frankfort, 77.
Haydn, compoſer, 214, 253, 293, 324, 364.
Hiller, compoſer of Leipſic, 84.

Hofmann,

[372]

Hofmann, composer, 214, 239, 322, 324, 364.
Holtzbauer, chapel-master at Schwetzingen, 86.
Holtzbogn, violin player at Munich, 173.
Hoole, Mr. 297.
Huber, composer at Vienna, 230, 264.

I.

Jesuits college at Munich, 144.
Instruments, ancient, at Antwerp, 41.
Jomelli, 104, 329, 348.
Journey, down the Iser and Danube, from Munich to Vienna, 175 to 202.
JULIERS, 67.

K.

Keiser, 346.
Kenedy, father, 142, 143, 161
Kennis, violin player at Lovain, 62.
Kohaut, lutanist at Vienna, 324, 365.
KOR NEUBURG, 201.
Kramer, violin player at Schwetzingen, 86.
————, Madame, singer at Schwetzingen, 87.
KREMS, 197.
Kröner, violin player at Munich, 133, 138, 169.
Kuckelkorn, organist at Aix la Chapelle, 66.

L.

Lamey, M. librarian at Manheim, 85.
La Motte, violin player at Vienna, 324, 365.
Language, frequent change of it in the Netherlands, 11.
L'Augier, M. 244, 247, 278, 282, 322.
Lessing, M. Ephraim, his play of Emilia Galotti, 208.
Library, Burgundy, at Brussels, 57. Manheim, 84. Ludwigsburg, 108. Munich, 128. Vienna, 270, 317. Musical, 335.
LIEGE, 63.
Lion of Cologn, 69.
L'ISLE, 4.
Lobst, violin player at Munich, 173.
Lodi, Signora, singer at Munich, 127, 147, 172.
Lolli, leader of the opera at Ludwigsburg, 97.
Lotti, 329.
LOVAIN, 61.
Lucchese, *maestro di capella* of the Elector of Cologn, 71.
LUDWIGSBURG, 97. Performers there, 100.

M.

Maestrick, 63.
Mancini, Signor, singing-master at Vienna, 324, 332.
Manheim, 80.
Manservisi, Signora, singer at Munich, 147.
Marmontel, his Zemire and Azor, 23.
Martinetz, M. librarian at Vienna, 317.
——— Mademoiselle, 306, 341, 348, 350, 358.
Martini, Padre, 127.
Metastasio Signor Abate, 223. Sketch of his life, 224. Dislike of extempore verses, 225. Not partial to the ancients, opinion of blank verse, 226. His regular life, 227, 245. Visited by the author, 293, 305, 341, 358. Laughs at poetic inspiration, 359. Instance of generosity, 361.
Meyer, organ builder, 74.
Michel, composer, 170.
Migliavacca, 306.
Millico, Signor, 259.
Minelli, Giorgio Battista, 334.
Mingotti, Signora, 123, 142. Sketch of her life, 150, 169, 173, 236.
Misliwiceck, composer, 365.
Mittermeir, organist at Vienna, 239.
Mozart, 126.
Montague, lady M. W. her account of the theatre at Vienna, 211, 366.
Munich, 121, 142.
Music, military, in France, 5, 6, 10. At Ghent, 17. At Darmstadt, 77. At Manheim, 80.
Mut, performer on the harp at Vienna, 279.
Müthel, composer, 353.

N.

Nardini, 104, 365.
National music, 108, 202, 249.
Naumann, *maestro di capella* of the Elector of Bavaria, 130, 138.
Newton, father, 32, 45, 46.
Noverre, M. ballet-master at Vienna, 220.
Nymphenburg, 130, 166.

O.

Omer's, St. 1.

[374]

Opera, at Bruffels, 23, 27. At Manheim, 82. At Schwetzingen, 89. At Munich, 127, 147. At Vienna, 237, 240.
Operation, a curious one performed at Naples, 334.
Orcheftra, at Bruffels, 22, 26, 56. At Manheim, 84. At Schwetzingen, 92. At Vienna, 213, 219.
Organ, at St. Omers, 2. At Courtray, 12. At the Jefuits church, in Ghent, 18. At Aloft, 20. At Antwerp, 31, 32, 37. At Cologn, 69. At Frankfort, 74, 76. At Ulm, 112. At Vienna, 214, 272.
Ottane, compofer, 127.

P.

Panzachi, Signor Don, 122, 131, 138, 142.
Paleftrina, 329.
Pafi, Antonio, 334.
PASSAU, 186.
Pfeil, M. 77.
Pergolefi, 329.
Perti, 329.
Pefarini, finger at Schwetzingen, 86.
Piety, appearance of, along the Danube, 192.
Piftocco, 232, 306.
Plain-chant, finging of the common people tinctured with it in French Flanders, 9.
Plas, hautbois players, 104.
Polifh mufic, 145, 162, 163.
Ponta, M. French horn player, 71.
Poor fcholars, at Munich, 140, 144, 149. At Vienna, 206.
Porpora, 139, 143, 154.
Pofitif, fmall organ at St. Omer's, 3.
Poftmafters and poftilions in Germany, 73.
Prat, at Vienna, 206.
Premiums no longer given at Vienna to actors who fubmit to be kicked and cuffed, 218.
Proceffion, through the ftreets of Vienna, 356.
Proceffions, Auftrians addicted to, 305.

R.

Rauzzini, finger at Munich, 126, 138, 140, 148, 171.
——— Matteo, compofer, 147.
Ravanni, finger at Munich, 127.
Reflexions, on national characters, 88. On travelling in Germany, 89. On Italian and French mufic, 53. Upon the abufe of mufic, 105.

Reuter, composer, 357.
Rheiner, bassoon player at Munich, 169.
Roncaglio, singer at Schwetzingen, 87.
Rousseau, M. 125, 283, 300, 345.
Ruckers, famous harpsichord makers, 47.

S.

Sacchini, 90, 171.
Salieri, composer, 240, 364.
Sales, *maestro di capella* at Coblentz, 72.
Sarazin, violin player at Frankfort, 77.
Soporosi, singer at Schwetzingen, 87.
Scarlatti, Domenico, 247, 347, 353.
———— Alessandro, 329, 343, 345, 347.
———— Nephew to Dom. Scarlatti, 324, 365.
Scheppen, M. carilloneur at Lovain, 62.
Schmahl, organ builder of Ulm, 112.
Schobert, 353.
SCHWETZINGEN, 85.
School of arts, at Solitude, 104.
Schubart, organist at Ludwigsburg, 101, 105.
Sechi, hautbois player at Munich, 169, 171.
Senesino, 251.
Seyfurth, cantor at Augsburg, 116, 113.
Serpent, 4, 36.
Simon, inventor of the harp with pedals, 59.
Silbermann, organ builder, 21.
Snetzler, Mr. 75, 187, 272.
Stephani, harpsichord player at Vienna, 365.
Startzel, violin player, and composer at Vienna, 288, 290.
Shops, brought to the inhabitants of Vienna, 205.
Singing in parts in Roman catholic countries, 200.
———— why common at Vienna, 222.
Stamitz, 91, 93.
Strafe, organist at Brussels, 50.
Street music at Frankfort, 74. At Vienna, 330.
Symphonies, at Manheim, *manierées*, 220.
Soldiers, their mechanical exactness at Ludwigsburg, 103.

T.

Tallis, 392.
Tartini, 138, 173, 180.
Taruffi, Abate, 244, 278, 305, 343.

[376]

Tefi, Signora, 318.
Teuberinn, Signora, 319.
Theatre, at Bruffels, 22. At Manheim, 82. At Schwetzingen, 90. At Ludwigfburg, 102. At Munich, 127, 143. At Vienna, 213, 217, 241.
Thomas, father, organift of St. Omer's, 2.
Toefchi, Charles, leader of the French and German operas at Schwetzingen, 86.
————— John, violin player at Schwetzingen, 86.
Traetta, 140, 174, 258.
Tragedy, German, at Vienna, 207, 354.

V.

Vanden Bofch, organift at Antwerp, 31, 37, 41.
Vanderelche, harpfichord maker, 48.
Vanhall, compofer, 214. Vifited by the author, 350, 364.
Vanhelmont, *maeftro di capella* at Bruffels, 52.
Vanmaldere, leader of the band at Bruffels, 23.
Vanpetigham, organ builder, 20.
Venturini, hautbois player at Vienna, 324, 365.
Verteil, Madame, actrefs at Bruffels, 55.
VIENNA, 202. The imperial feat of mufic in Germany, 364.
Voice, writing prejudicial to it, 343.
Voluntary playing in Germany unnatural, and why, 114.
Urot, M. librarian at Ludwigfburg, 103, 109.

W.

Wagenfeil, vifited by the author, 324, 336, 353, 363, 364.
Walther, French horn player, 104.
Waterfall, famous, 195.
Wegerer, organift of Vienna, 273.
Weigel, violoncello player at Vienna, 290.
Weitz, M. his tragedy, 354.
Wendling, J. B. principal flute player at Schwetzingen, 84.
————— Francis, violin player at Schwetzingen, 86.
————— Charles, violin player at Schwetzingen, 86.
————— Mademoifelle, finger at Schwetzingen, 87.
Wenzlaer, violin player at Aix la Chapelle, 66.
Weftmann, organift at Cologn, 69.
Women, allowed to fing in the church at Bruffels, 60.
————— their drefs at Darmftadt, 79. At AUGSBURG, 118.

Z.

Zonca, finger at Schwetzingen, 90.

London, April 20th, 1773.

PROPOSALS

FOR

PRINTING by SUBSCRIPTION,

A

GENERAL HISTORY of MUSIC,

From the EARLIEST AGES to the PRESENT PERIOD,

CONDITIONS.

I. That the work shall be elegantly printed in Two Volumes Quarto, illustrated with examples of national music, and compositions of different ages, and in different styles, as well as with original drawings of ancient and modern instruments, engraved by the best artists.

II. That the price to subscribers shall be two guineas; one to be paid at the time of subscribing, and the other on the delivery of the second volume, in sheets.

III. It is the author's intention to publish the first volume in the course of next year, 1774. But, as the printing of it will be attended with too great an expence for him to risk it against the public opinion, though the work is in great forwardness, he cannot venture to send it to the press before *five hundred copies*, are subscribed for. He therefore entreats those who may be inclined to honour this undertaking with their patronage, to send in their names early. And in order to render security reciprocal, between the public and the writer, if the number of copies specified be not ascertained by next Christmas, he will abandon the enterprize, and return the money to the subscribers.

SUBSCRIPTIONS will be taken in, and Receipts delivered, by the AUTHOR, at his house in Queen's Square, Bloomsbury; T. BECKET and Co. Strand; J. ROBSON, New Bond Street; G. ROBINSON, Paternoster-Row; Messrs. FLETCHER and PRINCE, Oxford; Messrs. MERRIL and WOODYER, Cambridge; and at the music shops of R. BREMNER, in the Strand; and P. WELCKER, Gerrard-Street, Soho.

THE PRESENT STATE OF MUSIC IN GERMANY, THE NETHERLANDS, AND UNITED PROVINCES.

OR,

The JOURNAL of a TOUR through those Countries, undertaken to collect Materials for

A GENERAL HISTORY OF MUSIC.

By CHARLES BURNEY, Muf. D.

IN TWO VOLUMES.

VOL. II.

Auf Virtuosen sey stolz, Germanien, die du gezeiget;
In Frankreich und Welschland sind größere nicht.

Zachariä.

LONDON,

Printed for T. BECKET and Co. Strand; J. ROBSON, New Bond Street; and G. ROBINSON, Paternoster Row. 1773.

ADVERTISEMENT.

AS it may probably have been expected that this work, like the account of The Present State of Music in France and Italy, *should have been comprised in one volume, it may be necessary to account for its having swelled into two. As the author proceeded in arranging his materials, he soon found that one volume would not contain those which related merely to music, without such retrenchments, or compression, as would justly subject him to censure, either for totally neglecting, or too slightly mentioning several persons and things, which merit particular attention. It was, therefore, the opinion of several of his friends, whose judgment he has reason to respect, that by intermixing with his account of music and musicians,*

musicians, a few miscellaneous memorandums, he would connect the several parts of his narrative, and, by rendering the whole a more uniform series, carry his reader with him wherever he went.

This indeed a little breaks into his original design, of confining his remarks wholly to musical matters. However, to give the Present State of Music, *in the several countries through which he travelled, is still the object of this publication, as to acquire materials for the* History of its Past State *was that of his voyage.*

ERRATA to Vol. I.

Page 36. *for* baffoons players, *read* baffoon player; p. 52. laſt line, *for* Toinetti, *read* Toinette; p. 57. *for* it it, *read* it is; *for* into there claſſes, *read* into their claſſes; p. 65. *for* theogiſt, *read* theologiſt; p. 78. *for* thril, *read* ſhrill; p. 83. *for* defect, *read* defects; p. 85. *for* Etrennes Palatine, *read* Etrennes Palatines; p. 97. *for* forms the judgment, and eſtabliſhes a taſte, *read* form the judgment, and eſtabliſh a taſte; p. 100. *for* Gurreieri, *read* Guerrieri; p. 211. *for* focias, *read* foſias; p. 244. *for* inperial, *read* imperial; p. 269. *for* dilineated, *read* delineate.

Vol. II.

Page 8. *and elſewhere, dele* e *after* Wolfe; p. 19. *dele* s *after* impoſition; p. 35. *for* chemical, *read* chymical; p. 152. laſt line but one, *for* fincc, *read* fince; p. 157. *for* paſſes, *read* paſſages; p. 171. *for* Hienſchen, *read* Heinichen; p. 173. *for* rational, *read* national; ib. *for* performances, *read* performance; p. 183. *for* coutryman, *read* countryman; p. 231. *dele* s *after* motion; p. 232. *dele* s *after* opinion; p. 234. *for* preſcribes, *read* preſcribes; p. 244. *dele* s *after* object; ib. p. 9. *after* at, *dele* comma.

THE
PRESENT STATE
OF
MUSIC, &c.

BOHEMIA.

MY journey through this country, was one of the moſt fatiguing I ever took in my life; for though the road, in general, is very good, for a German road, yet my want of time, which obliged me to travel night and day; the exceſſive heat and cold of the weather, occaſioned by the preſence and abſence of the ſun; together with bad horſes, and diabolical wagons, used as chaises, exhausted both my spirits and my patience.

The country is flat, naked, and disagreeable to the eye, for the most part, all the way through Austria, Moravia, and Bohemia, as far as Prague, the situation and environs of which are very beautiful.

The dearness and scarcity of provisions, of all kinds, on this road, were now excessive; and the half-starved people, just recovered from malignant fevers, little less contagious than the plague, occasioned by bad food, and by no food at all, offered to view the most melancholy spectacles I ever beheld.

No refreshments of any kind were to be found, till I arrived at Colin, a village rendered famous, by the battle fought near it in the last war; here a pigeon, and half a pint of miserable sour wine, cost me three or four shillings; till now I had subsisted on bread and water, except

cept one pint of milk, which I obtained with difficulty, and which coſt me fourteen *creuzers*, about ſeven-pence Engliſh.

I had frequently been told, that the Bohemians were the moſt muſical people of Germany, or, perhaps, of all Europe; and an eminent German compoſer, now in London, had declared to me, that if they enjoyed the ſame advantages as the Italians, they would excel them.

I never could ſuppoſe effects without a cauſe; nature, though often partial to individuals, in her diſtribution of genius and talents, is never ſo to a whole people. Climate contributes greatly to the forming of cuſtoms and manners; and, it is, I believe, certain, that thoſe who inhabit hot climates, are more delighted with muſic than thoſe of cold ones; perhaps, from the auditory nerves being more irritable in the one than in the other, and from ſound being propagated with greater

greater facility: but I could, by no means, account for climate operating more in favour of mufic upon the Bohemians, than on their neighbours, the Saxons and Moravians.

I croffed the whole kingdom of Bohemia, from fouth to north; and being very affiduous in my enquiries, how the common people learned mufic, I found out at length, that, not only in every large town, but in all villages, where there is a reading and writing fchool, children of both fexes are taught mufic.

At TEUCHENBROD, JANICH, CZASLAU, BÖMISCHBROD, and other places, I vifited thefe fchools; and at Czaflau, in particular, within a poft of Colin, I caught them in the fact.

The organift and cantor, M. Johann Dulfick, and the firft violin of the parifh church, M. Martin Kruch, who are likewife the two fchool-mafters, gave me me all the satisfaction I required. I went into the school, which was full of little children of both sexes, from six to ten or eleven years old, who were reading, writing, playing on violins, hautbois, bassoons, and other instruments. The organist had in a small room of his house four clavichords, with little boys practising on them all: his son of nine years old, was a very good performer.

After this, he attended me to the church, which is but a small one, and played an admirable voluntary on the organ, which is likewise but small, though well-toned; its compass was from C to C, and there were no reed stops; but it had pedals, and an even good chorus. He played an extempore *fugue*, upon a new, and pleasing subject, in a very masterly manner; and I think him one of the best performers on the organ, which I heard throughout my journey. He complained of loss of hand, for want of practice, and said, that he had too many learners to instruct, in the first rudiments, to be allowed leisure for study, and that he had his house not only full of other people's children, but his own;

"Chill penury repressed his noble rage:"

which is the case of many a musician, whose mind and talents are superior to such drudgery! yet, thus circumstanced, there is no alternative, but a jail.

PRAGUE.

This city is extremely beautiful, when seen at a distance. It is situated on two or three hills, and has the river Mulda running through the middle of it. It is divided into three different quarters, or districts, which are distinguished by the names of Alt Stadt, Neue Stadt, and Kleine Stadt or Old Town, New Town, and Little Town; the Kleine Stadt is the most
mo-

modern, and the beſt built of the three. The houſes are all of white ſtone, or ſtucco, in imitation of it, and all uniform in ſize and colour. The hill of St. Laurence, the higheſt about the town, commands a proſpect, not only of the whole city, but of all the adjacent country: the declivity of this hill is covered with wood, confiſting chiefly of fruit-trees, and vineyards. A great part of the town is new, as ſcarce a ſingle building eſcaped the Pruſſian batteries, and bombardment during the blockade, in the laſt war. A few churches and palaces only, that were ſtrongly built, and of leſs combuſtible materials than the reſt, were proof againſt their fury; and in the walls of theſe, are ſtill ſticking innumerable cannon balls, and bombs, particularly, in the ſuperb palace of count Czernin, and in the Capuchin's church. This palace, which is of the Ionic order, and built of white ſtone, has thirty windows in front; the chapel, at the Capuchins, is an exact copy, in stone, of that at Loretto, in marble.

The inhabitants are still at work throughout the city, in repairing the Prussian devastations, particularly at the cathedral and imperial palace, which were both almost entirely demolished; these are situated on a high hill, facing that of St. Laurence. The organ of the cathedral, which, as well as the building, has been newly constructed, since the last war, is very large, and finely toned; it was well played on during the morning service, though the principal organist, M. Wolfe, was ill in bed of a fever. I went to his house, in order, if he had been well enough, to have conversed with him concerning the present state of music at Prague; but the messenger I sent in before me, in order to negotiate the visit, returned quite pale with fear, telling me, that it would be very dangerous for me to enter the house, as M. Wolfe was ill of the malignant and contagious

contagious fever, which had lately raged with so much violence, and swept off such a number of the inhabitants of this city.

M. Wolfe, who is esteemed one of the best organists in Germany, is called am Schloß Organiſten, or organist of the castle; for the cathedral of Prague is built within the castle or royal palace walls, of which it makes a part.

There are three large colleges of Jesuits in Prague; that of St. Nicholas has a very beautiful church, in which the organ is divided into two parts, placed one on each side the gallery; and the keys, with a *positif*, or small choir organ, are in the middle, but placed so low, as to leave the west window clear: instead of wood, the frame-work, pillars, base, and ornaments of this instrument, in front, are of white marble; the organ and church seem quite new. I never saw a more rich or noble front to an organ than this; it was constructed by one

of

of the Jesuits, and is well-toned; but has a very heavy touch.

An itinerant band of street-musicians came to salute me at the inn, the 𝕰𝖎𝖓=𝖍𝖔𝖗𝖓, or Unicorn, during dinner; they played upon the harp, violin, and horn, several minuets and Polonoises, which were, in themselves very pretty, though their performance of them added nothing to the beauty of the compositions; and it will, perhaps, appear strange to some, that this capital of so musical a kingdom, in which the genius of each inhabitant has a fair trial, should not more abound with *great* musicians. It is not, however, difficult to account for this, if we reflect, that music is one of the arts of peace, leisure, and abundance; and if, according to M. Rousseau, arts have flourished most in the most corrupt times, those times must, at least, have been prosperous and tranquil. Now, the Bohemians are never tranquil long together; and even in the short intervals of

peace,

peace, their firſt nobility are attached to the court of Vienna, and ſeldom reſide in their own capital; ſo that thoſe among the poorer ſort, who are taught muſic in their infancy, have no encouragement to purſue it in riper years, and ſeldom advance further than to qualify themſelves for the ſtreet, or for ſervitude.

Indeed many of thoſe who learn muſic at ſchool go afterwards to the plough, and to other laborious employments; and then their knowledge of muſic turns to no other account, than to enable them to ſing in their pariſh-church, and as an innocent domeſtic recreation, which is, perhaps, the beſt and moſt honourable uſe, to which muſic can be appropriated.

It has been ſaid by travellers*; that the Bohemian nobility keep muſicians in their houſes; but, in keeping ſervants, it is impoſſible to be otherwiſe, as all the children of the peaſants and

* Nugent's Grand Tour, vol. ii.

trades-

trades-people, in every town and village throughout the kingdom of Bohemia are taught music at the common reading schools, except in Prague, where, indeed it is no part of school-learning; the musicians being brought thither from the country.

In these common country schools, now and then a great genius appears, as was the case at Teuehenbrod, the birth-place of the famous Stamitz. His father was *cantor* of the church in that town; and Stamitz, who was afterwards so eminent, both as a composer and performer, was brought up in the common school, among children of common talents, who lived and died unnoticed; but he, like another Shakespeare, broke through all difficulties and discouragements; and, as the eye of one pervaded all nature, the other, without quitting nature, pushed art further than any one had done before him; his genius was truly original, bold, and nervous; invention,

vention, fire, and contraſt, in the quick movements; a tender, graceful, and inſinuating melody, in the ſlow; together with the ingenuity and richneſs of the accompaniments, characteriſe his productions; all replete with great effects, produced by an enthuſiaſm of genius, refined, but not repreſſed by cultivation.

M. Seger, is organiſt of the Kreutzherrn, or convent of the Holy Croſs in Prague. I was deſired by M. Gaſman, to enquire after him, as he is the beſt player in this city; he favoured me with a long converſation, and I found him to be a ſenſible man, as well as an excellent performer. He remembers Tartini, and Vandini, at Prague, fifty years ago; and ſeems well acquainted with the character and works of all the great muſicians in Europe.

He informed me, that at the convent of the Holy Croſs, where he is organiſt, there are now three or four boys, brought thither from country ſchools, who ſing most admirably; having good voices, and good shakes, with good taste and expression. I arrived at Prague one day too late, for a great musical performance in the church of this convent.

It was with great difficulty that I acquired information from the Bohemian musicians, as even the German language is of little use in that kingdom, throughout which the Sclavonian dialect is generally used. M. Seger, indeed, spoke Italian, and was very communicative; it was from him that I obtained a confirmation of my discovery, that not only in Bohemia, but in Moravia, Hungary, and part of Austria, children are taught music at the common reading schools. The Bohemians are remarkably expert in the use of wind instruments, in general; but M. Seger says, the instrument upon which their performers are most excellent, on the Saxon side the kingdom, is the hautbois; and on that of Moravia, the tube, or clarion.

The

The celebrated Misliwiceck was brought up at a village school in Bohemia, and afterwards studied counterpoint, at Prague, under M. Seger.

The best violin players in this city, at present, are M. Joseph Strobach, Johan Galli, of the Amschlofs, and Wenzel Braupner, who is an admirable solo player. The best, and indeed, the only violoncello player in this city, is M. Hetes; and on the hautbois, Stiestni is an excellent performer.

There have been no operas here lately; however, German and Sclavonian plays are performed three times a week, which are, at present, the only public exhibitions at Prague, of any kind. The nobility were now, for the most part, out of town; but in winter, they are said to have great concerts frequently at their hotels, and palaces, chiefly performed by their own domestics and vassals, who have learned music at country schools.

※ ※ ※ ※ ※ ※

I quitted

I quitted Prague, Thurſday morning, September 17th, after many delays and plagues, incident to travellers in a foreign country; among the reſt, my good landlord at the 𝔈𝔦𝔫𝔥𝔬𝔯𝔫, inſtigated the poſt-maſter's ſervant to inſiſt on my having an additional horſe to my poſt wagon; and threw all the difficulties in my way, he poſſibly could, in hopes of keeping me longer in his *ſpunging* houſe. After theſe ſquabbles were over, and I had run the gauntlet through the gates and barriers, where my baggage was narrowly ranſacked, by cuſtom-houſe inquiſitors, I got away about ſeven o'clock.

The firſt poſt, to SDIEPS, I travelled through a mountainous country, and cold thick fog; the ſecond, to WELTRUS, through a good road, and level, though naked country; here the weather was again very hot. Sour milk, and black ſour bread, 𝔓𝔬𝔪𝔭𝔢𝔯𝔫𝔦𝔠𝔨𝔢𝔩 were thus far, all the refreſhments that could be obtained.

At BUDIN, the next ſtage, I found a muſic ſchool; and heard two of the poor boys

boys perform in the street, one on the harp, and the other on the triangles, tolerably well.

At LOBESCHUTZ, two or three stages from the confines of Saxony, there is likewise another school, with more than a hundred children, of both sexes, of which number all learn music who chuse it. I visited the church, which is small and neat, with a little plain organ in it; here the children, vocally and instrumentally, perform. I heard a considerable number of the boys practising on the fiddle, at school, but in a very coarse manner.

I hope I shall be excused, if I here relate a few of the hardships which I underwent, in the course of my journey through these parts of Germany; as the account of them may put future travellers on their guard, or, at least, prevent surprize, under similar circumstances.

And first, I must inform them that I did not meet with a chaise, or carriage, of any kind, that had a top, or covering, to protect paſſengers from heat, cold, wind, or rain, in my whole journey; and ſo violent are the jolts, and ſo hard are the ſeats of German poſt-wagons, that a man is rather kicked than carried from one place to another. Yet, for theſe wretched conveyances, when I travelled in them alone, *extra-poſte*, as it is called, it coſt me frequently at the rate of eighteen pence for each Engliſh mile: ſo great is the number of fees and taxes on this occaſion: Poſtgeld, Wagengeld, Schoſſegeld, Schwagergeld, Schmiergeld, Barriergeld, and Drinkgeld, to hundreds, but particularly to the Stallknecht, for getting Pferden, horſes, ready in ſomewhat leſs than than three hours*.

* For ſuch of my readers as may be unacquainted with the language of their progenitors, the Saxons, it may be neceſſary to tranſlate the names of the impoſts above mentioned, into their Engliſh equivalents, of *horſe-hire, chaiſe-hire, turnpikes, poſtilion, greaſing wheels, toll at the gates*, on both ſides each town, as well as *drink* to the oſtler, and a ſwarm of helpers,

But such as are provided with a comfortable carriage, with beds, provisions, and a number of servants, and are so indifferent about expence, that they calmly submit to all kinds of impositions, as things of course, may be utterly ignorant of the sufferings of others who dread expence; and who are exposed to all the plagues of bad vehicles, bad horses, bad inns, and worse provisions, or who are unable to find either inns or provisions of any kind.

The excellent roads, inns, and carriages, throughout Great Britain, make an Englishman very unfit to encounter such hardships; but indeed they exceed those of most other countries in Europe so much, that to travel with a *Vittorino*, a *Procaccio*, or a *Corriere*, through the worst *Italian* roads, is ease and luxury,

---

helpers, who, in removing baggage, steal cordage, straps, and every thing which they can carry off undiscovered.

compared with what is suffered in Germany.

At Lobeschütz, which is situated on the Elbe, I quitted the chaise, and hired a boat down that river to Dresden, in order to escape two or three terrible posts, and indeed postilions, for every German 𝕾𝖈𝖍𝖜𝖆𝖌𝖊𝖗 is such a friend to surgery, that I always wished to get out of his hands; and, besides personal safety, the country is so mountainous, and road so full of holes, and great loose stones, that both carriage and baggage frequently suffer. It was now six o'clock in the evening, when I arrived at the waterside; I was much disturbed at seeing the boat, in which I was to perform the voyage; it was long, narrow, and quite open at the top. There was straw to lye on, but nothing to cover me or my baggage in case of rain; at this time, indeed, the weather was hot, and I nestled into my straw, accommodating myself to my circumstrances as well as I could.

The boat moved so very slow, there being only one waterman, that it frequently seemed to stand still. The weather as yet continued calm, but as we proceeded lower down the river, through an amazingly wild and rocky country, there were frequent waterfalls that made a violent noise, and seemed very likely to overset our little boat; about midnight it grew totally dark, and began to rain; I protected my head as well as I was able, with a *parapluye*, or small umbrella; but was very wet elsewhere.

The rain continued till day-break, after which, the wind got up, and became quite furious, just in our teeth; in this kind of hurricane, the boat could make no way. Distress on distress! the *parapluye*, my only defence, was forced from my hands, in a violent gust of wind, and blown into the river, where it instantly sunk; and we tried in vain, a considerable time, to fish it up: I was now wet, cold, hungry, and totally helpless;

less; for the boatman himself was in despair of ever getting to Dresden during this storm!

At length, however, we reached KÖ-NINGSTEIN, a village and castle, on one of the highest rocks in Europe; this was but half way from Lobeschütz to Dresden. I sent my servant and the boat-man to try if they could procure a chaise, a cart, a wheelbarrow, or any thing, to carry me to Pirna, the first post-town, and after keeping me shivering with cold and wet, more than an hour, they returned with the news of having procured a wagon.

Here I got some bread, which revived me a little, and enabled me to clamber up this terrible rock, on foot, to warm myself; which it did as effectually, before I reached the summit, as if I had had recourse to a warm bed and sudorific. After this I had twelve English miles to Pirna, through the most stony and jumbling road I ever travelled.

At

At PIRNA, the place where the king of Pruffia took all the Saxon troops prisoners, at the beginning of the laſt war, I was detained two hours before I could get horſes, for each of which, by a new *reglement,* or regulation, I was obliged to pay a rixdollar, inſtead of a florin, the uſual price.

At Köningſtein and Pirna, there are ſchools for muſic, though both are in Saxony. At Pirna, there is one for the children of officers, and one for thoſe of the poorer ſort, where they learn, as elſewhere, muſic, with reading and writing.

It would be tireſome to the reader were I minutely to deſcribe all the muſic-ſchools which I entered in my way through Auſtria, Moravia, Bohemia, and Saxony. I ſhall only ſay, that in general, the performance of the ſcholars in them was rude and coarſe, and that perfection ſeems never aimed at amongſt them. Metaſtaſio is of opinion, that the children learn ſo ill in theſe ſchools, as to be ever afterwards incorrigible; indeed, moſt of them are intended for ſervants, and mean employments; and as, in many parts of Bohemia and Saxony, the Gothic power over vaſſals ſtill ſubſiſts, theſe people have ſeldom any ambition to excel in muſic, as they have no opportunities of mending their condition by it; now and then, indeed, a man of genius among them, becomes an admirable muſician whether he will or no; but when that happens, he generally runs away, and ſettles in ſome other country, where he can enjoy the fruit of his talents.

Upon the whole, however, it is manifeſt from theſe ſchools, that it is not *nature*, but *cultivation*, which makes muſic ſo generally underſtood by the Germans; and it has been ſaid by an accurate obſerver of human nature, who has long reſided among them, that " if " innate genius exiſts, Germany cer- " tainly is not the ſeat of it; though it " muſt be allowed, to be that of per- " ſeverance and application".

The road from Pirna to Drefden is good; the country on the left hand is flat, naked, and unpleafant to the eye, when the grain is off the ground; but on the right, the hills, covered with vines and houfes, all along the banks of the Elbe, are delightful.

DRESDEN.

The approach to this city through the Elector's Gardens, by a beautiful *Chateau*, or Villa, and pavilions, in a very good tafte, is extremely ftriking; but the city itfelf has fuffered fo much in the laft war, that it is difficult for a ftranger to imagine himfelf near the celebrated capital of Saxony, even when he fees it from the moft favourable eminence in the neighbourhood, fo few of it's once many cloudcapt towers are left ftanding; only two or three remain intire, of all the ftately edifices which formerly embellifhed this city: fo that here, as well as at
Prague,

Prague, the inhabitants are still repairing the ravages of the Prussians; of whom it is remarkable, that though, during the last war, they ruined many a noble city, they never took one by a regular siege.

They were in possession of Dresden three years: it was taken from them during the absence of the king of Prussia, by the prince of Deux-ponts, who commanded the army of the empire. In 1760; that monarch invested it again, and did incredible damage by his batteries, and bombardments, till it was relieved by general Lacy.

The river Elbe divides the city into two parts, which are called the Old and New Town; these have a communication by one of the finest bridges in Europe, built of white stone, and consisting of eighteen arches; it is 540 feet long, and 36 broad. There is a rule observed in passing this bridge, worthy of imitation; one side being appropriated to the use of those who are

are going to the Old Town, and the other to those who are going to the New; so that each passenger moves without interruption, and has his right hand constantly next the parapet wall.

The first thing I did, after my arrival, was to wait on Mr. Osborn, our minister at this court, who received me so well, and honoured me with so many kind offices, and marks of regard, during my residence at Dresden, that, to forget, or conceal them, would be the highest ingratitude.

He was no sooner informed of my musical curiosity, than he made me acquainted with Signor Bezozzi, the celebrated hautbois player, in the service of this court; and, upon conversing with this able performer, I found that he was not only possessed of an excellent understanding, but that he had thought more profoundly concerning the theory of his art, than most practical musicians with whom I had conversed, who had devot-

ed

ed so much time to any one instrument, as he must have bestowed upon the hautbois, in order to acquire that high degree of perfection upon it, to which he has attained. The father of signor Bezozzi, who is still living, and in the service of the elector of Saxony, is brother to the famous Bezozzis of Turin.

Mr. Osborn was so kind, during this interview with Signor Bezozzi, as to desire him to collect together in a few days the best band of musical performers which Dresden could furnish, in order to afford me an opportunity of hearing, in a concert at his house, whatever that city could furnish most perfect in practical music.

The day after my arrival, Mr. Osborn did me the honour of carrying me to dine with several of the foreign ministers, at the house of Dr. Bayley, a worthy English physician, no less remarkable for skill in his profession, than for hospitality: and in the evening to the prime minister,

minister, count Sachen, who occupies the first floor of the late count Brühl's palace, of which his eldest son, the Starost, has only the second. Here we staid till the Electoral family arrived from the country, to go to the opera.

It was only a burletta, that was represented to-night in the little theatre, which is small, but neat; it has four rows of boxes, nineteen in each. *L'Amore innocente* was the name of the piece, of which Signor Salieri was the composer. The music was as innocent of design, as the drama and performance: nothing in the least seducing or inflammatory was to be heard or seen; but all was tranquil, unmeaning, and as truly soporific as a nurse's lullaby.

The best singer in this placid pastoral, was Signora Calori, who, twelve or fourteen years ago, when in England, wanted only spirit to make her an excellent performer; for then her voice, shake, and execution, were good; her person
ele-

elegant, and features regular; but now, some of these particulars being rather impaired by time, her performance passed as unnoticed as that of the rest, which was insipid to a very tiresome degree.

I must, however, mention, that in the second act of this opera, Signora Calori sung a long *bravura* song, accompanied on the violin, *obligato*, by M. Hunt, the principal violinist of this place, in which both these performers executed many great difficulties with little effect. He has indeed a very strong hand, and clear tone; but neither his taste nor expression are of the most delicate or touching kind.

Sunday, 20th September. I went this morning to the *Frauen Kirche*, or great Lutheran church of our Lady, placed on the side of a spacious square; it is a very noble and elegant building, of white stone, with a high dome in the middle; this church is square without, but formed into an amphitheatre within. There is is a projection for the communion table, over which is placed a moſt magnificent organ. This is the only inſtance I can recollect, of an organ being placed at the *eaſt* end of a church. I had hitherto only ſeen it at the weſt window, at the weſt end of the choir, or on one ſide.

The ſinging here, with ſo fine an inſtrument, has a very ſtriking effect. The whole congregation, conſiſting of near three thouſand perſons, ſing in uniſon, melodies almoſt as ſlow as thoſe uſed in our pariſh churches; but the people being better muſicians here than with us, and accuſtomed from their infancy to ſing the chief part of the ſervice, were better in tune, and formed one of the grandeſt choruſſes I ever heard.

The building is very high and ſpacious, and there are four galleries in elegant forms, one over the other, between the columns: the ſeats below are circular, and all facing the organ and communion table; upon the whole, this was
one

one of the moſt decent and reſpectable congregations which I had ever ſeen.

The King of Pruſſia, in his laſt bombardment of Dreſden, tried every means in his power to beat this church, as well as the other public buildings, about the ears of the inhabitants, but in vain, for the orbicular form of the dome threw off the balls and ſhells, and totally prevented their effect: however, he ſucceeded better in five or ſix other churches, which he totally demoliſhed. This of our Lady conſtitutes the great feature of the city, like St. Peter's at Rome, and St. Paul's in London.

When I quitted this church, I ſtepped into the Elector's chapel, which is a new, large, and elegant building, adorned with ſeveral capital paintings, by Mengs, and Battoni. I was too late to hear the organ, or any thing but the ordinary ritual of the Romiſh church *.

* The court is of a different religion from the people, who are Lutherans.

At noon Mr. Osborn carried me to court, where, after waiting about an hour, in the drawing-room, among the ambassadors and great officers of state, for the arrival of the Elector, I had the honour of being presented to his highness as soon as he entered: he was pleased to enquire, " from whence I " came last?" I answered, from Vienna; but Mr. Osborn informed his highness, that I had been at Munich, and had had the honour of being presented to the Electress dowager, his mother, and added something concerning my musical enquiries; this seemed to awaken curiosity. " You love music?" "Yes Sir." " Have you " been in Italy?" and upon my answering in the affirmative, his Electoral highness appeared to be pleased, and desirous of entering into a more particular conversation; but, throwing his eyes around, and seeing the foreign ministers, officers of state, and a number of strangers, and people of condition eager for notice, and expecting their share of his attention, he turned about, and spoke two or three words to prince Beloselsky, the Russian minister; then one or two to the Prussian and Austrian ministers, after which he retired.

His Electoral highness was born 1750, and succeeded to the electorate, upon the death of his father, in 1763; he is of a reserved disposition. Naumann, his *maestro di capella*, and Gasman, had informed me, that his highness was so good a musician as to accompany readily, and in a masterly manner, on the harpsichord, at sight; but was so shy of playing before company, that even the Electress, his consort, had hardly ever heard him. His favourite amusement is dancing, and, to oblige him, his subjects and courtiers are dancing for ever.

When the Elector quitted the drawing-room, every one hastened up another pair of stairs, to the apartment of the Electress. I had the honour of being presented

sented to her highness, as she passed by, in her way to dinner; she was a princess Palatine of Deuxponts, and born in 1752; she is tall and thin, of a fresh rosy complexion, and has strong indications of good humour in her countenance.

After dinner, Mr. Osborn honoured me so far as to carry me with him in a round of visits to all the foreign ministers, and to the houses of several other persons of distinction.

There was at this time in Dresden, an Englishman, Mr. Tunnerstick, who was born at Pool, in Dorsetshire, but brought up in France, and who, last summer, in several parts of Germany, had undertaken to perform a very curious experiment: it was no less, than to drive a nail through the brain of a horse, by which he would be, to all appearance dead; but, after extracting the nail, and pouring into the wound a chemical liquor prepared by himself for that purpose, the horse in five or six minutes time, was to recover sufficiently to carry any one of the spectators.

Mr. Tunnerstick was at Vienna at the same time as myself, and performed before thousands of spectators; but the account of the operation seemed to me so extraordinary, that imagining there was some quackery or deception in it, I would not make one of the number. However, upon my arrival at Dresden, I found that he had repeatedly performed the same thing there, before physicians, anatomists, and the whole court; one of the horses that had undergone this singular operation, and was recovered, had been killed by command of the Elector, in order, by dissection to ascertain the fact, whether the nail had really penetrated the brain; and it was allowed by all the physicians and surgeons of the place, to have passed through the most dangerous part of it. Another horse that had been *assassinated* in the same barbarous manner,

ner, at the same time and place, was recovered, and continued perfectly well, when I left Dresden.

The Elector wishing to have this medicine turned to some useful account, and not merely employed in healing wounds made through wanton cruelty, had asked this equestrian operator, whether it would be equally efficacious if applied to fresh wounds in other parts of the body? Dr. Tunnerstick answered in the affirmative; but afterwards, pretending to take offence at some doubts, that had been expressed, concerning the success of this second experiment, evaded making it, and went away in a pet.

In the evening I was again carried to court, where the Electoral family, with their principal attendants were at cards. I here had the honour of being presented to the Elector's three brothers; prince Charles Maximilian, presumptive heir to the Electorate, born in 1752; prince Anthony Clement, born in 1755, intended

tended for the church; and prince Maximilian Emanuel, born in 1759. The eldest of these princes has the misfortune to be so lame, that he is obliged to wheel himself about in a chair; having not only lost the use, but almost the appearance of his legs; he seems, however, very intelligent and curious in conversation. The other two are far from robust.

The next day I was presented to the two princesses, sisters of the Elector; the eldest, though but fifteen, is formed, and perfectly well-bred; she honoured me so far as to speak a considerable time to me concerning the Electress dowager, her mother, whom Mr. Osborn had told her, I had seen frequently at Munich. The youngest sister, about twelve years of age, is very pretty, and has a sharp and intelligent countenance; she spoke but little, however that little was pertinent and obliging.

Dresden

Dresden still affords matter of great amusement to the eye of a stranger, though much less to the *ear*, than formerly. If I quit my musical remarks for a moment, in order to give the reader an idea of the contents of the Elector's celebrated picture gallery, I hope I shall be pardoned; as the catalogue is but in few hands, and the collection is, without doubt, the first, and most considerable in Europe, both for the number and excellence of the paintings it contains *.

The collection was begun by Augustus II. but was greatly augmented by his successor, Augustus the III. who, in 1745, purchased, for sixty thousand pounds, the whole gallery of the duke of Modena, in which were all the paintings of Correggio, as well as most of those by

* The collection of prints, commonly called, the Dresden gallery, was never finished, and only contains engravings from a small number of these pictures.

Anibal Carrach, which enrich the prefent collection; and, in 1748, he added to it the imperial gallery of Prague, which he purchafed of the Emprefs queen; this collection he acquired at a very eafy rate, having had fixty-eight capital pictures of eminent mafters for fixty thoufand florins, which is lefs than fix thoufand pounds fterling; but, even fince that time, the collection has been augmented by fuch a number of different purchafes, that many hundred excellent pictures are placed againft the wainfcot of the gallery three or four deep, for want of room to hang them up; and though the printed catalogue makes the outward gallery contain only eight hundred and thirty, and the interiour three hundred and fifty-feven, I was affured by the Cicerone, or Interpreter, that the Elector was in poffeffion of two thoufand original paintings, and two thoufand four hundred copies.

In the cabinet of crayon paintings, there are no lefs than a hundred and fifty-feven portraits by Rofalba, among which, is that of Fauftina, when young, and in the fervice of this court. She was very handfome when this was painted, or was very much flattered; there is likewife in this cabinet, a portrait, in crayons, by Mengs, of Mingotti, when young, with a mufic paper in her hand; and if the refemblance was exact, fhe was then nearer a beauty, than it is now eafy to imagine her ever to have been; fhe is here painted in youth, plumpnefs, and with a very expreffive countenance.

There are only two Raphaels, in this immenfe collection; the St. George is the beft; the other, an afcenfion of the Virgin, with the *Bambino* in her arms, and pope Sextus Quintus and St. Barb, in the act of adoration, has fuffered greatly in the colouring; the heads, however, are charming. There is not one piece by Domenichini in the gallery, though
there

there are eleven capital works by Guido; eleven by Albano, twelve by Guercino, seventeen by Paul Veronese, ten by Anibal Carracci, seventeen by Vandyke, four by Parmegiano, thirteen by Nic. Poussin, eleven by Spagnolet, thirty-nine by Rubens, and fifteen by Titian, with three by Leonardo da Vinci.

But the most precious pieces of this collection, are the Correggios, of which charming painter, there are six capital pictures.

First. The *Virgin* sitting on a throne, with Jesus on her knee; she is surrounded by St. John the Baptist, St. Catherine, St. Anthony of Padua, and St. Francis d'Assisi, all as big as the life; this is in his first manner; he has written his name on it: the colouring is less bright than in his succeeding works; but the elegance and grace of the figures are very striking.

Second. The *St. George*, exquisite in colouring and keeping.

Third.

Third. The *Magdalen*, which is beautiful and delicate beyond description.

Fourth. The *Nativity*, known by the name of the *Night-piece* of Correggio; all the light comes from the child: it is the most perfect of his works. The King of Prussia stopped half an hour to admire it, when he first entered Dresden. The Electress Queen offered it to him, but he declined taking it; however, he had a fine copy made of it by Dietrich, at a very high price.

Fifth. The *St. Sebastian*, a large and capital picture, in which the Virgin and Child are in glory, surrounded by a choir of angels: below are St. Sebastian, St. Geminiano, and other figures.

Sixth. A *Portrait* of Coreggio's physician; and supposed to be the only portrait that he ever painted.

There are in the cabinet, copies of the capital pictures of Raphael and Correggio, in water colours, and in enamel, uncommonly large, by Mengs, father, son,

and

and daughter, which are delicious. To examine and defcribe this vaft collection, minutely, would require ten years, and ten folios.

I had the honour of dining, to-day, with a large company, at Mr. Ofborn's. After dinner, Signor Bezozzi, and a band of muficians, which he had provided, were ready to begin a concert in a different part of the houfe from that where the company had dined. During the performance, all the foreign minifters came in and out, and, at times, the rooms were full of the firft people in Drefden.

The concert was opened by a fymphony of Haffe; after which, a folo on the violin by M. Hunt, who, as was before obferved, has a clear tone, and ftrong hand; but he wants high finifhing, and plainly difcovered that he was not much accuftomed to folo playing: the mufic which he performed was by Tartini.

The next piece was a German flute concerto, played by M. Götfel. I did not

not much like the compofition, there was noife in the choruffes, and, in the folo parts, there were repetitions of old and common paffages; but it was not compofed by the performer, who manifefted, in the courfe of it, great execution, a clear and fweet tone, always even, and perfectly in tune; though not fo full above the middle D as below it.

After this, Signor Bezozzi played an extremely difficult concerto on the hautbois, in a very pleafing and mafterly manner; yet I muft own that the lefs one thinks of Fifcher, the more one likes this performer. However, I tried to difcriminate, and to difcover in what each differed from the other: and firft, Fifcher feems to me the moft natural, pleafing, and original writer of the two, for the inftrument, and is the moft certain of his reed; which, whether from being in lefs conftant practice, or from the greater difficulty of the paffages, I know not, more frequently
fails

fails Bezozzi in rapid divisions, than Fischer: however, Bezozzi's *messa di voce*, or swell, is prodigious; indeed, he continues to augment the force of a tone so much, and so long, that it is hardly possible not to fear for his lungs.

His taste and ear are exceedingly delicate and refined; and he seems to possess a happy and peculiar faculty of tempering a continued tone to different bases, according to their several relations: upon the whole, his performance is so capital, that a hearer must be extremely fastidious not to receive from it a great degree of pleasure.

The second part of the concert began with an admirable symphony of Vanhall, produced in those happy moments of effervescence, when his reason was less powerful than his feeling.

After this, a solo of Nardini, by M. Hunt, which he executed correctly; but the composition was full of repetitions of passages, neither very new nor interesting;

teresting; and these were not meliorated by any thing remarkable in the taste or expression of the performer.

This solo was succeeded by another concerto on the German flute, by M. Götsel, which he played much better, and, indeed, it was a much better composition than the former.

Signor Bezozzi performed, after this, a new concerto on the hautbois, which was very graceful and ingenious. The *Allegro* was more rapid, and of a still more difficult execution, than that in his preceding piece. He exerted himself very much in this performance, which ended with a pleasing rondeau, and left the company in great good humour. He afterwards was prevailed on, though not without difficulty, to play, by way of *bonne bouche,* Fischer's well-known rondeau minuet, which he had performed here so frequently, and with such applause, that I had been assured he made more of it than the author himself; but
I can-

I cannot say that his present performance of it convinced me of the truth of this assertion. However, after being accustomed to the exquisite manner in which Mr. Fischer has played it in England, it is no small praise to say, that I heard Signor Bezozzi perform it with great pleasure.

On Tuesday the 22d September. At nine o'clock in the morning, I went to the *Frauen Kirche*, to hear the organ played by M. Hunger, the organist, who met me there, by appointment. This instrument, of which the largest pipe in the pedals, is thirty-two feet long, was made by old Silbermann, of Neuburg: it is one of the best works of this celebrated builder, and was constructed about twenty-three years ago. There are forty-eight stops, three sets of keys, in the manual, which extend from double D, in the base, to D in alt; and two octaves in the pedals; there is likewise a spring of communication, by which the three

sets

sets of keys may be played together, in order to augment the force of the chorus; but this renders the touch so heavy, that each key requires a foot, instead of a finger, to press it down.

The reed stops in this instrument are but seven in number, so that the imitations and changes are very few. The best solo stops it contains are the viol da gamba, bassoon, vox humana, trumpet, schalmo, tremulant, and Schwebung: this last, as the name implies, is to imitate a close shake.

M. Hunger possesses neither great fancy nor finger: but his performance was masterly, and manifested a perfect knowledge of his instrument.

This being the first organ which I had met with, that was built by Silbermann, I entered the inside case, and found the work strong, neat, and well disposed: it is remarkable that to so immense a machine, there are but five bellows.

On Sundays and festivals, the school singers frequently perform in this church

Cantatas, which in Germany is a different word for anthems; at other times the whole congregation sings in unison, accompanied only by this organ, of which the chorus, assisted, perhaps, by the form of the building, is the most noble I ever heard.

From hence I went to the great theatre, where the serious opera used to be exhibited. It was built in 1706, by Augustus the second; but was afterwards decorated, and the stage much enlarged, by Augustus the third.

I was extremely curious to see this celebrated scene of action, where *general Hasse*, and his well-disciplined troops, had made so many glorious campaigns, and acquired such laurels; all his best works having been expressly composed, as some of Metastasio's dramas were written, for its use *.

* Italy is very desirous of adopting Hasse for her son. Count Algarotti, in an epistle addressed to Augustus the third, speaking of this theatre, says,

Ivi *d'Italia l'armonia divina*
Ne' bei concenti suoi varia, e concorde
Risuona

No money was ever taken for admiſſion into this theatre, which is nearly as large as that at Milan. It has five rows of boxes, thirty in each, is of an oval form, like the theatres of Italy, and has an orcheſtra capable of containing a hundred performers.

In the year 1755, the late king of Poland had in his ſervice, for this theatre, ten *ſoprano* voices, four *contralto*, three tenors, and four baſes. Among theſe, were Fauſtina, Mingotti, Pilaia, Monticelli, Pozzi, Anibali, Amorevoli, and Campagnari. The inſtrumental performers were of the firſt claſs, and more numerous than thoſe of any other court in Europe; but, now, not above ſix or

<blockquote>
Riſuona d'Haſſe ſotto all' agil dito,
Che gli affetti del cuor, del cuor Signore,
Irrita, e molce a un ſol toccar di lira,
E pietà, com' ei vuol, ſdegno, od amore
Nuovo Timoteo in ſen d'Auguſto inſpira.

Op. del Conte Algarotti, tom. viii.
</blockquote>

eight

eight of these are to be found at Dresden*.

It was from the dispersion of this celebrated band, at the beginning of the last war, that almost every great city of Europe, and London among the rest, acquired several exquisite and favourite performers.

At present, this theatre is shut up, for œconomical reasons, no use having been made of it since the marriage of the present Elector, three years ago; at which time two operas were performed in it, one set by Hasse, and another by Naumann, the present chapel master of this court.

The opera house being in the neighbourhood of the picture gallery, I could not resist the desire of entering it again,

---

* Signor Bezozzi was so obliging as to furnish me with a list of the court and chapel musicians, now at Dresden; but, by comparing it with that published by Marpurg, in 1756, I find only the two Bezozzis, Binder, Götsel, Hunt, Neruda, and Adam, remaining of the old corps.

in order once more to contemplate the divine Coreggios; but in the way to them, through the interior gallery, my eye was caught by the magic of Battoni's Magdalen, and Pordenone's queen of Cyprus, both of which are exquifitely beautiful. The *Night-Piece* of Correggio ſtruck me more now than before; though the three figures on the left fide feem ill drawn, and one of them is too much hidden: however, the light from the Child is thrown on them fo admirably, and the expreffion of the third of thefe figures is fo natural, her eyes blinking, and hand held up to keep off the glare, that a little defect in the drawing may be well excufed. The figures in the air, are truly divine; and the Virgin and Child feem fuperior to any thing I ever faw expreffed on canvafs.

The little *Magdalen* is all beauty, foftnefs, expreffion, and grace. The frame is ornamented with precious ftones; and the late duke of Modena prized this piece fo much,

much, that he never quitted his capital without taking it with him, nor could sleep if it was not in his chamber.—— But, as I had little time to spare from my musical pursuits, for these *pictoresque* enjoyments, after this slight mention of them, I shall return to business.

Mr. Osborn, whose friendly offices supplied me every hour with opportunities of gratifying my curiosity, had engaged M. Binder, the court organist, to meet me this afternoon, at the Elector's chapel, where there is a still larger organ than that at the *Frauen Kirche*.

This instrument was begun by old Silbermann, who dying before it was finished, his nephew of Strasburg was called to Dresden to put the last hand to it. I entered the inside case of this as well as of the other organ, found the work well finished, very ingeniously arranged, and the pipes so highly polished, that they had the appearance of silver, even when nearly examined.

The

The chorus is amazingly rich and powerful; but so great is the echo, and long the continuance of the sound in this building, particularly when empty, that no melody can be heard distinctly.

M. Binder, the organist, was a scholar of the famous Hebenstreit, inventor of the *Pantaleone*, an instrument much celebrated in the beginning of this century, in the practice of which M. Binder spent all his youth; but though he applied to the organ and harpsichord late in life, he is a very able performer on both. He played three or four *fugues* in a very full and masterly manner, making great use of the pedals. I did not indeed find him possessed of much fancy; but in the German full manner of playing, there is not much opportunity of shewing it. To use the pedals of these huge instruments much, at the same time as two hands are fully employed on the stiff and heavy manuals, is a very laborious business.

The multiplicity of stops in this organ, amounting to 54, only augments noise, and adds to the weight of the touch. The *vox humana* is bad; and there are very few solo stops that are agreeable; no *swell* has ever been heard of in an organ at Dresden; and the echos to common stops, are all that can be called sweet, by themselves. The great merit of all the German organs that I had yet seen, was in the richness and power of the chorus; indeed little else is wanted, for voluntaries, like those in our parish churches, are unnecessary, where there is singing; as are imitative stops to play *retornellos*, where the real instruments abound.

Signor Bezozzi and M. Hunger, with several other masters were in the chapel to hear M. Binder; who, when he had done, was in as violent a heat with fatigue and exertion, as if he had run eight or ten miles, full-speed, over ploughed lands in the dog-days.

At

At night I went to M. Binder's houſe to ſee the ruins of the famous *Pantaleone.* This inſtrument, and the performance upon it, at Paris, in 1705, gave birth to a very ingenious little work, under the title of *Dialogue ſur la Muſique des Anciens,* by the Abbé Chateauneuf,: the inventor went by the name of his inſtrument ever after; it is more than nine feet long, and had, when in order, 186 ſtrings of catgut. The tone was produced by two *baguettes,* or ſticks, like the dulcimer; it muſt have been extremely difficult to the performer, but ſeems capable of great effects. The ſtrings were now almoſt all broken, the preſent Elector will not be at the charge of furniſhing new ones, though it had ever been thought a court inſtrument in former reigns, and was kept in order at the expence of the prince. M. Binder lamented, that he could not poſſibly afford to ſtring it himſelf, as it was an in-

ſtrument

strument upon which he had formerly employed so much of his time.

Every one here is in the utmost indigence; this poor man has a small nominal pension, as court organist, but it is ill-paid; and most of the nobility and gentry are too much impoverished, to be able to afford to learn, or to let their children learn music.

The Saxons of old, so remarkable for patience, industry, and probity, are now reduced to knavery and chicane, beyond the inhabitants of any other country. Dresden is at present a melancholy residence; from being the seat of the Muses, and habitation of pleasure, it is now only a dwelling for beggary, theft, and wretchedness. No society among the natives can be supported; all must retrench; the court is obliged to abandon genius and talents, and is, in turn, abandoned by them!

Except the wretched comic opera, there is no one spectacle, but that of misery, fery, to be feen at Drefden; no *guinguette*, no public diverfion in the city or fuburbs, for the people, and not a boat or veffel either of pleafure or bufinefs can be defcried on the river Elbe, which is here nearly as wide as the Thames at Londonbridge *.

The horfes in this Electorate have had no corn allowed them, nor the foldiers powder for their hair, thefe three years; but though every fpecies of oeconomy feems now put in practice, yet, it is thought with little effect, as to reftoring the inhabitants and ftate to their ancient affluence and fplendor.

During the reign of Auguftus the IIId this city was regarded by the reft of Eu-

* The Saxon traffic *up* this fine river, is faid to be ruined by fome commercial difputes with Auftria; and *down* it, by the king of Pruffia not permitting a fingle veffel from Drefden to pafs by his fortrefs at Magdeburg; fo that befides paying heavy duties, all goods muft be removed into Pruffian veffels before they are fuffered to proceed to Hamburg.

rope, as the Athens of modern times; all the arts, but particularly, those of music, poetry, and painting, were loved and cherished by that prince, with a zeal and munificence, greater than can be found in the brightest period of ancient history; but, perhaps, some part of the late and present distresses of this country, have originated in this excessive magnificence.

The gardens of the late minister, count Brühl, which are situated on the banks of the Elbe, and open to the public, command a delightful prospect of that river, of its hilly and fertile banks, towards Pirna, and of the New Town, and beautiful bridge, leading to it.

A most magnificent and elegant temple in these gardens was reduced to a heap of rubbish, in which it still lies, during the Prussian bombardment; and the Saxons accuse his Prussian majesty of carrying personal resentment against their minister so far, as to order his engineer to point his artillery at the temple and other

other buildings, as well as statues in these gardens. However this may have been, not a street of this once charming city has recovered the devastations of the last war.

The present Elector is a great encourager of honesty and good morals in his subjects; and has manifested himself to be susceptible of the tender feelings of humanity, by the abolition of racks and tortures, to which criminals were exposed in his dominions, during former reigns.

The late minister, count Brühl, left three sons at his decease, of whom the eldest only, known by the name of the *Starost**, now resides at Dresden. I had the honour of being presented to this nobleman, whose figure and appearance are the most perfect and pleasing I ever saw; he is said to be very accomplished, and a great musician; he condescended to desire Mr.

---

* *Starost* is a Polish title given to the lord, and principal judge of a *starosty*, or fief. Count Bruhl, is starost of Warsaw, *starosta* Warszawski.

Osborn

Osborn to bring me with him to one of his country residences, to see his books, hear music, and converse about it at leisure; but the tasks I had assigned myself would allow of no such tranquil enjoyment.

However, I remained one day longer at Dresden than I intended, at the obliging instance of his excellency count Sachen, minister for foreign affairs, who did me the honour to invite me in the most pressing manner to dine with him. This nobleman gives a public dinner once a week to the foreign ministers, to persons of condition, and to strangers, in a truly hospitable and splendid manner; and though his appointment is not great, so considerable is his private fortune, that he is able to support the dignity of his office at his own expence, without aggravating the present miseries of the people, by appropriating the public money, either to enrich himself or maintain magnificence.

The

The count's entertainment was one of the moſt ſumptuous I ever ſaw; the company confiſted of near forty perſons, of both ſexes, moſt of whom were of high rank and condition; each courſe was ſerved on the moſt elegant plate, and beautiful Dreſden china,—But to return to muſic.

I have had frequent occaſion, in the courſe of my journey, to mention the Singſchüler or ſinging boys of the *muſic ſchool*, commonly called *poor ſcholars*; and during my reſidence at Dreſden, I procured all the information I could concerning the origin of this inſtitution, and the following is the reſult of my enquiries.

When the Roman catholic religion was the only one profeſſed in this country, the clergy, who officiated in cathedrals and collegiate churches, uſed to employ boys, that had good voices, to ſing part of the divine ſervice in the choirs, in nearly the ſame manner as the choriſters,

risters, in English cathedrals, sing at present. In recompense, the clergy maintained and educated these boys, and prepared all such as had a literary genius for the priesthood.

The change of religion propounded to the Saxons, by Martyn Luther, though supported by powerful protectors, and forwarded by favourable circumstances, had great obstacles to surmount: the chief part of the people of the city of Dresden were so far from having a propensity to embrace the new preached doctrine, that they obstinately refused to give into any religious innovations. This is so true, that the custom of shutting the city gates, during divine service, which custom is observed to this day, had its rise from the people's dislike to the new liturgy: for the citizens having been observed to go in great numbers to walk in the fields while the public prayers were performing, rather than assist at them, the gates were ordered to be shut, to prevent the inhabitants from going out, and they were forced to church by the foldiers then in garrifon. At prefent, the army is never made ufe of for that purpofe, for the Saxons are now as ftrongly attached to the tenets of Luther, as they were then to the Roman catholic religion.

Upon the fecularization of bifhopricks, the fuppreffion of abbies, and the alienation of their lands, the finging boys loft the only means of fubfiftance that they had. But the clergy of the new religion foon began to employ thefe voices, by making them fing canticles in the ftreets, which dwelt on the impropriety of fuch articles, in the Roman catholic religion, as were to be rejected, and extolled the tenets they began to preach, in order to accuftom and familiarize, by degrees, the ears of the people to Luther's religious fentiments, and infenfibly to gain them univerfal approbation.

It is generally thought, that thefe fcholars or finging boys contributed greatly to the rapid progrefs of the Lutheran religion in Saxony. There being no fixed foundation to provide for the continual fupport of thefe fingers, fuch families as favoured the reformation, readily confented to contribute towards it, by voluntary gifts; and when the people became all Proteftants, thefe difcretionary charities encreafed. The method prefcribed to them to follow and obferve, is this: the town is divided into certain wards; when they begin to fing, the firft of the month, for inftance, before the doors of the principal ward, they fing the fecond of the month at the next; and fo on, till they have fucceffively made their finging rounds over all the wards of the city, which they commence again in a perpetual rotation.

Befides the ufual turn, it is cuftomary with families of diftinction, and fome

citizens

citizens who maintain the strictest appearance of devotion, to appoint these scholars to sing before their houses once or twice in the week, for which they receive extraordinary payment, and although that is discretionary, yet it is so far regulated, that no one should give them less than two *groschen*, or four pence for every canticle they sing. Some families employ them to sing gay genial airs on birth-days and name-days; and they are frequently engaged to sing mournful ditties and dirgies at night, with lighted torches in their hands, before the houses of the rich and opulent, when they die; and they accompany the funerals to the place of interrment, singing the *neniæ*, in the same manner the *præficæ*, or weeping women, at the burials of the ancients, used to do.

It is to be observed, that besides the laborious way of singing in the streets during the whole winter, in a severe climate, they are obliged to sing in different churches every Sunday and festival.

val. They are generally divided into troops of sixteen or eighteen together, and what they collect during the whole week, is put into a common box, which is opened every Saturday by the rector of the school, and what remains over and above their necessary expences, he divides into small sums among them, in proportion to their musical merit; for when he that leads the vocal band gets a dollar to his share, the next that excels gets but a florin, or two thirds of a dollar. These shares are not entrusted into their own hands immediately, but are kept for them by the rector, till they have also finished their classics, and then, at their quitting the school, they respectively receive their savings.

Those who know Latin and Greek tolerably well, become school-masters in the different parishes throughout Saxony; but they must be able to play upon the organ, because every parish church, even the smallest, in Saxony,

is

is furnished with an organ, and a set of such instruments as are usually employed in church-music.

Those, among the singing scholars, who are found to have the best genius, and the greatest disposition to the learned professions, are sent either to the university of Leipsic, or to that of Wittemberg, where they are established, as vacancies happen, on the foundation, in those seminaries of literature called *Convectorium*, where they are maintained without any expence to their friends.

The two universities support above 300 of these poor students; when they have finished the common course of philosophy, they apply themselves, as their different inclinations lead them, either to divinity, law, or physic, and often become very useful in different branches of learning. Those who discover a particular genius and propensity to music, confine themselves entirely to that art, as a regular profession.

Even at the common boarding-schools of this city, children are taught to sing hymns in parts. The school singers who frequent the streets, not excepting the little boys, wear a black undertaker-like uniform, and large grizzle wigs; and as every house pays annually something towards their support, the ambassadors generally give them a crown a quarter, for *not* singing at *their* doors.

Musical airs, known by the name of *Polonoises*, are very much in vogue at Dresden, as well as in many other parts of Saxony; and it is probable, that this was brought about during the long intercourse between the Poles and Saxons, during the reigns of Augustus the second and third.

The *strofil*, which is a musical instrument, made of pieces of glass of different lengths, instead of wood or metal, and is played on by sticks, like the *sticcado*, is much used by the common people throughout Saxony.

M. Ho-

M. Homilius, cantor of the *Kreuz-kirche* in this city, is a great contrapuntift, and church-compofer, and in high efteem throughout Germany; and M. Adam, a veteran mufician, one of the few remaining performers in the celebrated opera-band, under the direction of Signor Haffe, has eftablifhed a great reputation by his compofition of the mufic to the dances performed at this opera in its moft flourifhing ftate.

LEIPSIC.

This city has not yet recovered its rigorous treatment during the laft war; and its celebrated fair, which ufed to be the rendezvous of the rich, the gay, and the induftrious citizens of every quarter of the globe, as well as an affembly of the fovereign princes and nobility of all the northern parts of Europe, feems now dwindled into a common mart, or quarterly fair, fuch as is held in a fmall Englifh market-town.

M. Ebe-

M. Ebeling, of Hamburg, a man of letters, and an extremely well-informed *dilettante* in music, on the publication of my account of *The present State of Music in France and Italy*, had voluntarily favoured me with several very intelligent letters, and useful communications, concerning the musical History of Germany; and, upon his being informed of my intention to travel through that country, he carried his zeal so far as to write to several of his friends, and to able professors in the different cities of my route, pressing them, in the most urgent manner, to afford me all possible information and assistance in my enterprize.

On coming to Leipsic, I experienced the good effects of his friendship, in the reception I met with from M. Hiller, music-director of this city, whom he had prepared, by letter, for my arrival. This gentleman, who is not only an eminent writer on the subject of music, but the first and most popular composer of comic

comic operas in the German language, was indefatigable in his endeavours to serve me the whole time I remained at Leipsic.

I expected to receive much information concerning music and musicians from M. Breitkopf, the most considerable vender of musical compositions in Europe, whom I visited immediately on my arrival in this city; but I found him rather taciturn than communicative. He claims the honour of being the inventor of musical types, and seems entitled to it, as he has, for thirteen or fourteen years, furnished his own country, as well as other parts of Europe, with a prodigious quantity of music from his press, of all kinds, by the greatest composers of the present age, of which he prints catalogues quarterly; he seems likewise to have been the first who gave to his catalogues an index *in notes,* containing the *subjects,* or two or three first bars, of the several pieces in each musical work;

by

by which a reader is enabled to difcover not only whether he is in poffeffion of an *entire* book, but of any part of it's contents.

Befides *printed* copies of works of the moſt celebrated compoſers of all nations, he ſells in manuſcript, at a reaſonable price, ſingle pieces of any work already printed, as well as of innumerable others which have never been publiſhed.

M. Hiller, who hardly ever quitted me from my arrival to my departure, was ſo obliging, the firſt evening, as to take me with him into his box at the comic opera. This city, before the laſt war, uſed to find conſtant employment for a company of comedians; but ſince that time no one has been long ſtationary there: the preſent company was juſt arrived from Berlin, where they had been during eighteen months. The piece they repreſented this night, was the *Déſerteur*, in German; but to M. Gretry's original muſic. The performers

mers did not charm me, either by their finging or acting; all were out of tune, out of time, and vulgar. I hardly ever was more tired; but indeed, after travelling all night in an open wagon, a better performance would with difficulty have kept me awake. However, from hence, I went home with M. Hiller, whofe great good nature and intelligence, furnifhed a much better and more interefting entertainment than the theatre had done.

The next morning, September 25, M. Hiller was fo obliging as to conduct me to the play-houfe, where one of his comic operas was rehearfing The overture, and one fong, had been performed when we entered, but all was begun again. I found this mufic very natural and pleafing, and deferving of much better performers than the prefent Leipfic company can boaft; for, to fay the truth, the finging here is as vulgar and ordinary as our common finging in England,

among

among those who have neither had the advantage of being taught, nor of hearing good singing. There is just the same pert snap in taking the high notes, which they do with a kind of beat, and very loud, instead of a *messa di voce*, or swell. The instrumental parts went ill; but as this was the first rehearsal, they might have been disciplined into good order, if M. Hiller had chosen to bounce and play the tyrant a little; for it is a melancholy reflection to make, that few composers are well treated by an orchestra, till they have first used the performers roughly, and made themselves formidable.

I endeavoured to account for the bad manner of singing which prevails so generally among the performers on the Leipsic stage, and I could suggest nothing that was so likely to explain it, as the distance which this town is at present from an Italian opera, which being usually supplied by Italians, is an excellent school for singing, to the inhabitants of

places

places where operas are constantly performed: as at Manheim, Ludwigsbourg, Munich, Vienna, and Dresden, where I found the common singing very pleasing, the expression natural, and the carriage of the voice far from vicious; in all these places, Italian operas have long been established, which have certainly had an effect on the public taste, and manner of singing.

At the latter end of the last century, and in the beginning of this, Italian operas very frequently made a part of the public amusements at Leipsic, during the three annual fairs, at New Year's tide, Easter, and Michaelmas: and so great was the passion for these exhibitions, in 1703, that six new operas were performed there within the compass of that year. In 1720, these representations were discontinued; and I do not find any memorial of their having been revived since that time.

When

When the rehearsal of M. Hiller's burletta was over, he was so kind as to attend me through the town, in search of books. It seems, by the catalogues published in this city, at the two great fairs of Easter and Michaelmas, that more books are printed in Germany, than in any other country of Europe: and perhaps Leipsic has a greater share in these publications, than any other city of Germany.

In a second visit to Breitkopf, I mounted his printing office, and found a great number of presses at work, of various kinds, for his publications are not confined to music. Among the several questions which my curiosity put to the workmen, one was, how many different characters were used for letter-press, and what proportion they bore in their number to the types used in printing? and I was much surprised to find, that the different characters employed in the music-press, were upwards of three hundred, and that there were not more than one hundred ufed in common printing.

I entered fome of the principal churches here, and found them in general very fine, and very dirty*. There are, however, in feveral of them good organs, particularly in the reformed church; but I heard no great player in any one of them, nor did I find, upon enquiry, that this city is at prefent in poffeffion of many performers of the firft clafs, upon any inftrument. It muft not be inferred from hence, that Leipfic has been lefs the refidence of genius than other places, as it would not be difficult to trace a fucceffion of able mafters with which it has

* In Charles the fifth's time, before religious difputes were adjufted, a kind of truce was agreed on between the catholics and reformers, under the title of *Interim*, which ftipulated, that the ornaments and veftments of the church, as well as fome of the ceremonies, fhould remain in *ftatu quo*, till, by a general council, religious peace was finally concluded; and this *Interim* was afterwards adopted in fome of the free cities, where the churches, though ftill in the poffeffion of Lutherans, retain all the ancient ornaments of the Roman catholic times.

been supplied for near a century past; but the musical history of this city can furnish no circumstance more interesting to the lovers of harmony, than its having been the residence of the great Sebastian Bach, father of the present eminent musicians of that name, from the year 1723, to his death in 1754.

This celebrated master, who was successively cantor, organist, and music-director, at Leipsic, was born at Eisenach, in Saxony, 1685. There has been a constant succession of great musicians in his family, for more than two hundred years. All the musical writers of Germany, for these last fifty years, have given testimony to his abilities: M. Quantz, in his *Art of Playing the Flute*, written during the life of Sebastian Bach, says, that this admirable musician had brought organ-playing to the highest degree of perfection; and M. Marpurg, in his *Treatise upon Fugues*, published soon after his death, in speaking of him, says, that

that he united in himself the talents of many great men: deep science, a fertile and lively genius, an easy and natural taste, and the most powerful hand that can be imagined.

The challenge which he received, and accepted, from the celebrated French organist, Marchand, at Dresden, is well known in Germany. Upon the arrival of Marchand in that city, after he had vanquished all the organ players of France and Italy, he offered to play, extempore, with any German whom the King of Poland could prevail upon to enter the lists against him; no one at Dresden had the courage to encounter so successful a champion, but an express being sent to Sebastian Bach, who was at that time a young man, and residing at Weymar*, he came away immediately, and, like another David, vanquished this Goliah. It must not, however, be concluded from hence, that

---

* Sebastian Bach resided at Weymar, from the year 1708, to 1717.

Marchand was a mean performer; if that had been the cafe, the victory over him would have added nothing to the fame of his competitor. It was an honour to Pompey that he was conquered by Cæsar, and to Marchand to be only vanquished by Bach.

Besides many excellent compositions for the church, this author produced *Ricercari,* consisting of preludes, and fugues, for the organ, upon two, three, and four subjects; in *Modo recto & Contrario,* and in every one of the twenty-four keys. All the present organ-players of Germany are formed upon his school, as most of those on the harpsichord, clavichord, and *piano forte* are upon that of his son, the admirable Carl. Phil. Emanuel Bach; so long known by the name of Bach of Berlin, but now music-director at Hamburg.

As Leipsic was the last considerable town in Saxony to which I extended my musical enquiries, it seems here the place to remark, that this Electorate has been extremely fertile in muficians of extraordinary genius and abilities: for it has given birth to Keifer, Handel, the Bach family, to Haffe, and to Graun.

* * * *

A word or two more of travelling in Germany, and I have done with defcription and complaints.

The road to knowledge is rough and rugged in every country, but in none more than Germany.

> ———Alpeftre, fcofcefo, erto e felvaggio,
> Degno d'un alma audace.

After fuffering the ufual hardfhips of bad fare, bad roads, bad carriages, and bad horfes, for two days and a night, in my way from Leipfic to Berlin; and being obliged, during that time, to wait three or four hours, either in my open vehicle, or the open air, at each pofthoufe, while horfes were fought and fed with ftraw, wheels greafed, and inevitable fquabbles about the number of horses which I was to have, were adjust-eft, I arrived at SCHWARMUTH, within one poſt of Berlin.

When a traveller comes to a poſt-houſe, in this part of the world, with two horſes, he is rudely teaſed to go out with *three*; and if he arrive with three, *four* are forced upon him, if poſſible, at his departure, and ſo on, *creſcendo*, let the firſt number be what it will; and all this is tranſacted on the part of the poſt-maſter and his people, with an inſolence and brutality ſo deter-mined, that reaſoning and remonſtrating operate no otherwiſe than in rendering them more obſtinate and malevolent. It ſeems a thing of neceſſity, for poſtilions, in every part of the world, to be greater brutes than thoſe they drive: here, it is the caſe, *par excellence*; and ſo inſatiable in their demands and expectations, are theſe ſworn foes to man and beaſt, that I have frequently tried to part in peace and good humour with them, by more than doubling their ſtated and accuſtomed

customed fees, but in vain: each claim was a hydra.

I quitted Schwarmuth at seven o'clock in the evening, in hopes of getting to Berlin before midnight. The weather was now extremely disagreeable; rain was coming on, with a cold and furious north wind full in my face. The wagon with which I had been furnished, at the last post-house, was the worst and most defenceless that I had hitherto mounted; before nine o'clock, it rained violently, and became so dark, that the postilion lost his way, and descended from his place, in the front of the wagon, in order to feel for it with his hands; but being unable to distinguish any track of a carriage, he mounted again, and, in driving on, at a venture, got into a bog, on a bleak and barren heath, where we were stuck fast, and obliged to remain from eleven o'clock at night, till near six the next morning; when day-light enabled us to disentangle the horses

horses and carriage, and discover the road to the capital of Brandenburg. It had never ceased raining and blowing the whole night; the cold was intense; and nothing could be more forlorn than my condition.

BERLIN.

When I arrived at the gates of this city, about nine o'clock in the morning, Sept. 28th, I had hopes that I should have been suffered to pass peaceably to an inn, having received a passport at Trauenbritzen, the first Prussian town I entered on the Saxony side, where I had submitted to a thorough rummage of my baggage, at the persuasion of the custom-house officers, who had assured me that it would prevent all future trouble upon entering Berlin. But this was merely to levy fees upon me, for, notwithstanding my passport, I was stopped three quarters of an hour at the barrier, before I was taken into the custody of a centinel; who mount-

mounting my post-wagon, with his musket on his shoulder, and bayonet fixed, conducted me, like a prisoner, through the principal streets of the city, to the custom-house. Here I was detained in the yard more than two hours, shivering with cold, in all my wet garments, while every thing was taken out of my trunk and writing box, and examined as curiously as if I had just arrived at Dover, from the capital of France.

As I had long wished to visit the capital of a prince, no less renowned for his protection and cultivation of the liberal arts, than for his military skill and heroism; so I was impatient to begin my musical enquiries in a place where operas had long been established, and where both the theory and practice of music had been more profoundly treated than elsewhere, by professors of great and acknowledged abilities, who are still living; and who have published the result of their long experience and superior skill in treatises which are regarded throughout Germany as classical. Among these, *The Art of Playing the Flute*, by M. Quantz; *The Art of Playing upon Keyed Instruments*, by M. C. P. E. Bach; *The Art of Singing*, by M. Agricola; the numerous and well-written dissertations, *Practical, Historical, and Critical*, by M. Marpurg; *Musical Institutes*, by M. Kirnberger; and *The Theory of Polite Arts*, by M. Sulzer, stand foremost *.

* The original titles of the above books are as follow: Johann Joachim Quantzens, Königl. Preußischen Kammermusicus, Versuch einer Anweisung die Flötetraversier zu spielen. Berlin 1752. Versuch über die wahre Art das Clavier zu spielen, von Carl Philip Emanuel Bach. Berlin. this work is in two vols. of which the first was published in 1753, and the second in 1762. Anleitung zur Singkunst aus dem Italiänischen, mit Erläuterungen und Zusätzen von Joh. Friedr. Agricola. Berlin 1757. Marpurgs Anleitung zur Singecomposition. Berl. 1758. *Traité sur la Fugue*. Handbuch bey dem Generalbasse, und der Composition. 1762. ꝛc. ꝛc. Die Kunst des reinen Satzes in der Musik. Berl. 1771. Allgemeine Theorie der schönen Künste, von Joh. Geo. Sulzer, Mitglied der Königl. Academie der Wissenschaften in Berlin. 1771.

My

My zeal for the business in which I had embarked, was not so much cooled by the sufferings of the night, as to prevent me from hastening, as soon as I had obtained my liberty at the custom-house, to Mr. Harris, his majesty's envoy extraordinary at the court of Berlin. Mr. Harris received me with the utmost politeness, and honoured me in the kindest manner with his counsel concerning the most expedient methods to be pursued in making my enquiries.

In the afternoon I visited M. Nicolai, an eminent and learned bookseller, who had been previously apprised of my journey, and its object, by my zealous friend, M. Ebeling, of Hamburg; so that he expected my arrival, and entered upon business directly. After a long conversation, concerning the state of music in Berlin, M. Nicolai was so obliging as to conduct me to M. Agricola, the present composer of his Prussian majesty's serious opera; a station which he has held ever since the death of the late chapel-master, Graun.

John Frederic Agricola was born at Dobitzen, a village near Altenburg, in Upper Saxony, in the year 1720. His mother was a near relation of the late Mr. Handel, and in correspondence with him till the time of his death. M. Agricola was educated at Leipsic, and studied music there, under the famous Sebastian Bach. He has resided at Berlin ever since the year 1741; and in 1751 he was taken into his Prussian majesty's service, under the title of Hof-componist, or composer to the court. His life has been very active in the exercise of his profession, and the number of his compositions, both for the church and stage, are a proof of the fertility of his genius.

He is more corpulent than Jomelli, or than his relation Handel ever was. He received me very politely; and though he was indisposed, and had just been blooded, he obligingly sate down to a fine *piano forte*, which I was desirous of

hear-

hearing, and touched it in a truly great ſtyle. He is regarded as the beſt organ-player in Berlin, and the beſt ſinging maſter in Germany. He ſhewed me ſome of his compoſitions for the church, in ſcore, which were very maſterly; but he ſaid that it was a ſtyle of writing which was but little cultivated, at Berlin, as the King will not hear it. Indeed, I had been told before my arrival that his Pruſſian majeſty carries his prejudice againſt this kind of muſic ſo far, that when he hears of any compoſer having written an anthem, or oratorio, he fancies his taſte is contaminated by it, and ſays, of his other productions, every moment, *Oh! this ſmells of the church*.

From hence I went to the French theatre, more to ſee the building than to hear ſinging. However, as actors, the company is excellent: they were performing *le Mercure Galant*; and though I had ſeen this piece at Paris, more than once, I was very much pleaſed with it now.

now. For *Petite Piece*, the comic opera of the *Cadi Dupé*, was said and sung. The piece itself has very little musical merit, and the performers of to-night contrived to make that little, still less.

Sept. 29th. This morning M. Nicolai did me the favour of introducing me to M. Joseph Benda, brother of the celebrated violin-player of that name, who is master of his Prussian majesty's band. This able musician was so obliging as to play to me a very pleasing solo, composed by his brother, which he executed with great neatness and delicacy. He was accompanied by his son, under whose direction there is an *Academia* of *Dilettanti*, every Friday night, to which I had the honour of an invitation.

Upon quitting M. Benda, we called on M. Lindner, an eminent performer on the German flute, and scholar of M. Quantz. His Prussian majesty's attachment to this instrument has rendered the practice of it very general at Berlin. M. Lindner

Lindner invited me to another concert that was to be on the enſuing Sunday, to which he was ſo kind as to promiſe to conduct me.

After this I made a ſecond viſit to M. Agricola, accompanied ſtill by my obliging friend M. Nicolai, who dedicated this whole day to my ſervice. I was now preſented to Signora Agricola, whoſe name before marriage, was Benedetta Emilia Molteni; ſhe is now near fifty years of age, and yet ſings ſongs of *bravura*, with amazing rapidity. The thinneſs of ſome parts of her voice, diſcovers the loſs of youth, but yet ſhe has fine remains of a great ſinger; her compaſs extends from A in the baſe, to D in *alt*; and ſhe has a moſt perfect ſhake and intonation; ſhe was born at Modena, and had inſtructions from all the great maſters of her time; among whom ſhe numbers Porpora, Haſſe, and Salinbeni. She has been upwards of thirty years ſettled at Berlin, and in the ſervice of the court.

she now performs the second woman's part in his Prussian majesty's serious opera. During this visit, she was so obliging as to favour me with three airs in different styles, a *Grazioso*, an *Allegro*, and an *Adagio*, all composed by M. Agricola.

From hence we went to the great opera-house; this theatre is insulated in a large square, in which there are more magnificent buildings than ever I saw, at one glance, in any city of Europe. It was constructed by his present majesty soon after his coming to the crown. The principal front has two entrances; one level with the ground, and the other by a grand double escalier; this front is decorated with six Corinthian pillars, with their entablature entire, supporting a pediment ornamented with *reliefs*, and with this inscription upon it.

FRIDERICUS REX,
APOLLINI ET MUSIS.

This front is decorated with a considerable number of statues of poets, and
dramatic

dramatic actors, which are placed in niches. The two sides are constructed in the same manner, except that there are no pillars.

A considerable part of the front of this edifice forms a hall, in which the court has a repast on ridotta days; the rest is for the theatre, which, besides a vast pit, has four rows of boxes, thirteen in each, and these severally contain thirty persons. It is one of the widest theatres I ever saw, though it seems rather short in proportion.

The orchestra is very large, and arranged after that at Dresden. The band consists of about 50 performers, among whom are.

   Two composers.
   The concert-master.
   Eleven violins.
   Five violoncellos.
   Two double bases.
   Two harpsichord-players.
   One harp.

Four tenors.
Four flutes.
Four hautboys.
Four baſſoons, and
Two French horns.

The moſt eminent profeſſors in his majeſty's ſervice, are:

M. John Johachim Quantz, compoſer and chamber-muſician in ordinary to the king; no leſs celebrated for his performance and compoſitions, than for having had the honour of inſtructing his Pruſſian majeſty on the German flute. But few of his *Concertos* for that inſtrument are publiſhed; however, he has compoſed more than three hundred for the uſe of his royal ſcholar.

M. Joh. Frederic Agricola, compoſer and director of the opera, mentioned above; his name is as well known in Germany by his writings on the ſubject of muſic, as by his compoſitions.

M. Francis Benda, muſician, in ordinary to his majeſty, and maſter of his concert

concert, has acquired a great reputation in his profession, not only by his expressive manner of playing the violin, but by his graceful and affecting compositions for that instrument.

His Prussian majesty's favourite operas, are those of his late *maestro di capella*, Charles Henry Graun, to which he is so much attached, as to hear, unwillingly, those of any other master; and the overtures and concertos for violins of his brother, the concert master, M. Joh. Gottlib Graun, but lately deceased, are still in high reputation at Berlin, though not of the first class for taste or invention.

The chief singers of this serious opera, in the female parts, are Mademoiselle Schmeling, Signora Agricola, and Signora Gasparini, seventy-two years of age; a time of life, when nature seldom allows us any other voice, than that of complaint, or second childhood.

The principal male parts are performed by Signor Ant. Uberti Porporino, whose voice is a *Contralto*; he has been more than twenty years, in the service of his Prussian majesty, and is extremely admired for his taste and expression, particularly in singing *adagios*. And Signor Carlo Concialini, a *soprano*; his voice is feeble, but extremely sweet, and his manner of singing slow movements is delicate and touching.

Besides the composers and performers just mentioned, the theatre royal employs twenty-four chorus singers, a ballet-master, a great number of dancers of both sexes, and the Abate Landi, as poet.

The king being at the whole expence of this opera; the entrance is *gratis*, so that any one, who is decently dressed, may have admission into the pit. The first row of boxes is set apart for the royal family and nobility; the boxes that are even

with

with the pit, and those of the second and third row, are appropriated to the use of the ministers of state, foreign ministers, and persons of rank, who have offices about the court; and a stranger of distinction, by application to the baron Pölnitz, chamberlain and director of public spectacles, is sure of being accommodated with a place in the theatre, according to his rank.

The performance of the opera begins at six o'clock; the king, with the princes, and his attendants, are placed in the pit, close to the orchestra; the queen, the princesses, and other ladies of distinction, sit in the front boxes; her majesty is saluted at her entrance into the theatre, and at her departure thence by two bands of trumpets and kettle drums, placed one on each side the house, in the upper row of boxes *.

* This species of music, as it is the most ancient, so it seems to be that for which the

The king always stands behind the *maestro di capella,* in sight of the score, which he frequently looks at, and indeed performs the part of *director-general* here, as much as of *generalissimo* in the field.

Such is the *present state* of the opera at Berlin, and history must shew what it *has* been in times past. I shall only just mention, that from the death of Frederic the First, in 1713, till the year 1742, there were no operas performed in this capital. Soon before the accession of his present majesty to the throne, in 1740, a new theatre was constructed, which was opened on the birth-day of the queen-mother, in 1742; at which

---

northern inhabitants of Europe have, in spite of new fashions and refinements in music, the greatest passion. There is scarce a sovereign prince in Germany, who thinks he can dine comfortably, or with proper dignity, without a flourish of drums and trumpets; and this love of noise, perhaps first introduced music at our city entertainments, at my lord mayor's feast, and at the feast of every mayor in the kingdom.

time.

time, the moſt able German inſtrumental performers, Italian ſingers, and French dancers, were engaged, and muſic ſaw herſelf eſtabliſhed in more than her former ſplendor.

Ever ſince this period, operas have been exhibited in the theatre royal at each carnival with ſpirit and magnificence; the brilliancy of their ſucceſs has ſomewhat varied according to the talents of the vocal performers, which have been in general, very numerous, and very eminent; however, one of the moſt ſhining periods in the muſical annals of Berlin ſeems to have been in 1752, when Careſtini and the Aſtrua performed the two principal parts. At this time, the whole band of vocal and inſtrumental performers was the moſt ſplendid in Europe; among the latter, we find the celebrated names of Bach, Benda, Czarth, Graun, Heſſe, Quantz, and Richter.

A conſiderable part of this afternoon was ſpent in viſiting ſuch churches, as are the moſt remarkable for good organs. In general, I found the organs of Berlin large, coarſe, and crowded with noiſy ſtops, which, if they had been in tune, would have produced no pleaſing effects; but as it was, ſuch a number of diſſonant and ill-voiced pipes, more tortured that tickled my ears.

Before I left England, M. Snetzler had told me, that I ſhould doubtleſs find *ſwells* in Berlin organs, though he was not certain that this improvement, which was Engliſh, had been adopted in other places on the continent; for Mr. Handel, ſeveral years ago, had deſired him to deſcribe, in writing, the manner in which the ſwell was produced, that he might ſend it to a particular friend in Berlin, who very much wiſhed to introduce it there.

But I enquired in vain of muſical people in that city, whether they knew of any ſuch machine, as a ſwell, worked by pedals, in any of their organs; no ſuch
contri-

contrivance had ever been heard of, and it was difficult to explain it.

At the *garrison church* built in 1722, which is an oblong square, supported by massive pillars, there are eight doors, and over each there is a black eagle, which is the crest of the Prussian arms, taking his flight, towards a golden sun, with a thunder-bolt in his talons; and above, is this inscription, *non soli cedet*.

I found a large organ in this church, built by Joachim Wagner; it is remarkable for compass, having 50 keys in the manuals, and for its number of pipes, amounting to 3220; but still more so, for the ornaments and machinery of the case, which are in the old Teutonic taste, and extremely curious.

At each wing is a kettle drum, which is beat by an Angel placed behind it, whose motion the organist regulates by a pedal; at the top of the pyramid, or middle column of pipes, there are two figures,

figures, representing Fame, spreading their wings, when the drums are beat, and raising them as high as the top of the pyramid; each of these figure sounds a trumpet, and then takes its flight.

There are likewise two suns, which move to the sound of cymbals, and the wind obliges them to cross the clouds; during which time, two eagles take their flight, as naturally as if they were alive.

I was much more pleased with four monumental pictures, which are placed in the same church, than with this ecclesiastical puppet-shew. They were presents from M. Bernard Rode, history-painter, and member of the royal academy, who in 1762, painted them in honour of four Prussian heroes, who fell in battle during the last war.

I. Marshal Schwerin, dying, and embracing Victory, by whom he is crowned. The colours are leaning against him,

which

which he had in his hand when he was flain at the battle of Prague, in 1757*.

II. The monument of general Winterfeld, upon which the hiftorical Mufe is feated, and writing his hiftory.

III. Marfhal Keith, whofe monument Glory is covering with laurels.

IV. Major Kleift, the celebrated poet, killed at Kunnerfdorf, upon whofe urn Friendfhip is weeping. Beneath the monument, his fword and lyre are entwined in a laurel wreath.

This evening I had the pleafure of being introduced to the acquaintance of M. Marpurg, a perfon who had fo long laboured in the fame vineyard as myfelf, that he was a perfect judge of the difficulties I had to encounter. Nothing could be more flattering than the manner in which he received me. I found him

---

* There is a marble ftatue of this brave general, lately erected at Berlin, in the fquare called *Place Guillaume*, where the foldiers are daily exercifed; an animating fight to military men.

to be a man of the world; polite, accessible, and communicative. His musical writings may justly be said to surpass, in number and utility, those of any one author who has treated the subject. He was perhaps the first German theorist that could patiently be read by persons of taste; so addicted were former writers to prolixity and pedantry.

This author, besides the works which I have already mentioned, p. 88. has published five volumes of Essays and Dissertations towards the history and practice of music; A History of Ancient Music; and a great number of correct and pleasing compositions of various kinds, both vocal and instrumental. It is a misfortune to music, that he has now wholly quitted his former studies, being invested, by his majesty, with the title of counsellor of war, and the office of director of the royal lottery.

His History of Music was intended to be general, and to comprise modern times; and

and he had projected a continuation of Walther's Musical Dictionary, and several other interesting works to lovers of music; but he is prevented from executing these designs, by his new office.

He kindly undertook to furnish me with several books and papers, of which I was in search; and offered, in a most obliging manner, to conduct me to such persons and things, as the nature of my enquiries rendered the most essential for me to see, during my residence at Berlin.

After this visit, I went home with my guide, M. Nicolai. He had provided a small concert of *dilettanti*, his friends, with whom I spent a very agreeable evening.

Wednesday, 30th. This morning was fixed upon, by previous arrangement, for visiting mademoiselle Schmeling. How much my expectations had been raised concerning this performer, the reader will be enabled to judge, by the following extract of a letter which I had received from a very intelligent musical cor-

correspondent, in Germany, before my departure from England.

"At Berlin there is now a German
"opera singer, that astonishes every one
"who hears her. People who have been
"a long time in Italy, and who have for-
"merly heard Faustina, Cuzzoni, and
"Astrua, assure me that she surpasses
"them all. Indeed, when I heard her
"at Leipsic, two years ago, I was en-
"raptured. I never knew a voice so
"powerful and so sweet, at the same
"time: she could do with it just what
"she pleased. She sings from G to E
"*in altissimo,* with the greatest ease and
"force, and both her *portamento di voce,*
"and her volubility are, in my opinion,
"unrivalled; but when I heard her, she
"seemed to like nothing but difficult
"music. She sung at sight, what very
"good players could not play, at sight,
"on the violin; and nothing was too
"difficult to her execution, which was
"easy and neat. But, after this, she re-
"fined

" fined her taste, insomuch that she was
" able to perform the part of *Tisbe*, in
" Hasse's opera, which requires simpli-
" city and expression, more than volu-
" bility of throat; and in this she per-
" fectly succeeded, as Agricola, the
" translator of Tosi's *Arte del Canto*,
" and our best singing master in Ger-
" many, assures me. The King of Prus-
" sia, a great connoisseur, was astonished
" at it. Her name is *Schmeling*, she is
" about twenty-four years of age, and
" was in England, when a child, where
" she played the violin; but she quitted
" that instrument, and became a singer,
" by the advice of English ladies, who
" disliked a *female fidler*."

This account had been corroborated since my arrival on the continent, where I had been informed that his Prussian majesty was at first, with difficulty, prevailed on to hear mademoiselle Schmeling: " A German singer? I should as
" soon expect to receive pleasure from the
" neigh-

"neighing of my horse." However, after he had heard her sing one song, his majesty is said to have sought among his manuscript music for the most difficult airs in his collection, in order to try her powers, as much as to gratify his own ear; but she executed, *at sight*, whatever he commanded her to perform, in all styles, as well as if she had practised each of these compositions during her whole life.

Mademoiselle Schmeling received me very politely and unaffectedly. She is short, and not handsome, but is far from having any thing disagreeable in her countenance; on the contrary, there is a strong expression of good nature impressed upon it, which renders her address very engaging. Her teeth are irregular, and project too much, yet, altogether, her youth and smiles taken into the account, she is rather agreeable in face and figure.

I found

I found that she had preserved her English; indeed she sometimes wanted words, but, having learned it very young, the pronunciation of those which occurred, was perfectly correct. She was so obliging as to sing, at my request, very soon after my entrance. She began with a very difficult *aria di bravura*, by Traetta, which I had heard before at Mingotti's. She sung it admirably, and fully answered the great ideas which I had formed of her abilities, in every thing but her voice, which was a little cloudy, and not quite so powerful as I expected. However, she had a slight cold and cough, and complained of indisposition: but with all this, her voice was sweetly toned, and she sung perfectly well in tune. She has an excellent shake, a good expression, and facility of executing and articulating rapid and difficult divisions, that is astonishing.

Her second song was a *Larghetto*, by Schwanenberg, of Brunswick, which was very pretty in itself; but she made it truly

truly delightful by her taste and expression: she was by no means lavish of graces, but those she used, were perfectly suited to the style of the music, and idea of the poet.

After this, she sung an *Andante*, in the part which she had to practise for the ensuing carnival, in Graun's *Merope*; and in this acquitted herself with great taste, expression, and propriety.

His Prussian majesty very seldom resides at Berlin, except during the carnival, which generally commences about the middle of December, and terminates with the month of January.

When his majesty and the court arrive at Berlin, every day of the week, except Saturday, which is a day of rest, has its particular amusements allotted to it, according to the following regulations.

On *Sunday*, the Queen has a great court. On *Monday*, there is an opera. *Tuesday*, a ridotta, or masqued ball, in the opera-house. *Wednesday*, a French play,

play, at the court theatre. *Thurſday*, the princeſs dowager has a drawing-room; and on *Friday*, there is another opera.

At other times, his majeſty's uſual reſidence is at Sans-Souci, a palace near Potſdam, five German miles from Berlin, where he is attended by his muſicians in ordinary, who are there in monthly waiting, by turns.

The celebrity of his majeſty's performance on the German flute, had long excited in me a ſtrong deſire to hear him play, and I had now, in concert with ſeveral friends, taken the moſt likely meaſures for gratifying that wiſh. I was furniſhed with letters to ſeveral perſons of diſtinction at Potſdam, who were entreated to uſe their utmoſt endeavours to procure me the honour of being admitted into the royal apartments, at Sans-Souci, during the performance of his majeſty's uſual evening concert.

As the court was now at Sans-Souci, and ſeveral of the moſt eminent muſicians of the King's band were there in waiting, I was impatient to go thither, in hopes of satisfying my curiosity relative to his majesty's musical abilities. I therefore set off for Potsdam this morning, immediately after quitting mademoiselle Schmeling, and taking leave of my worthy friend, M. Nicolai, who, unluckily for me, was going to Leipsic fair; which I regarded as a real loss to myself, for his knowledge of music, and musical people, joined to his zeal for my service, rendered him a most agreeable and useful acquaintance.

POTSDAM.

The road from Berlin hither, is through a deep running sand, like the worst parts of Norfolk and Suffolk, where there are no turnpikes, till within a few miles of the town; and then it is through a wild forest of fir-trees, with lakes frequently in sight. Upon a nearer approach, there is a fine opening on the

left

left hand, to a very large piece of water, and a beautiful view of the town, in which three towers, of the fame fize and fhape, only appear, but thefe are elegant. The reft of the way is through a wood, cut into walks and rides, which interfect each other, and lead to different towns and villas.

The examination at the gates of this city, is the moft minute and curious, both in going in, and out, which I have ever experienced in my travels; it could not be more rigorous at the poftern of a town befieged. Name, character, whence, where, when, to whom recommended, bufinefs, ftay, and feveral other particulars, were demanded, to which the anfwers were all written down.

However, a ftranger, upon his entrance into this city, is made fome amends, by the variety and fplendor of new objects, for the bad road, and difficulty of admiffion, which he has previoufly encountered.

The streets are the most regularly beautiful which I ever remember to have seen; the houses all seem to be built of white stone, though they are only of brick, stuccoed over, in imitation of stone. A canal, supplied by the river Havel, runs through the middle of the town, which is situated on an island, called the *Werder* of Potsdam, which implies *an island in a river*. This island is four German miles in circumference: the approach to Potsdam is over a very wide piece of water, by a stone bridge.

The number of houses in this city has been very much encreased during the reign of his present majesty, and that of his father. At the beginning of this century, there were only two hundred houses, and at present there are at least two thousand, and seventeen thousand inhabitants, exclusive of the military, which amount to about eight thousand men.

Four battalions of foot guards, with the squadron of life guards, and the regiment

regiment of the prince of Pruſſia, compoſe the conſtant garriſon of Potſdam. The uniform of the firſt battalion of foot-guards, is blue, embroidered with ſilver, and turned up with red; the waiſtcoats are of pale yellow; The hats, which are extremely large, have a very broad ſilver lace, in imitation of *point d'eſpagne*, and are cocked in the old Kevenhuller faſhion, which, added to huge black whiſkers, give the men a moſt formidable appearance. The fourth battalion, called the Leſtewitz battalion, is formed of the remains of the late king's *tall* grenadiers.

The ſquares, public buildings, and houſes of individuals, in this city, are elegant and noble. The architecture of Palladio, in the Venetian ſtate, is here very frequently and ſuccefsfully copied. His majeſty's preſent paſſion is for architecture, in which he is ſaid to expend 200,000 l. ſterl. a year. Potſdam is almoſt entirely new built, from his own.

own designs, besides his new palace, near Sans-Souci, and innumerable houses and palaces in Berlin, constructed since the last war. Whenever a citizen is about building a house, either in his capital, or at Potsdam, his majesty furnishes the design, and is at the expence of building the front.

The instant I arrived at Potsdam, I went to M. Benda, in hopes of seeing him before his duty called him to the king's concert; but he was already gone thither, and I was told that the performance was begun, so that there was no possibility of my hearing his majesty that evening. It was now near seven o'clock, and rather late for a first visit, to a great personage; however, time was so precious, that I could not be exact in observing forms; in defiance of which, I ventured to wait upon lord Marshal, to whom Mr. Harris had kindly honoured me with a letter.

His

His lordship lives in a neat small house, in the suburbs, built for him by the king, as the coachman, unasked, informed me. The porter, an honest Scotsman, asked immediately if I spoke English, and told me that his lord was at home, but in his night-gown. I acquainted him with the letter which I had to deliver, sent in my name, and said if my visit would at all incommode his lordship, I would return in the morning. The porter soon came back, and desired me to walk in.

I was instantly conducted to my lord; it was so dark that I could hardly see him. He desired me to sit down, with a very benevolent tone of voice, in a Scots accent. I presented to him my letter, and acquainted him that I was extremely pressed in time, or should not have broke in upon his lordship at so late an hour: he said he was glad to see me at any time. When lights were brought in, I was as much pleased with his face, as I had been before by his voice; it is the moſt pleaſing, elegant, and benign that can be imagined.

I continued with his lordſhip three hours, during which time he entertained me with a great number of anecdotes, many of which related to muſic. When he had peruſed Mr. Harris's letter, in which mention was made of my Italian tour, and the tranſlation of it into German, he told me, that he had ceaſed to go to court on account of his age, though the king frequently told him, that he kept a cover for him conſtantly at his table; but he would ſend what I had in German of my book*, and my plan, to his majeſty, in the morning. His lord-

---

* At this time I was in poſſeſſion of only a few looſe ſheets of the German tranſlation of my former tour, which has ſince been publiſhed at Hamburg, under the title of, Burneyiſches Tagebuch einer Muſikaliſchen Reiſe durch Frankreich und Italien, aus dem Engliſchen überſetzt von C. D. Ebeling, Aufſeher der Handlungs Akademie zu Hamburg. Bey Bode 1772.

ſhip

ship did me the honour of inviting me to dine with him at twelve o'clock the next day, and informed me of whatever was best worth seeing at Potsdam and Sans-Souci; as to music, he said, that I was unfortunate in being addressed to him, for he was such a Goth, as to know nothing of it, nor to like any music, but that of his own country bagpipes. On this occasion, he was very pleasant upon himself: here ensued a discussion of Scots music, and Erse poetry; after which, his lordship said, "but lest you "should think me too insensible to the "power of sound, I must tell you, that I "have made a collection of *national tunes* "of almost all the countries on the globe, "which I believe I can shew you." After a search, made by himself, the book in which these tunes were written, was found, and I was made to sing the whole collection through, without an instrument; during which time, he had an anecdote for every tune. When I had
done,

done, his lordship kindly wrote down a list of all such tunes as had pleased me most by their oddity and originality, of which he promised me copies, and then ordered a Scots piper, one of his domestics, to play to me some Spanish and Scots tunes, which were not in the collection; "but play them in the garden, says he, "for these fine Italianised folks cannot "bear our rude music near their delicate "ears".

The conversation afterwards turned upon French music, and the comparative merit of that and the Italian, upon which subject his lordship told me a story, that very much resembled one related by Rousseau, in his *Lettre sur la musique Françoise*.

A young Greek lady being brought from her own country to Paris, some years since, was, soon after her arrival in that city, carried to the opera by some French ladies, supposing, as she had never heard any European music, that she would

would be in raptures at it; but, contrary to thefe expectations, fhe declared, that the finging only reminded her of the hideous howlings of the Calmuc Tartars; and as to the machinery, which it was thought would afford her great amufement, fhe declared her diflike of many parts of it, and was particularly fcandalized, by what fhe called, the impious and wicked imitation of God's thunder. Soon after this experiment, fhe went to Venice, where another was made upon her uncorrupted ears, at an Italian opera, in which the famous Gizziello fung; at whofe performance fhe was quite diffolved in pleafure, and was ever after paffionately fond of Italian mufic.

Upon mentioning this ftory to an excellent judge of mufic and of human nature, who had been at Paris when M. de Bougainville brought thither a native of the new difcovered ifland of Otaiti, he told me, that the effects of *French* mufic
had

had been fairly tried upon *Putaveri* immediately on his arrival. "I wish", said my friend, "you had been there, "to have observed with me, what a "strange impression the French opera "made upon him; as soon as he returned "to his lodgings, he mimicked what "he had heard, in the most natural and "ridiculous manner imaginable; this he "would repeat only when he was in "good humour; but as it was just be- "fore his departure that I saw him, he "was melancholy, and would not dance, "however entreated. I proposed to send "for music, and one of the servants was "ordered to play on his bad fiddle just "without the door of the room; upon "hearing this, *Putaveri* suddenly sprang "up, and seizing two of the candle- "sticks, placed them on the floor, and "danced his own country dance; after "this, he gave the company a specimen "of the French opera, which was the "most natural and admirable parody
"that

" that I have ever heard, and accom-
" panied with all its proper geſtures. I
" wiſhed at this time to try the power
" of *Italian* muſic upon him; but there
" was no opportunity, for how could it
" be properly executed at Paris?"

Among the anecdotes relative to the ſtrange effects of muſic, which were given to me by lord Marſhal, he told me of a Highlander, who always cried, upon hearing a certain ſlow Scots tune, played on the bagpipe. General G. whoſe ſervant he was, ſtole into his room one night, when he was faſt aſleep, and playing the ſame tune to him very ſoftly, on the German flute, the fellow, without waking, cried like a child.

His lordſhip next confirmed to me, the account of the *Maladie du Païs*, or home-ſickneſs, being brought on by the tune, called the *Rens de Vache*, if heard by any of the Swiſs troops in foreign ſervice. Five ſoldiers at Valadolid, in Spain, who had heard one of their countrymen

trymen play this tune, on the top of the steeple, were all seized with this distemper, and obliged to be sent home. An effect which can only be accounted for, by reminiscence of former liberty and happiness, in their native country.

The Tarantula story, his lordship allowed to be all a lye, as to the musical cure; but not the bite, which was to his knowledge certain; however, some of the inhabitants of Apulia had confessed to him, that the only salutary effect of music, was to keep the patient awake, as sleep was usually fatal, if indulged before the poison is extracted.

I had frequently been told by persons who were well acquainted with lord Marshal many years ago, that his character approached nearer to perfection, than that of any other human being; and this became now my own opinion. It was with great reluctance that I quitted him, in order to return to my inn; he had attached me as much
during

during this visit of three hours, by his sociable, entertaining, easy, and benign manner, as any one else had ever done in as many years.

Thursday, October 1st. My first visit this morning was to M. Benda, whom I found to be a plain, obliging, sensible man, and possessed of all the modesty of a truly great genius. I was furnished with a letter to him from Mr. Giardini, with whose remembrance he appeared to be much pleased, and said, that though it was more than twenty years since he had seen or heard him, he had not forgot his fine tone, so remarkably clear, full, and sweet; and added, that he should always retain a precise and pleasing idea of his graceful manner of playing, of his fancy in extempore cadences, and facility in executing whatever was possible to be performed on the violin.

Mr. Giardini, in his letter, had desired M. Benda to indulge me with the pleasure

sure of hearing him perform; when he read this request, he shook his head, and said, *non sum qualis eram*, " I have "ceased to play *solos* even to the king "my master, these five years; however, "such as they are, you shall hear my "feeble endeavours to oblige you."

He performed to me an admirable solo, of his own composition, *con sordino*; his hand, he said, wanted force sufficient to play without. The gout has long enfeebled his fingers; however, there are fine remains of a great hand, though I am inclined to suppose him to have been more remarkable at all times for his feeling than his force. His style is so truly *cantabile*, that scarce a passage can be found in his compositions, which it is not in the power of the human voice to sing; and he is so very affecting a player, so truly pathetic in an *Adagio*, that several able professors have assured me he has frequently drawn tears from them in performing one. How he acquired

quired this style of writing and playing, it may be of some use to musical students to trace and develope: the productions and performance of this master are indeed so truly original and pleasing, that I hope every lover of music, among my readers, will excuse me if I here insert a sketch of his life, the principal incidents of which I obtained from himself, during my visit; the rest are extracted from a printed account of him, published at Leipsic, 1766; in a work which was then carried on by M. Hiller, under the title of *Weekly Intelligence, and Observations concerning Music**.

Francis Benda was born at Alt Benatky, in Bohemia, 1709. He was brought up in the choir at Neubenatky, as a singing boy. At nine years old, he was conducted to Prague, by one of his relations, and employed at the church of

* Nachrichten und Anmerkungen die Musik betreffend. 4to. This publication, which was begun in 1766, continued till 1769.

the Benedictines, as a *soprano*. Soon after this, his voice became so excellent, that he was enticed away to Dresden, without the consent of the Benedictines, in order to sing in the Elector of Saxony's chapel. After continuing a year and half in this service, he ran away with a lighterman, intending to return to his friends; but in going with him up the Elbe, he was stopt at Pirna, and carried back to Dresden; however, not being used to the water, and the night before having been very cold, he lost his treble voice.

This misfortune immediately removed the difficulty of obtaining his dismission: he now found himself at full liberty to go whither he pleased; and, returning to his parents, they were much perplexed what to do with him: but, at the performance of the Easter music, he was persuaded to attempt a *contralto* part in the church. At first, his voice was coarse, but it very soon grew so much better, that the same afternoon M. Benda found himself able to sing the counter-tenor, as well as he had formerly done the *soprano*.

Having discovered his new voice, he went to Prague, where he was engaged at the Jesuit's seminary, though there were already six counter-tenors in that service. But his manner of singing, together with his having performed in the chapel-royal at Dresden, were two cogent reasons for his being well received.

In 1723, Benda was one of the chorus singers in the music performed at Prague, on occasion of the Emperor Charles the sixth being crowned king of Bohemia. An event which forms a very important æra in the life of this eminent musician, who had now attained his fifteenth year. He confessed to me, that the excellent singing which he then heard, was of the utmost use to him in his future studies, and particularly the performance of Gaetano Orsini, a *contralto*, with which he was beyond measure affected. Soon after this solemnity was over, a drama was performed, at the Jesuit's college, by young Bohemian noblemen, in which music was introduced; it was composed by the famous Zelenka, the King of Poland's chapel master.

Benda, with another descanter of the Kreuzhern, and an Italian, with a base voice, were the singers employed on this occasion: three airs were given to each of them, but Benda was so superior to the rest, that he not only acquired great applause by his performance, but a new appointment, with a large salary, at the Kreuzhern convent; which being extremely rich, and appropriated to the reception of the nobility who devote themselves to the defence of the christian religion against the Turks, is regarded by musicians at Prague, as the post of honour.

Here he first applied himself to composition, and set to music the *Salve Regina* twice; once accompanied by the organ only, and once by two violins. Heaven

ven knows, says Benda, how many of the rules of counterpoint were broken in this attempt! not long after this, he lost his counter-tenor voice, and was again obliged to return to his friends at Benatki.

Being now deprived of all hope of gaining a livelihood by singing, and unable to bear the thoughts of becoming a burden to his relations, he applied himself seriously to the violin, upon which he had made a beginning, but he knows not when, nor under what master. It must, however, have been early in his life, as he was remembered to play the tenor, in the concerts performed by the singing boys at Dresden, and to work hard on the violin, at Vivaldi's concertos.

After losing his voice, he had no other means of turning his musical talents to account, than by playing dances about the country with a company of strolling Jews; in which, however, there was a blind

blind Hebrew, of the name of Löbel, who, in his way, was an extraordinary player. He drew a good tone from his inftrument, and compofed his own pieces, which were wild, but pretty: fome of his dances went up to A in *altiffimo*; however, he played them with the utmoft purity and neatnefs.

The performance of this man excited in Benda fo much jealoufy, that he redoubled his diligence in trying to equal him; and not to be his inferior in any part of his trade, he compofed dances, for his own hand, which were far from eafy. He often fpeaks of his obligations to the old Jew for ftimulating him to excel on the violin.

After ftrolling about in this manner, for fome time, he fhut himfelf up in a garret at Prague, where he practifed two things, mufic, and temperance: here he obtained a few leffons from Konyczek, violinift to prince Lobkowitz, by which he qualified himfelf for the fervice of a noble-

nobleman, with whom he travelled to Vienna: here he was transferred to a new master, count Uhlefeld, with whom he had frequently the advantage of hearing the famous Francischello, who taught the count, and of playing trios with him and his patron *.

When he quitted this service, he travelled on foot to Breslau, with three other musicians, who afterwards became very eminent. These were M. Höckh, the present chapel-master to the prince of Zerbst, the late M. Weidner, and M. Czarth, formerly in the Prussian service, but now at Manheim.

* Francischello was the greatest performer on the base-viol of his time. Geminiani related of him, that in accompanying Nicolini, at Rome, in a cantata composed by Alessandro Scarlatti, for the violoncello, the author, who was at the harpsichord, would not believe that a mortal could play so divinely; but said, that it was an angel who had assumed the figure of Françischello; so far did his performance surpass all that Scarlatti had conceived in composing the cantata, or imagined possible for man to express.

After staying a short time at Breslau, these four adventurers set off in the 𝔉𝔲𝔥𝔯𝔰 𝔚𝔞𝔤𝔢𝔫, or common wagon, for Warsaw. Within four miles of this capital of Poland, they found, in a forest, a well-furnished portmanteau; and, after trying, in vain, to discover the owner of it, they divided the contents among them. By this partition, a coat luckily fell to the share of Benda, of which he was in great want, and which fitted him as well as if it had been made by a Paris taylor.

Being arrived at Warsaw, they took possession of an apartment in the old Cassimir palace, which, for fifty years before, had had no other inhabitants than rooks and jackdaws: none of the primitive saints ever practised the virtue of abstinence more rigidly than these three young sinners did now, though guests of a royal palace; without a plan of future conduct, without money, and without friends, their heads had as yet furnished no
em-

employment for their hands, but that of amusing themselves on their several instruments in their retirement; so that they practised incessantly. During this time the palace was supposed to be haunted, but by what kind of spirits, none of the neighbours had the courage to examine; till the Starost Suchaczewski, Szaniawski, being told that the ghosts were musical, was sufficiently intrepid to wish to hear them, and being pleased with their performance, he engaged them in his service.

It is a rule in Poland, when a nobleman has more than four musicians in his service, to appoint a *maestro di capella* over them; and as the band of the Starost Suchaczewsky now consisted of nine performers, this honourable office was forced upon Benda by his new patron.

Our hero remained at Warsaw two or three years, after which, returning to Germany, he was a short time employed in the Elector of Saxony's chapel at Dresden;

den; during which period, he received a letter from M. Quantz, inviting him to enter into the service of the prince of Prussia, at Ruppin, where his present majesty usually resided before his accession to the crown.

It was by stealth, that this prince indulged his passion for music, during the life of his father, the late king, who had forbid him, not only to study and practise music, but to hear it. M. Quantz told me afterwards, that it was the late queen mother, who at this time encouraged the prince in his favourite amusement, and who engaged musicians for his service; but so necessary was secrecy in all these negociations, that if the king his father had discovered that he was disobeyed, all these sons of Apollo would have incurred the danger of being hanged. The prince frequently took occasion, to meet his musicians a hunting, and had his concerts either in a forest or cavern.

.M. Benda

M. Benda, who entered into the service of Prussia, in 1732, found already with his royal highness the two Grauns, with whom he studied, and from whom he confesses to have received signal services, as well as from M. Quantz.

He still leads the band at the great opera, where he is seconded by his brother Joseph; and he can boast of having had the honour of accompanying his majesty, during the forty years he has been in his service, in near 50,000 different concerts.

The father of M. Benda was a linen manufacturer, but not less musical than other Bohemians, his countrymen; for he played a little on several instruments, particularly the hautbois, bagpipe, and dulcimer. In 1742, being the second year of his present majesty's reign, M. Benda had the satisfaction of bringing his parents to Berlin, and of establishing them there, under his roof. In 1756, this venerable pair celebrated the Hoch-

𝖅𝖊𝖎𝖙 𝕵𝖚𝖇𝖎𝖑ä𝖚𝖒 or marriage jubilee, usually solemnized in Germany, by persons who have lived together in wedlock, *fifty years.*

M. Benda has two sons, both able musicians; his three brothers all applied themselves to music, in consequence of his success. John, the eldest, whose instrument was the violin, died in the service of his Prussian majesty; George, the second brother, is at present an eminent chapel-master, and elegant composer in the service of the duke of Saxe-Gotha; and Joseph, the third, is one of his Prussian majesty's band.

A word more, concerning the musical abilities of the worthy concert-master, Francis, shall terminate this long article. His style is not that of Tartini, Somis, Veracini, nor that of the head of any one school or musical sect, of which I have the least knowledge: it is *his own,* and formed from that model which should be ever studied by all instrumental performers, *good singing.*

When I quitted M. Benda, I waited on Col. Quintus Icilius *, to whom I was honoured with letters; he is member of the royal academy of sciences, author of a celebrated treatise, written in French, upon the military art of the ancients, and a great collector of *Virtu*; he is a *connoiſſeur* in all the arts, except muſic; and has a well-choſen library, in which I found ſeveral ſcarce and curious books.

After this I had the honour to viſit Col. de Forcade, to whom I had likewiſe letters. I had been recommended to this gentleman, who is court-marſhal,

---

* This officer's original name is Guichard, and that of Quintus Icilius, only his *Nom de Guerre*, given to him, in pleaſantry, by his majeſty, who when he conferred upon him a command in a regiment, haſtily raiſed and collected from the refuſe of all nations, during the heat of the laſt war, honoured him with the appellation of the commander of Cæſar's tenth legion, a name which has ſince been adopted by the whole Pruſſian nation.

with

with a view to his doing me the honour of presenting me to his royal highness, the prince of Pruffia, to whom I had been charged with a parcel of books from England.

It was now twelve o'clock, the general hour for dining at Potsdam; at my lord Marshal's, I was so fortunate as to see and converse with the Grecian lady, who had been so offended with French music, and so pleased with Italian, upon her first arrival in Europe. The dinner was quite English, and the conversation of his lordship was entertaining to a very uncommon degree.

After dinner I went to see the king's *new palace*, das neue Schloß, built since the last war. The ground on which it is erected, was a morass eight years ago, as was the whole country round it, which is a dead flat, and still very naked and barren; it was however in consequence of the rapidity with which this palace was constructed, and the face of the

the country changed, that a German wit said, "it must be allowed, that his majesty performs miracles, though he believes none."

It is not my design to give a minute description of this superb palace; I shall only observe, in general, that it appeared to me, one of the most elegant and perfect, which I had seen in Europe. It is constructed, as well as most of the magnificent buildings in Potsdam, from his majesty's own designs; the front is decorated with fluted pilasters, of the Corinthian order, before each of which there is a statue; these pilasters are of a pale yellow colour, and the rest of the wall in imitation of red brick. A cupola appears above the pediment, upon which are placed on a high pedestal, the three Graces; and the statues and groupes of figures which embellish the Attic story, and the balustrades, are scarcely to be numbered.

The

The apartments are fitted up with the utmoſt magnificence and taſte. There is a *ſuite* of rooms appropriated to almoſt every branch of the royal family. Thoſe of the king, of his ſiſter princeſs Amelia, and the prince of Pruſſia, are the moſt ſplendid. In each of theſe apartments, there is a room dedicated to muſic, furniſhed with books, deſks, a harpſichord, and with other inſtruments.

His majeſty's concert room is ornamented with glaſſes of an immenſe ſize, and with ſculpture, partly gilt, and partly of the moſt beautiful green varniſh, by Martin of Paris; the whole furniture and ornaments of this room, are in a moſt refined and exquiſite taſte. There is a *piano forte* made by Silbermann of Neuberg, beautifully varniſhed and embelliſhed; and a tortoiſe-ſhell deſk for his majeſty's uſe, moſt richly and elegantly inlaid with ſilver; on the table lay a catalogue of concertos for the

new

new palace, and a book of manuscript *Solfeggi*, as his majesty calls them, or preludes, composed of difficult divisions and passages for the exercise of the hand, as the vocal *Solfeggi* are for the throat. His majesty has books of this kind, for the use of his flute, in the music room of every one of of his palaces.

In another apartment, there is a most magnificent harpsichord, made by Shudi, in England; the hinges, pedals, and frame are of silver, the case is inlaid, and the front is of tortoise-shell; this instrument which cost 200 guineas, was sent to Hamburg by sea, and from thence to Potsdam, up the Elb and the Havel, which, I was told, had injured it so much, that it has been useless ever since; however, it is natural to suppose, that some jealousy may have been excited by it, and that it has not had quite fair play from those employed to repair it; for I never heard of any one of the great number of harpsichords, which are annually sent from England to the East and West Indies by sea, receiving so much damage as this is said to have done, in a much shorter passage. And now I am upon the subject of musical instruments, I must observe, that the Germans work much better out of their own country, than they do in it, if we may judge by the *harpsichords* of Kirkman and Shudi; the *piano fortes* of Backers; and the *organs* of Snetzler; which far surpass, in goodness, all the keyed instruments that I met with, in my tour through Germany.

But to return to his Prussian majesty's *new palace*: in every apartment through which I was conducted, there appeared a studied elegance and delicacy in the furniture, which I had never met with before; the taste, indeed, is rather that of France than Italy; however, it is the best of the kind, and includes both elegance and convenience. The hall, called the *Marble Gallery*, is truly superb, and worthy of royalty; it is extremely spacious,

cious, and lofty, and is totally encrusted with red spotted marble, called *Red Caro-line,* mixed with white Italian marble. The pavement likewise is of white marble, and the ceiling is ornamented with three large pictures, in gilt stucco frames, painted by Rode, the subjects of which, are *morning, noon,* and *night.*

Though his majesty's principal collection of paintings, is in the picture-gallery at Sans-Souci, yet there are two or three rooms in the new palace, very rich in works of capital Italian masters; but it is out of my province to enumerate these; and for the costly gold and silver hangings; the exquisitely varnished wainscots; rich ceilings, or Mosaic floors, they are not to be described.

Opposite to the great front of this palace, there are two elegant buildings of white stone, joined together, by a superb semi-circular colonade of fluted pillars, of the Corinthian order. These buildings are called, The *Great Commons;* in the

lower

lower part of which, are the kitchens, cellars, and other offices; and in the upper ftories, lodging-rooms for the king's attendants, and for foreigners of diftinction. At the front of each building there is a double circular efcalier, which leads to a colonade of infulated and fluted Corinthian pillars, which fupport a pediment, ornamented with ftatues: at each wing, is placed a fmall tower, with a cupola. The idea of thefe buildings, is taken from the ruins of Palmyra; indeed, his Pruffian majefty has made as frequent ufe of the remains of Athens, Palmyra, and Balbec, in the temples ruins, and other buildings, in his gardens as he has at Potfdam, of the defigns of Palladio, Sanfovino, and Scamozzi.

There were innumerable things in and about this palace, which merited a minute examination; but I was obliged to haften away, in order to be prefent at his majefty's evening concert, at Sans-Souci. I was carried thither between five and six o'clock in the evening, by an officer of the houshold, a privileged person, otherwise it would have been impossible for a stranger, like myself, to gain admission into a palace where the king resides; and even with my well-known guide, I underwent a severe examination, not only at going out of the gates at Potsdam, but at every door of the palace. When we arrived at the vestibule, we were met by M. de Catt, lecturer to his majesty, and member of the royal academy, to whom I had been furnished with a letter, who very politely attended my conductor and me the whole evening.

I was carried to one of the interior apartments of the palace, in which the gentlemen of the king's band were waiting for his commands. This apartment was contiguous to the concert-room, where I could distinctly hear his majesty practising *Solfeggi* on the flute, and exercising himself in difficult passages, previous to his calling in the band. Here I met with M. Benda, who was so obliging as to introduce me to M. Quantz.

The figure of this Veteran musician, is of an uncommon size:

> The son of Hercules he justly seems,
> By his broad shoulders, and gigantic limbs;

and he appears to enjoy an uncommon portion of health and vigour, for a person arrived at his 76th year. We soon began a musical conversation; he told me, that his majesty and scholar played no other concertos than those which he had expressly composed for his use, which amounted to 300, and these he performed in rotation. This exclusive attachto the productions of his old master, may appear somewhat contracted; however, it implies a constancy of disposition, but rarely to be found among princes. The compositions of the two Grauns and of Quantz, have been in favour with his Prussian majesty more than forty years; and, if it be true, as many assert, that music has declined and degenerated since that time, in which the Scarlattis, Vincis, Leos, Pergolesis, and Porporas flourished, as well as the greatest singers that modern times have known, it is an indication of a sound judgment, and of great discernment, in his majesty, to adhere thus firmly to the productions of a period which may be called the Augustan age of music; to stem the torrent of caprice and fashion with such unshaken constancy, is possessing a kind of *stet sol*, by which Apollo and his sons are prevented from running riot, or changing from good to bad, and from bad to worse.

These reflections, which occurred to me while I was conversing with M. Quantz, were interrupted by the arrival of a messenger from the king, commanding the gentlemen of his band to attend him in the next room.

The concert began by a German flute concerto, in which his majesty executed the solo parts with great precision; his *embouchure* was clear and even, his finger brilliant, and his taste pure and simple. I was much pleased, and even surprised with the neatness of his execution in the *allegros*, as well as by his expression and feeling in the *adagio*; in short, his performance surpassed, in many particulars, any thing I had ever heard among *Dilettanti*, or even professors. His majesty played three long and difficult concertos successively, and all with equal perfection.

It must be owned, that many of the passages, in these pieces of M. Quantz, are now become old and common; but this does not prove their deficiency in novelty, when they were first composed, as some of them have been made more than forty years; and though M. Quantz has not been permitted to publish them, as they were originally composed for his majesty, and have ever since been appropriated to his use, yet, in a series of years,

years, other composers have hit upon the same thoughts: it is with music as with delicate wines, which not only become flat and insipid, when exposed to the air, but which are injured by time, however *well-kept*.

M. Quantz bore no other part in the performance of the concertos of to-night, than to give the time with the motion of his hand, at the beginning of each movement, except now and then to cry out *bravo!* to his royal scholar, at the end of the solo parts and closes; which seems to be a privilege allowed to no other musician of the band. The cadences which his majesty made, were good, but very long and studied. It is easy to discover that these concertos were composed at a time when he did not so frequently require an opportunity of breathing as at present; for in some of the divisions, which were very long and difficult, as well as in the closes, he was obliged to

take

take his breath, contrary to rule, before the paſſages were finiſhed.

After theſe three concertos were played, the concert of the night ended, and I returned to Potſdam; but not without undergoing the ſame interrogatories from all the centinels, as I had before done in my way to Sans-Souci.

I have already given an account of the regularity with which the pleaſures of the court ſucceed each other every week, during the king's reſidence at Berlin: and as ſome of my readers may, perhaps, be curious to know in what manner his majeſty ſpends his time each day, at Sans-Souci, I ſhall here preſent them with a detail of that regular diſpoſition of it, to which he has ſtrictly adhered, during peace, ever ſince he began his reign: indeed, the evolutions of his ſoldiers, on the parade, cannot be more exact than his own diurnal motions.

His majeſty's hour of riſing, is conſtantly at four o'clock in the morning,

during

during summer, and at five in winter; and from that time till nine, when his ministers of different departments attend him, he is employed in reading letters, and answering them in the margin. He then drinks one dish of coffee, and proceeds to business with his ministers, who come full fraught with doubts, difficulties, documents, petitions, and other papers, to read. With these he spends two hours, and then exercises his own regiment on the parade, in the same manner as the youngest colonel in his service.

At twelve o'clock he dines. His dinner is long, and generally with twelve or fourteen persons; after this he gives an hour to artists and projectors; then reads and signs the letters, written by his secretaries, from the marginal notes which he had made in the morning. When this is over, he thinks the *business* of the day is accomplished; the rest is given to amusement; after his evening concert, he gives some time to conversation, if
dis-

disposed for it, and his courtiers in waiting constantly attend for that purpose; but whether that is the case or not, he has a lecturer to read to him, every evening, titles and extracts of new books, among which he marks such as he wishes to have purchased for his library, or to read in his cabinet. In this manner, when not employed in the field, reviewing his troops, or in travelling, he spends his time: always retiring at ten o'clock, after which, however, he frequently reads, writes, or composes music for his flute, before he goes to bed.

Friday 2d. I this morning visited M. Quantz; he was so obliging as to play, at my request, three solos of his own composition, and, notwithstanding his advanced age, he still executes rapid movements with great precision. His music is simple and natural; his taste is that of forty years ago; but though this may have been an excellent period for composition, yet I cannot entirely subscribe to the opinion

of

of those who think musicians have discovered no refinements worth adopting, since that time. Without giving into tricks and caprice, and even allowing composition to have been arrived at its *acme* of perfection, forty years ago, yet a simple melody may surely be embellished by the modern manner of taking *appogiaturas*, of preparing and returning shakes, of gradually enforcing and diminishing whole passes, as well as single notes, and, above all, by the variety of expression arising from that superiority in the use of the bow, which the violin players of this age possess over those of any other period since its invention.

But even at the best time of M. Quantz, the elder musicians, and those in years, cried out against the innovations and levity of the younger. And no period can be named since the time of Plato, who likewise complained of the degeneracy of music, in which it has not been said to be corrupted by the moderns. Things of of sentiment, and mere objects of taste and feeling, cannot, I fear, be reduced to any standard of perfection. In painting, we have nature to copy, and to judge by; in poetry, though there is a fashion in language, and the newest and least debased by vulgar use, are the best words, yet grammar and common sense must remain the same.

As to *simplicity* in music, there are degrees of it, which border upon dryness, rusticity, and vulgarity; and these, it is the business of every composer to avoid. However, some who call themselves lovers of simplicity, would reduce music to the same metrical laws as poetry, and make long and short syllables determine melody; which would be neither suffering more than one sound to be given to one syllable, nor a longer or shorter duration to that sound, than the poetical rhythmus requires; but in this case, what would vocal music be, but a mere *Recitative*, with which every one is tired and disgusted! Mankind will certainly

tainly judge of their own pleasures; and it is natural to suppose, that when a new style of composition or performance *generally* prevails among the refined part of them, that it has something more captivating in it than that which they quitted. However, caprice, vanity, and a fondness for singularity, on one side; and obstinacy, pride, and prejudice, on the other, will always make it difficult to reconcile different sects, or to draw a line between truth and falsehood.

M. Quantz told me, that the first concerto which his Prussian majesty had played the night before, was made twenty years ago, and the other two had been made forty years. Considering this, and the great desire that every composer has to deviate from his predecessors, these pieces have stood their ground very well. There were *traits* both of melody and harmony, which must be good to unprejudiced ears, at all times, and in all places.

Be-

Besides the three hundred concertos which his majesty plays, in turn, he has nearly as many solos, which he performs in the like rotation. Upwards of a hundred of these have been composed by himself, the rest by M. Quantz.

M. Quantz, and his royal scholar, use only two keys to the German flute; and these, with a method of lengthening the mouth-piece, correct, they say, all the imperfections of this instrument, in point of bad notes and false tuning.

In the year 1754, M. Quantz drew up, in the German language, an account of his own life, which was printed in Marpurg's Musical Essays: and, as it contains several circumstances relative to music, as well as to himself, I shall make no apology to my readers, for giving them an abstract of it; selecting only such parts as are most interesting, and connecting them with such particulars as I obtained in my conversations with the author.

John Joachim Quantz was born at Oberscheden, a village in the Electorate of Hanover, in 1697. His father, who was a blacksmith, obliged him to work at the anvil before he was nine years old; which must have afforded him an early opportunity of making the famous Pythagorean experiment, mentioned by Jamblicus, *de Vit. Pythag.* and by all the musical writers of antiquity. Indeed, the ear of our young Ardalus * had been already formed, in his excursions with his brother, a village musician, that used to play about the country, on holydays and festivals, whom he accompanied upon these occasions, on the base-viol, when but eight years old, and without knowing a note of music; but this performance, bad as it was, pleased him so much, that he determined to chuse music for his profession; though his father,

* Ardalus was the son of Vulcan, by Aglaia, one of the Graces, and inventor of the pipe called *tibia*.

who died when he was only ten years of age, recommended to him, on his death-bed, to continue in the honourable profession of his anceſtors.

Quantz, after loſing his father, had no other friends to depend upon for counſel and protection, than two uncles, who lived at Merſeberg in Saxony; and theſe, ſending for him, gave him the choice of their ſeveral profeſſions, the one being a taylor, and the other a Kunſtpfeifer, or town-wait.

Upon this occaſion, the paſſion for muſic in the young Quantz overpowered all other conſiderations, and, preferring the fiddleſtick to the ſhears, he bound himſelf apprentice to his uncle, the muſician, for five years; but this uncle dying three months after, he was transferred to his ſon-in-law, Fleiſchhack, who was of the ſame profeſſion; and it was under him that he firſt practiſed the violin, an inſtrument to which his inclination at this time impelled him, preferably to any other.

Soon after this, however, he practiſed the hautbois, and the trumpet, with which inſtruments, and the violin, he chiefly filled up the term of his apprenticeſhip; but as a true town muſician, in Germany, is expected to play upon all kinds of inſtruments, he had been obliged, occaſionally, to apply himſelf, during this period, to the ſackbut, cornet, baſe-viol, French-horn, common-flute, baſſoon, viol da gamba, and the lord knows how many more. Theſe were in the way of buſineſs, but for pleaſure, he now and then took leſſons on the harpſichord, of the organiſt, Kieſewetter, who was likewiſe his relation; by which he laid the firſt foundation of his knowledge in harmony, and love for compoſition.

Luckily for Quantz, his maſter Fleiſchhack, was not like other country muſicians, fond only of old, dry, ſtiff, and taſteleſs compoſitions, but had ſufficient diſcernment to chuſe his pieces out of the newest and best productions of the times, by Telemann, Melchior, Hofmann, and Heinechen, which were published at Leipsic; from the perusal, and practice of which, our young performer derived great advantage.

The duke of Merseburg's band not being very numerous, the town-waits, at this time, were often called in, to assist at the musical performances, both of court and chapel. Here Quantz frequently heard foreigners play and sing, in a manner far superior to any professors whom he had hitherto met with, which excited in him a strong desire to travel. Dresden and Berlin were at this time the most renowned cities in Germany, for the cultivation of music, and for the number of able musicians. He eagerly wished to visit one of those cities, but was destitute of the means. However, he now began to feel his strength, and trusting to his feet and his fiddle, he boldly set off for Dresden.

It was in the year 1714 that he arrived in this city. His firſt entrance was not auſpicious, being wholly unable to procure employment: on this account, he made an excurſion to Radeburg, where a journeyman fidler being wanting, he entered into the ſervice of the town-muſician, Knoll; but alas! he was ſoon driven from this poſt, by the fatal accident of the town being burnt down by lightning. Again reduced to the ſtate of a fugitive, and a wanderer, he levied contributions round the country, by the power of his violin, which was now his principal inſtrument, till he reached Pirna.

Here, deſtined ſtill to be *ſervus ſervorum*, he could procure no other means of exerciſing his profeſſion, than by accepting the office of deputy to a ſick journeyman muſician of the town. It was during this time, that he firſt ſaw Vivaldi's concertos for the violin, which were ſo congenial to his own feelings and ideas of perfection, that he made them

them his model as long as he continued to practise that instrument.

Still regarding Dresden as his centre, he eagerly accepted an offer that was made to him, of being temporary assistant there, to one of the town-waits, who was then ill; an employment which he preferred, for the opportunities it afforded him of hearing good music and good musicians, to the more honourable post of being the best of bad musicians at Berenburg, where he might have been appointed first violin, with a good salary.

His second arrival at Dresden, was in the year 1716, where he soon discovered that it was not sufficient for a musician to be able to execute the mere notes which a composer had set on paper; and it was now that he first began to be sensible of the existence of taste and expression.

Augustus the second, was at this time King of Poland, and Elector of Saxony, and the orchestra of this prince at Dresden

den was in a flourishing condition; however, the style which had been introduced there, by the concert-master Volumier, was French; but Pisendel, who succeeded him, introduced a mixed taste, partly French, and partly Italian, which he afterwards brought to such perfection, that Quantz declares, he never heard a better band in all his future travels.

No orchestra in Europe could now boast of so many able professors, as that of the Elector of Saxony, among whom, were Pisendel and Veracini, on the violin; Pantaleone Hebenstreit, on the pantaleone; Weiss, on the lute; Richter, on the hautbois; and Buffardin, on the German flute; not to mention several excellent performers on the violoncello, bassoon, French horn, and double-base.

Upon hearing these great performers, Quantz was filled with such wonder, and possessed of such a rage for improvement, that he laboured incessantly to render him-

himself worthy of a place among such honourable associates.

For, however prejudiced he may have been in favour of his own reputable calling of *kunstpfeifer*, he began now just to think it possible for him to be prevailed upon, to relinquish that part of it, at least, which required him to play country dances, though in itself so jovial, pleasant, and festal an enjoyment.

He continued, however, to be the *kunstpfeifer*'s delegate in this city, till the death of Augustus the second's mother, in 1717, at which time, the general mourning proscribing the use of every species of convivial music, he again, in his usual manner, commenced traveller, and fiddled his way through Silesia, Moravia, and Austria, to Vienna; and in the month of October, of the same year, returned through Prague to Dresden; which journey, he thinks, contributed more to his knowledge, in

practical

practical geography than in any other art.

The jubilee of the reformation, brought about by Dr. Luther, happening to be celebrated soon after his return, he was called upon, among others, to perform a part upon the trumpet, at church, where the chapel-master Schmidt having heard him, offered to prevail on the king to have him regularly taught that instrument, in order to qualify him for the place of court trumpeter; but Quantz, however ardently he might have wished for an office at court, declined the acceptance of this, well-knowing that the good taste to which he aspired, was not to be learned upon that instrument, at least as it was then played in Dresden.

In 1718, the Polish or royal chapel was instituted; it was to consist of twelve performers, eleven were already chosen, and a hautbois-player, only, was now wanting, to complete the number. After undergoing the several trials, and giving

giving the requisite proofs of his abilities, he had the happiness to be invested with that employment, by the director, baron Seyfertitz, with a salary of 150 dollars, and a lodging.

This was an important period in his life, and in the exercise of his profession. The violin, which had hitherto been his principal instrument, was now laid aside for the hautbois, upon which, however, he was prevented from distinguishing himself, by the seniority of his brethren. Mortified at this circumstance, he applied himself seriously to the German flute, upon which he had formerly made some progress without a master; but his motive now for resuming it, was the certainty of his having no rival, in the king's band, as M. Friese, the first flute, had no great passion for music, and readily relinquished to him his place.

In order to work upon sure ground, Quantz took lessons at this time of the famous Buffardin, with whom, however, he he only played quick movements, in which this celebrated flute-player chiefly excelled. The scarcity of pieces, composed expresly for the German flute, was such, at this period, that the performers upon that instrument were obliged to adopt those of the hautbois, or violin, and by altering or transposing, accommodate them to their purpose, as well as they could.

This stimulated Quantz to compose for himself; he had not as yet ever received any regular instructions in counterpoint, so that, after he had committed his thoughts to paper, he was obliged to have recourse to others to correct them. Schmidt, the chapel-master, had promised to teach him composition, but delayed keeping his word from time to time, and Quantz was afraid of applying to Heincchen, his collegue, for fear of offending Schmidt, as these masters were upon bad terms together. In the mean time, for want of other assistance, he
dili-

diligently studied the scores of great masters, and without stealing from them, endeavoured to imitate their manner of putting parts together, in trios, and concertos.

About this time he had the good fortune to commence a friendship with Pisendel, now appointed concert-master, in the room of Volumier. Quantz is very warm in his praises of Pisendel, whom he calls a profound theorist, a great performer, and a truly honest man. It was from this worthy concert-master that he learned to perform an *adagio*, and to compose in many parts. Pisendel had in his youth been taught to sing by the famous Pistocchi, and had received instructions, on the violin, from Torelli; however, having travelled through France and Italy, where he had acquired the peculiarities in the taste of both countries, he so blended them together as to form a third genus, or mixed style of writing and playing, which was half French

French and half Italian. Influenced by his example, Quantz declares, that he always preferred this compound ſtyle, to the national one, or that of his own country.

At the marriage of the prince royal of Poland, in 1719, ſeveral Italian operas were performed at Dreſden. Lotti, the famous Venetian *maeſtro di capella*, together with the moſt celebrated ſingers of Italy, male and female, were called thither upon this occaſion; theſe were the firſt Italian operas which Quantz had heard, and he confeſſes, that the performances of them gave him a very favourable idea of the genuine and rational Italian taſte, from which he thinks later times have too much deviated.

The principal ſingers in theſe operas, were Seneſino, Berſelli, the wife of Lotti, the Teſi, Dureſtante, and Fauſtina. M. Quantz characteriſes ſeveral of them, in ſo diſcriminate and maſterly a manner,

manner, that I shall follow him more exactly than I have hitherto done.

Francesco Barnardi, called *Senesino*, had a powerful, clear, equal, and sweet *contralto* voice*, with a perfect intonation, and an excellent shake; his manner of singing was masterly, and his elocution unrivalled; though he never loaded *adagios* with too many ornaments, yet he delivered the original and essential notes, with the utmost refinement. He sung *allegros* with great fire, and marked rapid divisions, from the chest, in an articulate and pleasing manner; his countenance was well calculated for the stage, and his action was natural and noble: to

* M. Quantz calls it a low *mezzo soprano* voice, which seldom went higher than F; but as this account was drawn up, in the younger part of Senesino's life, before he went to England, it is natural to imagine, that his voice may afterwards have lost some of its high notes; for in all the airs which Handel made for him he is strictly confined to the limits of a true *contralto*.

these

these he joined a figure that was truly majestic, but more suited to the part of a hero than a lover.

Matteo Berselli had a thin, high, *soprano* voice, the compass of which was so extraordinary, that he could go from the lowest C, in the treble, to F in *altissimo*, with the greatest ease, by which he surprised the audience more than by his art in singing. In *adagios* he discovered very little passion, and in *allegros* he ventured at few difficulties; his countenance was rather disagreeable, and his action totally devoid of fire.

Santa Stella Lotti had a full, strong, *soprano* voice, a true intonation, and a good shake; high tones gave her little trouble; her principal excellence was in singing *adagios*. It was from her that Quantz first heard what professors call *tempo rubato:* her figure, on the stage, was full of dignity, and her action, particularly in elevated parts, could not be surpassed.

Vit-

Vittoria Tesi had by nature a masculine, strong, *contralto* voice. In 1719 she generally sung, at Dresden, such airs as are made for base voices; but afterwards, besides the majestic and serious style, she had occasionally something coquettish in her manner, which was very pleasing. The compass of her voice was so extraordinary, that neither to sing high nor low, gave her trouble. She was not remarkable for her performance of rapid and difficult passages; but she seemed born to captivate every spectator by her action, principally in male parts, which she performed in a most natural and intelligent manner *.

But, to return to Quantz. After describing the talents of the singers, he informs us, that this famous opera, at Dresden, was broke up by a quarrel between Heinechen, the King of Poland's chapel-master, and Senesino, who this same year, 1719, went to England, for the first time.

* See Vol. I. p. 318.

Nothing very interesting occurs in the life of Quantz, from this period, till the year 1723, when he took a journey with Weifs, the famous lutanist, and Graun, the composer, to Prague.

About this time, most of the great musicians of Europe were assembled together, in this city, by order of the emperor Charles VI, to celebrate the festival of his being crowned, king of Bohemia. History does not furnish a more glorious event for music, than this solemnity, nor a similar instance of so great a number of eminent professors, of any one art, being collected together.

Upon this occasion, there was an opera performed in the open air, by a hundred voices, and by two hundred instruments. There was not an indifferent singer among the principal performers, all were of the first class. The male parts were filled by Orsini, Domenico, Carestini, Gaffati, Borosini, and Braun, a German *baritono*; the female, by the two sisters,

Amberville, one of whom was afterwards married to Peroni, a famous player, on the violoncello, and the other to Borosfini, the finger.

The opera was called *la Constanza e Fortezza*, and composed by the famous old Fux, imperial chapel-master at Vienna. The music, which was in the old church style, was coarse and dry; but, at the same time, grand, and had a better effect, perhaps, with so immense a band, and in such an immense space, than could have been produced by more delicate compositions.

The chorusses were in the French style, and served for dances; Caldara beat the time; but Fux, who had the gout, was brought into the theatre, in a chair, and placed near the Emperor.

As it was upon the singing in this opera that Benda, formed his style, and as I have been told by the two Bezozzis, of Turin, and others who were present, that it surpassed all the vocal perfor-

mances

mances of other times, I shall here insert a character of the several singers, for the entertainment of such of my readers as have never heard them, nor are versed in the German language.

Gaetano Orsini was one of the greatest singers that ever existed; he had a powerful, even, affecting *contralto* voice, of a considerable compass; his shake was perfect, and his *portamento*, excellent. In *allegros*, he articulated divisions, particularly in triplets, most admirably, and always from the breast. In *adagios* he was so perfect a master of every thing which pleases and affects, that he took entire possession of the hearts of all that heard him; he was many years in the imperial service, and though he lived to an advanced age, he preserved his fine voice to the last *.

Domenico had one of the finest *soprano* voices that has ever been heard on the

---

* He died at Vienna, about the year, 1750.

stage; it was so clear and penetrating, as to make its way through all obstructions, and, with this great force, was sweet, and well toned; however he neither sung nor acted with much spirit.

Pietro Gassati was more remarkable as a great actor, than singer.

Borosini had a spirited, and flexible, tenor voice.

Braun, though his voice was that of a low pitch, from whence delicacy is not expected, had so much taste and expression, that he sung *adagios* in a most pleasing and affecting manner.

Giovanni Carestini had a strong and clear *soprano* voice, which, afterwards, changed into the fullest, finest, and deepest counter-tenor, that has ever been heard. When he performed at Prague, his compass was sixteen notes, from B in the base, to c in *alt*; he had a wonderful facility of executing difficult divisions from the chest, like Farinelli, and those of the Bernacchi school; and graced, and
varied

varied paffages, ufually, with great fuccefs, though in this he was fometimes a little licentious and extravagant. His action was admirable, and, like his finging, full of fire; but, after this time he improved, greatly, in his manner of performing *adagios*. He continued on the ftage, with the higheft reputation, for more than thirty years; in 1735 he was in England, and in 1750 went to Berlin, where he continued till 1755, after which, he retired to Italy, and there, foon ended his days.

M. Quantz, not long after the congrefs at Prague, went to Italy, in the *fuite* of count Lagnafco, with the confent of his royal mafter, the king of Poland. He left Drefden, in May 1724, and, when he arrived at Rome, he found that Vivaldi had juft introduced the Lombard ftyle, in that city, with which the citizens were fo captivated, that they would hear no other.

During his residence at Rome, he took lessons in counterpoint of the famous Gasparini, who was, at this time, 72 years of age; and whose good-nature and probity seem to have made as deep an impression upon M. Quantz, as his musical merit.

The cantatas and operas of Gasparini, which were more numerous than those of any other composer of his time, except Alef. Scarlatti, were in the highest estimation, at the beginning of the present century. M. Quantz attributes to him the invention of *accompanied recitatives*; he composed twenty-five operas for the theatre at Venice; and among his learned compositions, a mass in four parts, all in strict *canon*, is extremely celebrated.

M. Quantz, after studying counterpoint, which he calls music for the *eyes*, during six months, under this master, went to work for the *ear*, and composed
solos,

solos, duos, trios, and concertos; however, he confesses, that counterpoint had its use in writing pieces of many parts; though he was obliged to *unlearn* many things, in *practice*, which *theory* had taught him, in order to avoid that dry, and stiff style, which, too close an adherence to rules, is apt to produce; upon this occasion, he very judiciously observes, that *invention* is the first requisite in a composer, and that it behoves him to preserve a friendship between harmony and melody.

In 1725, he went to Naples, where he met with his coutryman Hasse, who then studied under Alef. Scarlatti. Hasse had not, as yet, distinguished himself by any compositions for the stage; however, it was at this time, that a considerable Neapolitan banker employed him to set a serenata for two voices, which he did in the presence of Quantz; the singers who performed in it, were Farinelli and Tesi. Hasse gained so much reputation by this production, that it paved the way to his future fuccefs, and he was foon after appointed compofer of the great opera at the theatre royal.

Quantz intreated Haffe to introduce him to his mafter, Scarlatti, to which he readily confented; but upon mentioning him to the old compofer, he faid, " my " fon, you know I hate wind inftru- " ments, they are never in tune." However, Haffe did not ceafe importuning him, till he had obtained the permiffion he required.

In the vifit which he made to Scarlatti, M. Quantz fays, that he had an opportunity of hearing him play on the harpfichord, which he did in a very learned manner; but obferves, that his abilities on that inftrument were not equal to thofe of his fon [*].

Before his departure from Naples, M. Quantz frequently heard concerts, at the

---

[*] Quantz had heard Mimo Scarlatti, during his refidence at Rome.

duke of Lichtenstein's, in which Hasse, Farinelli, Tesi, and Francischello, were employed.

In 1726, he was at Venice, during the performance of two rival operas, *Siface*, composed by Porpora, and *Siroe*, by Vinci; the latter was most applauded. The Cav. Nicolini, a *contralto*, la Romanina, a deep *soprano*, and the famous tenor, Paita, were the principal singers in these dramas.

San Martini, the celebrated performer, on the hautbois, who afterwards established himself in London, was now at Venice, as was Vivaldi.

At Turin, he met with Somis, under whom, Le Claire was at that time a scholar, on the violin.

From Turin he went to Paris, which with respect to music, was going from one extreme to another.

"I was displeased with the French "taste now," says M. Quantz, "though "I had heard it formerly with patience. "The

" The old, worn-out, second-hand
" thoughts, and passages ill expressed,
" disgusted me now, as much as a stale
" dish warmed again. The resemblance
" between recitative and air, with the
" affected and unnatural howling of the
" singers, particularly the women, shock-
" ed my ears."

M. Quantz was the first who applied an additional key to the German flute, in order to correct its imperfections; and it was in the course of this year, 1726, that he made the discovery.

In 1727 he arrived in London, where he found the opera in a very flourishing state, under the direction of Handel. The drama of *Admetus* was now in run, of which, he says, the music was grand and pompous. Senesino performed the first male part, and Cuzzoni and Faustina were the principal women.

I shall present the younger part of my readers with a character of these rival Syrens, Cuzzoni and Faustina, from

Quantz,

Quantz, whose judgment seems to be untainted by the partial rage of the times.

Cuzzoni had a very agreeable, and clear *soprano* voice; a pure intonation, and a fine shake; her compass extended two octaves, from C to c in alt. Her style of singing was innocent and affecting; her graces did not seem artificial, from the easy and neat manner in which she executed them; however, they took possession of the soul of every auditor, by her tender and touching expression. She had no great rapidity of execution, in *allegros*; but there was a roundness and smoothness, which were neat and pleasing. Yet, with all these advantages, it must be owned that she was rather cold in her action, and that her figure was not advantageous for the stage.

Faustina had a *mezzo-soprano* voice, that was less clear than penetrating. Her compass was now only from B b to G in alt; but after this time, she extended

tended its limits downwards. She possessed what the Italians call *un cantar granito*: her execution was articulate and brilliant. She had a fluent tongue for pronouncing words rapidly and distinctly, and a flexible throat for divisions, with so beautiful and quick a shake, that she could put it in motion upon short notice, just when she would. The passages might be smooth, or by leaps, or consist of iterations of the same tone, their execution was equally easy to her, as to any instrument whatever. She was doubtless the first who introduced, with success, a swift repetition of the same tone. She sung *adagios* with great passion and expression, but not equally well, if such deep sorrow were to be impressed on the hearer, as might require dragging, sliding, or notes of syncopation, and *tempo rubato*.

She had a very happy memory, in arbitrary changes and embellishments, and a clear and quick judgment in giving to
words

words their full power and expression. In her action she was very happy; and as she perfectly possessed that flexibility of muscles and features, which constitutes face-playing, she succeeded equally well in furious, amorous, and tender parts: in short, she was born for singing and for acting.

The violence of party, says M. Quantz, for the two singers, Cuzzoni and Faustina, was so great, that when one began to applaud, the other was sure to hiss; on which account operas ceased for some time in London.

If the frequenters of musical dramas had not then been enemies to their own pleasure, the merit of these singers consisted of excellencies so different and distinct, that they might have applauded each by turns, and, from their several perfections, by turns, have received equal delight.

Unluckily for moderate people, who seek pleasure from talents wherever they can be found, the violence of these feuds has

has cured all succeeding managers, of the extravagance of bringing over two singers of the same sex, at a time, of disputable abilities.

As it is natural to wish to know the opinion of strangers concerning our own country, I shall proceed a little farther with M. Quantz, in his account of the state of music in London, when he was there.

The opera orchestra, which consisted chiefly of Germans, with a few Italians, and two or three Englishmen, was led by Castrucci, and, being under Handel's direction, all went well.

The second opera which M. Quantz heard in London, was composed by Buononcini; but this was not so much approved as the other, for Handel's depth and solidity overpowered the lightness and grace of Buononcini.

Attilio and Tosi were now in London, which at this time did not abound in solo players upon any instrument. The principal

cipal were Handel, on the harpsichord and organ; Geminiani, a great master on the violin; Dubourg, his scholar, an Englishman, who was a pleasing performer on that instrument; the two Castrucci's, who were brothers, and tolerable solo players: Weidemann, a German, and Festing, an Englishman, on the German flute, with Mauro d'Alaia, who came to England with Faustina; he was a good performer on the violin, and an excellent leader; his manner of playing was clear and distinct, but he never ventured at great difficulties.

M. Quantz acquaints us, that he had the good fortune to be well received by several people of rank, who endeavoured to persuade him to settle in England; Handel advised him to this measure; lady Pembroke, a great judge and encourager of music, proposed to make him a benefit, in which baron Bothmar would have taken care of his interest, but he declined it; for, as he was still

a sera servant of the king of Poland, he did not chuse to perform in public, thinking it a duty to his prince to offer him the first fruits of his travels.

Upon his return to Dresden, he was established in the King's chapel, with an addition to his former salary of 250 dollars a year. He now entirely quitted the hautbois, supposing it hurtful to the *embouchure* of the flute, which, from this time, he made his sole study.

In 1728, he went to Berlin, with baron Seyfertiz, in the *suite* of the king of Poland; where he was obliged, at the command of the Queen of Prussia, and with the permission of his royal master, to remain for some months. Pisendel, Weiss, and Buffardin were, by the same order, called thither. After he had had the honour of playing before the queen, two or three times, he was offered a place and pension of 800 dollars a year. He was very willing to accept of them, but the King his master would not grant his
con-

consent: however, this prince gave him a general permission to go to Berlin, as often as he was desired.

This year, 1728, the prince royal, his present majesty of Prussia, determined to learn the German flute, and M. Quantz had the honour to teach him. On this account, he was obliged to go twice a year to Berlin, Ruppin, or Reinsberg, the several residences of his royal scholar.

After the death of the king of Poland, in 1733, his son, Augustus III. not chusing to dismiss M. Quantz, raised his appointment to 800 dollars, and confirmed the permission which had been granted by his royal father, for his going occasionally to Berlin.

In 1734, he published his first solos; but he does not acknowledge the sonatas, which were printed under his name, in Holland, about that time.

In 1739, M. Quantz finding a great scarcity of German flutes, undertook to bore them himself for the use of his pupils; an enterprize which, afterwards, he found to be very lucrative.

In 1741, he was again invited to Berlin, in order to enter into the service of his royal scholar, now King of Prussia, with offers of an annual pension of 2000 dollars for life; a separate payment for compositions; 100 ducats for every flute he should deliver; and an exemption from playing in the orchestra, or any where else, but in the King's chamber, as well as from dependance on any other commands than those of his majesty; which terms, as the King of Poland was too gracious longer to refuse his dismission, M. Quantz was unable to resist.

In 1752, he published his *Art of Playing the German Flute*; and it was this year that he invented the new joint for the upper-piece of the flute, by which means, without drawing out the middle piece, and without hurting the tone, the instrument may be raised or lowered, half a note.

And now, having traced our induſ-trious muſician through the troubleſome mazes by which he arrived at the temple of Fortune, we ſhall leave him to the enjoyment of that reputable eaſe, that *otium cum dignitate*, to which every artiſt in years, and in his ſenſes, aſpires.

Upon quitting M. Quantz, I went to the parade, in hopes of hearing military muſic, as well as of ſeeing military diſcipline, in its utmoſt perfection.

The parade at Potſdam is in a field, encloſed by a wall, where no ſtranger is permitted to enter, without leave from the captain of the guard. With reſpect to muſic, the ſame ſtability of ſtyle, and of taſte, is obſervable here as at court; and I did not find that the Pruſſians, in their marches, had advanced a ſingle ſtep towards novelty, or refinement, ſince the firſt years of his preſent majeſty's reign; for neither the airs that were played, nor the inſtruments that played them, had any peculiar merit: however, the old-faſhioned

fashioned march, of *dot and go one*, is perhaps, best calculated to mark the time, and to regulate the steps of the soldiers.

In visiting the principal streets and squares of this beautiful city, which is well-built, well-paved, magnificent, and new, I could not help observing, that foot passengers were here, as well as in every other city of Europe, except London, exposed to accidents from being mixed with horses and carriages, as well as from the insolence and brutality of their riders and drivers, for want of a *foot-path* *.

I know not whether it has been remarked by writers of travels, that on the *Via Appia*, and other ancient roads in Italy, a place was set apart, on each side, for the convenience of pedestrians; and in visiting Pompeia, where an entire antique Roman street has been dug out, I

* In Paris, a great number of citizens are annually killed and maimed for want of this retreat.

observed

observed the same thing. A Roman citizen, whether patrician, or plebeian, was a respectable character; and, perhaps, England is the only country, at present, where the common people are sufficiently respected, for their lives and limbs to be thought worth preserving.

The present rage for architecture, in his Prussian majesty, is carried on with such excess, that, in Potsdam, buildings which have all the external grandeur and elegance of palaces, are made the habitations of common soldiers, who rather exist than live in them, upon five *creuzers*, two pence half-penny, a day. However, this passion is hereditary, for the late King of Prussia made it a condition, in bestowing offices and employments about his court and person, that each incumbent should build a house; reserving to himself the pleasure of planning and constructing the front.

I did not quit Potsdam, before I had again had the honour to partake of Lord

Marshal's hospitality, by dining with his lordship a second time; where wit, good breeding, and good humour, crowned the board. After which, while I was preparing for my return to Berlin, I received a message from col. Forcade, to acquaint me that the prince of Prussia desired me to sup with him, at half an hour past six, and that he would present me to his royal highness. This great and unexpected honour somewhat embarrassed me, as it was my full intention to get to Berlin that evening, time enough to go to the *Accademia,* or concert, to which I had been invited, and which, I had been told, would be made as brilliant in performance as possible, on my account; but the fear of not appearing sufficiently sensible of the prince's condescension, and indeed of not executing properly the commission which I had undertaken concerning the books, determined me to stay.

At half an hour past six in the evening, I therefore went to the palace of
the

the prince royal, where I expected to hear music; but cards, and conversation, filled up the time, till supper. At my first entrance, I had the honour of being presented to his princess, who is fair, rather tall, and possessed of that pleasing degree of plumpness, which the French call *l'embonpoint charmant:* with a person infinitely less agreeable than falls to the share of this princess, her uncommonly gracious and condescending address and manner would captivate every one whom she honours with her notice.

Her royal highness had heard that I had been with Lord Marshal, and that I was attached to music; and upon these subjects she politely dwelt a considerable time. She plays the harpsichord well herself, as I was assured, and was very curious and conversible about music: even while at cards, she condescended to address herself to me very frequently, and at last asked me if I had known her brother, when he was in England?—I then recollected, and not before, that her royal highness was a princess of Hesse-Darmstadt, and sister to that prince of Hesse-Darmstadt, who last year made the tour of England, and to whom I had had the honour of being presented in London.

During this time, a young prince of two years of age, and his sister of only a year old, were brought into the card-room to the princess their mother; and, not long after, the prince of Prussia entered, to whom I had the honour of being presented. His royal highness is tall, and of a manly, plain, natural, and agreeable character. At supper, he was so gracious as to make me sit down on his left hand, and to address the discourse to me almost the whole evening. He was chearful and open, and seemed very well acquainted with the present state of the several countries of Europe, particularly England. Music had a considerable share in the conversation, and it was not difficult

cult to discover that his royal highness is less strongly attached to old music, and to old masters, than his majesty.

BERLIN.

The evening after my return to this city, October 3d, M. Lintner was so obliging as to conduct me to a private concert, composed of the principal professors, and gentlemen performers of Berlin. It was performed at the apartments of M. Kone, the King of Prussia's first violin, in one of the fine houses of the New Town, built by his majesty.

I here heard a concerto of the late concert-master Graun's composition, performed by M. Kone, with more force than delicacy; a difficult flute concerto, of Quantz, by M. Lintner, very neatly executed; and a concerto, on the same instrument, by M. Riedt, of his own composition, of which, both the style and performance, were rather ancient and coarse; with several symphonies of Hasse and Graun.

Without farther discussion of the merits of the several compositions which I heard at this concert, I must observe, that the musicians of many parts of Europe, have discovered and adopted certain refinements, in the manner of executing even old music, which are not yet received in the Berlin school, where *pianos* and *fortes* are but little attended to, and where each performer seems trying to surpass his neighbour, in nothing so much as *loudness*; a contention which very much resembles, the old naval sport of running the hoop, in which each spitefully strives to act with more force than those around him; for as the chief exertion of the sailor is to be *felt*, that of the Berlin musician is to be *heard*.

If I may depend on my own sensations, I should imagine, that the musical performances of this country want *contrast*; and there seems to be not only too many notes in them, but those notes are expressed

pressed with too little attention to the *degree* of force, that the instruments, for which they are made are capable of. Sound can only be augmented to a certain degree, beyond that, is *noise*. I have elsewhere said, I confess, that even *noise* is sometimes successfully made, in full pieces; but, when this is attempted, it should be for the sake of that contrast and opposition of passages and musical phrases, by which one contributes to the effect of another; for, when a piece is executed with such unremitting fury, as I have sometimes heard, it ceases to be music; and, instead of a part, the whole deserves no other appellation than that of *noise*.

At this concert I met with M. Rück, formerly musician to prince Henry, his Prussian majesty's brother. This performer visited England during the last war, at which time I frequently heard him play the solos of Benda, on the violin, with great feeling and expression; he has since relinquished music, as a profession,

sion, but, as a *dilettante*, he has not been idle; he has a strong hand on the violin, with great knowledge of the fingerboard; and has composed several concertos, solos, and symphonies, in a pleasing and brilliant style; but so *modern*, that, at Berlin, he is regarded as a heretic. I went home with him from the concert, and accompanied him in a great number of his own pieces.

Sunday 4th. This morning I was visited by M. Agricola, M. Reidt, the German flute-player, who has been more than twenty years in the service of his Prussian majesty, and M. Schüler, a *dilettante* of great merit, and intelligence in musical matters.

M. Agricola was so obliging as to go with me to St. Peter's church, which has the largest organ, and the best organist in Berlin; this instrument was begun in the time, and at the expence of the late king, and was intended to be the largest in the world. Since the death of this

prince

prince it has remained unfinished, as his present majesty's zeal for the church has not hitherto inclined him to complete it, after the original plan. The organ is placed over the pulpit; this instrument was to have contained 150 stops, and to have had six sets of keys, besides pedals; at present, its whole contents are 50 stops, with three sets of keys for the hands, and one for the feet; but, even in this diminished state, it is too powerful for the building, and each tone is continued so long, by the reverberation, after the hand is taken off, or removed to another, that all is confused and indistinct.

M. Bertuch, the organist, however, is a good player; he has a strong hand, and great knowledge of the instrument. After playing extempore, a very masterly introduction, he executed a very learned and difficult double *fugue*, composed by old Bach, expressly for the use of organs with pedals.

In

In the church of St. Mary, there is a fine organ, built by Wagner; M. Ringk, the organist, is much esteemed as a performer of extempore *fugues*, though he is possessed of less brilliancy of finger than the organist of St Peter.

I had this afternoon the pleasure of another conference with M. Marpurg. It was a mortifying circumstance to me, that the multiplicity and variety of my enquiries in this city, and the little time allotted me for making them, prevented me from more frequently enjoying the conversation of this gentleman, whose learning and intelligence, on the subject of music, are equally extensive and profound.

Upon quitting M. Marpurg, I made a second visit to mademoiselle Schmeling, who favoured me with several songs of uncommon rapidity, and compass; her powers, in these particulars, are truely astonishing; but she is frequently compelled to abuse these powers by the airs
that

that are given her to execute, in which she has passages, that degrade the voice into an instrument, indeed, often such as a player of taste would be ashamed to execute, upon any instrument.

Breaking a common chord into common *arpeggios* and passages of no meaning, such as may be seen in the second *allegro* of Corelli's third solo, does not seem to me an employment that reflects much honour, either upon a composer, or performer.

There was still a little want of brightness in the middle of mad^{lle} Schmeling's voice; and I can imagine it possible for her still to improve in singing *adagios*, though not in the execution of *allegros*. She does not seem, at present, to be placed in the best school for advancement in taste, expression, and high finishing; for, besides the partiality of the king, to particular compositions, the principal men singers of this opera are not now at their best period, and, if they were, variety is

perhaps

perhaps more neceffary to awaken genius, and ferment the latent feeds of tafte in a young performer, than the example of a few individuals, which infpires no other rage than that of mere *imitation*. If mademoifelle Schmeling were to go to Italy, fhe would not perhaps meet with greater powers than her own, in any *one* performer; but, by adopting the peculiar excellencies of *many* performers, of different fchools, and talents, her ftyle, like the Venus of Apelles, would be an aggregate of all that is exquifite and beautiful.

At the houfe of mademoifelle Schmeling, I heard this morning M. Mara execute, with great abilities, feveral pieces on the Violoncello; he is a young man, and the fon of a performer of the fame name, and upon the fame inftrument, whofe talents have been much celebrated in Germany.

October 5. I this morning vifited M. Sulzer, member of the royal academy
of

of gentlemen at Berlin; he is author of several works in literature, which are much esteemed. This gentleman is particularly attached to music, and has been very diffuse upon it in his *Theory of Polite Arts*, where he has manifested great taste and refinement, as well as depth and learning, in his manner of treating several of the musical articles; this work is written in the form of a dictionary, of which only the first volume, extending from the letter A to I, is, as yet, published; however, the second volume, which will complete the design, is in great forwardness.

We had a long musical conference together, and I found him to be, not only well-read in books concerning music, but, an ingenious and refined thinker, on the subject.

M. Schüler, the *dilettante*, whom I mentioned before, and who had been so obliging, as to introduce me to this gentleman, conducted me afterwards to M.

Kirnberger, a master whom I was very desirous to see, as I was well acquainted with many of his compositions, and had heard much of his musical controversies.

John Philip Kirnberger was born in 1721, at Saalfeld, in Thuringia, a province of Saxony; at the age of eighteen, he went to Leipsic, where he studied under Sebastian Bach, till 1741, when he went into Poland, where he was admitted into the service of several Polish princes; and afterwards, appointed director of the music at a convent. In 1751 he went to Dresden, where he studied the violin under Fickler, and some time after, entered into the service of the king of Prussia, as a performer on that instrument; at present, he is court musician to her royal highness, princess Amelia of Prussia. The harpsichord, which was his first, is likewise his best instrument; and his compositions for that, and for the organ, are very numerous, as well as his polemical and theoretical writings. Besides these

these publications, he has been editor of four collections of harpsichord pieces, which include several of his own; and of all these, he has marked the fingering, according to the rules of C. P. E. Bach.

He played at my request upon a clavichord, during my visit, some of his *fugues* and church music, which are very learned and curious; he likewise presented me with a copy of his *musical institutes*, and a short dissertation upon *temperament*, which he has lately published*, as well as of several manuscript compositions.

After this he had the complaisance to go with me to the house of Hildebrand, the best maker of harpsichords, and pianofortes, in Berlin; here M. Kirnberger played again, and discovered great strength of hand, as well as knowledge in harmony and modulation.

* The German title is, Construction der gleichschwebenden Temperatur, Berlin, gedruckt bey Fried. Wilh. Birnstiel.

these publications, he has been editor of four collections of harpsichord pieces, which include several of his own; and of all these, he has marked the fingering, according to the rules of C. P. E. Bach.

He played at my request upon a clavichord, during my visit, some of his *fugues* and church music, which are very learned and curious; he likewise presented me with a copy of his *musical institutes*, and a short dissertation upon *temperament*, which he has lately published*, as well as of several manuscript compositions.

After this he had the complaisance to go with me to the house of Hildebrand, the best maker of harpsichords, and pianofortes, in Berlin: here M. Kirnberger played again, and discovered great strength of hand, as well as knowledge in harmony and modulation.

* The German title is, Construction der gleichschwebenden Temperatur, Berlin, gedruckt bey Fried. Wilh. Birnstiel.

I was perhaps, the more flattered by the kindness and compliance of this ingenious professor, from his character, which is grave and austere; he is said to be soured by opposition and disappointment; his present inclination leads him to mathematical studies, and to the theory of music, more than the practice, in which he has such great abilities; and in his late writings, he appears to be more ambitious of the character of an algebraist, than of a musician of genius.

This afternoon I went to M. Marpurg for the last time, who was so obliging, on this occasion, as to throw out all the temptations which he could suggest, in order to keep me longer in Berlin; but my want of time rendered me inflexible; however, he kindly undertook to procure and transmit to me several interesting particulars relative to the history of German music and musicians, and furnished me with the description of a machine for writing down extempore pieces of

music,

music, commonly called voluntaries, of which I had been long in search.

To fix such fleeting sounds as are generated in the wild moments of enthusiasm, while "bright-eyed fancy——

"Scatters from her pictured urn,
"Thoughts, that breathe, and *notes*, that burn."

would be giving permanence to ideas which reflection can never find, nor memory retain.

I had been told, upon mentioning such a machine, among musical *desiderata*, to counsellor Reiffenstein, at Rome, that one had been constructed at Berlin; and, upon my arrival here, this interesting piece of mechanism was among the first objects of my enquiry. I was told, indeed, that such a one had been completed, to the satisfaction of the prinpal musicians of Berlin, but that it was soon neglected and thrown aside; and not long since, a fire happening in a house belonging to the royal academy where it was deposited, this ingenious piece of mechanism was burnt, and has never since been renewed.

Before I speak further concerning the machine in question, I must inform my readers, that the first idea of such a contrivance being practicable, was suggested to the Royal Society of London, in a paper written by the late revd. Mr. Creed, and sent to the president, 1747, under the following title.

A demonstration of the possibility of making a machine *that shall write* extempore voluntaries, *or other pieces of music, as fast as any master shall be able to play them, upon an organ, harpsichord, &c. and that in a character more natural and intelligible, and more expressive of all the varieties those instruments are capable of exhibiting, than the character now in use.*

This paper was published the same year, in The Philosophical Transactions, N°. 183, and, afterwards, in Martyn's

Abridg-

Abridgment, vol. x. p. 266; and the author's idea always appeared to me so feasible, that I have long wondered at its not having been executed by some ingenious English mechanic.

The first mention that I can find to have been made at Berlin, of such a contrivance, was in 1752, in a printed *Weekly Account of the most remarkable Discoveries in Nature and Science.* In 1753, an ample description of such a machine appeared in the same weekly publication: and here, in an elaborate preface, the author points out the great want of such a piece of mechanism, its utility, and properties; and concludes with saying, that this machine, so big with advantages to music and musicians, is the *particular invention,* besondere Erfindung, of M. Unger.

This description preceded the execution some time. The invention was here only recommended to the public, and offered to be completed, and applied to a keyed instrument, at a small expence.

It was M. Hohlfeld, who afterwards constructed the machine, and rendered it so perfect, that I was assured, by a great performer, who tried it upon a clavichord, that there was nothing in music which it could not express, except *tempo rubato*.

The description of the Berlin machine, so much resembles that proposed by M. Creed, that I shall not insert it here, but refer my reader to the Philosophical Transactions, where he will find that the machine was to consist of two cylinders, which were to be moved by clock-work, at the rate of an inch in a second of time; one of these was to furnish paper, and the other was to receive it when marked by pins, or pencils, fixed at the ends of the several keys of the instrument, to which the machine was applied. The paper was to be previously prepared with red lines, which were to fall under their respective pencils.

The chief difficulties in the execution, which have occurred to English mechanics, with whom I have conversed on the subject, were, the preparation of the paper for receiving the marks made by the keys; and the kind of instrument which was to serve as a pencil, and which, if hard and pointed, would, in the *forte* parts, tear the paper; and if soft, would not only be liable to break when used with violence, but would be worn unequally, and want frequent cutting.

In the Berlin machine, the pencils were approximated according to Mr. Creed's idea, and made to terminate in a very narrow compass, so that paper of an uncommon size was not requisite; but it was *not* found necessary to prepare the paper, as proposed in the Philosophical Transactions; for the degree of gravity, or acuteness, of each sound, was ascertained by a ruler applied to the marked paper, when taken off the cylinder.

I shall

I shall make no farther observations upon this subject, at present, except that though M. Unger seems to lose the honour of the *invention*, by Mr. Creed's more early publication of it; yet, that of the *execution* will wholly remain with M. Hohlfeld, till some Englishman shall participate it with him, by a like fortunate completion of the discovery of his countryman, Mr. Creed.

When I quitted M. Marpurg, I went to a concert, at the house of baron Seidlitz, one of his Prussian majesty's ministers, where I had the honour of being introduced by M. Jos. Benda. The baron is his scholar, and played a concerto, by M. Fran. Benda, reasonably well, for a *dilettante*. M. Grauel, a violoncello performer in the King's band, played a concerto; it was but ordinary music; however, it was well executed, though in the old manner, with the hand under the bow. After this, M. Joseph Benda
played

played one of his brother's concertos very neatly, with a good tone, and true intonation. This piece had no other fault, than that of being too long, which is ever the cafe here, in every fpecies of compofition, where each movement is fo protracted, that attention can never be kept awake to the end.

I found, upon enquiry, that the 𝕮𝖚𝖗=𝖗𝖊𝖓𝖉=𝕾𝖈𝖍ü𝖑𝖊𝖗, or chorus of children, who fing about the ftreets, ftill fubfifts in Berlin; they are furnifhed with a grey uniform and cloaks, and are twenty-four in number. The money which they collect is divided among them.

At the college of Cologne, in this city, the children are taught reading, writing, and *finging:* as are the children of the foldiers, at the garrifon church.

In moft parts of Germany, where the proteftant religion is eftablifhed, each parifh has a cantor to teach finging, and to direct the chorus.

Though

Though *cantor* is a general appellation for a finger, it is in a particular manner applied, in this country, to the person who has the direction of singing the psalms and hymns in parish churches. He is precentor, or leader of the psalm, which he likewise ends, by singing the last word of every line: so that he may be called the *alpha* and *omega* of sacred song.

The cantor, who is likewise frequently school-master, besides having a good voice, should necessarily understand counterpoint; if not in a high degree, at least sufficiently to correct such errors as may have crept into compositions, through the ignorance or carelessness of transcribers. He should likewise be able to make an accurate score, and from the score to figure the base, in such a manner as to include all the accidents of modulation. "Without these qualifications," says M. Walther, in his Musical Lexicon, " as a " German organist is not gifted with
" uni-

" universal knowledge, no perfect har-
" mony can be hoped."

In the market-towns and villages of Thuringia, in Saxony, where two persons are usually employed in a school, he who directs the music in the choir, or leads the psalm, or chorus, is called *rector*, or school-master, and the organist is commonly *cantor*.

The Italian comic operas are performed at the expence of the King, for which two women, and three men singers, are in salary. The instrumental performers are drawn from his majesty's band, as are the dancers, from his serious opera; the singers, male and female, reside at Potsdam. These operas are performed at no fixed time, but depend upon the King's pleasure to command them, in one of the theatres of his palaces, at Potsdam, Berlin, or Charlottenburg.

The Queen, and the princess dowager of Prussia, frequently give concerts at Berlin, to which the entrance is open,

and

and general. At these performances, the principal singers of the opera, and musicians of his majesty's band, are employed.

In assemblies, except minuets, the dances are almost constantly English; the Polonoise, so much in vogue formerly, are now no longer practised, but they still, some times, make use of French dances.

The night watch here, consists of a certain number of armed men, who are distributed in the several streets, throughout the city. They cry the hour in a kind of *chant*, with the sound of a horn, which is likewise the custom throughout Germany.

Among the principal musicians of Berlin, I have not yet mentioned M. Charles Fasch, chamber-musician to the King, and son of the celebrated chapel-master of that name. In our several attempts to meet each other at Berlin, I was always unfortunate; and his waiting time at Potsdam
coming

coming on, juſt when I quitted that city, I was not ſo happy as to hear him play: but, if I may judge by his reputation, and by his compoſitions for the harpſichord, in which the greateſt fire and delicacy are united, he muſt be an excellent performer.

M. Schale is likewiſe an organiſt and harpſichord-player of reputation in Berlin, whom I was not ſo fortunate as to hear.

M. Reidt, the performer on the flute, mentioned before, is deſcended from Engliſh parents; he is regarded as a learned muſician; but his ſtyle of compoſition and performance, is dry and uninterefting; he is author of *a Treatiſe upon muſical Intervals*, which has been celebrated in its day; it is full of calculations, which are uſeleſs to men of ſcience, and which men of refinement and genius will never ſubmit to ſtudy. It is, indeed, a ſpecies of learning, among muſicians, which is apt to degenerate

nerate into pedantry; and it is somewhat remarkable, that from all the learned and operose calculations of professed mathematicians, not a single piece of practical music has ever been produced, that is supportable to the ear of persons of taste; so true it is, that the operations of cool and deliberate reflection, have less power over our feelings, than those of passion and enthusiasm.

Musical controversies in Berlin have been carried on with more heat and animosity than elsewhere; indeed there are more critics and theorists in this city, than practitioners; which has not, perhaps, either refined the taste, or fed the fancy of the performers.

I must not quit Berlin without a more particular mention of the two Grauns, than I have hitherto had occasion to make; perhaps, in speaking of these composers, the fairest way would be to give the reader two characters of each, the one that of their partisans and admirers in

Berlin,

Berlin, and the other, drawn from the unbiassed judgment of those whom neither habit nor authority have influenced, but who examine their productions, with as little prejudice as they would those of anonymous composers.

The works of the chapel-master Graun, are very numerous; before his arrival at Berlin, he set three or four operas in the German language, at Brunswick, but the words were bad, and it is not fair to judge of his genius by these early productions.

He composed for the Berlin theatre, in the space of fourteen years, from 1742 to 1756, twenty-seven Italian operas; and for the church, a *Te Deum*, and a *Passione*, besides miscellaneous productions of less importance, as odes and cantatas, with the overture and recitatives of the pastoral opera of Galatea, of which his majesty, Quantz, and Nichelman, set the songs.

This composer died at Berlin 1759, at which time innumerable poems and panegyrics were written to his memory. Among the *critical Letters concerning Music,* published by M. Marpurg, there is an addrefs to M. Freid. Wilhelm Zachariä, the celebrated poet and musician of Brunswick, recommending the death of Graun to his muse. No great stress can be laid on panegyrics; however, there are few of Graun's admirers, who are not ready to burn with fire and faggot all those who dare to doubt of this author's veracity.

"Graun, the brightest ornament of
"the German muse, the noble master
"of sweet melody, is now no more!
"creator of his own taste, he spoke not,
"but to our hearts; tender, soft, com-
"paſſionate, elevated, pompous, and
"terrible, by turns;—he could force
"tears of admiration from us, at his
"pleafure; an artift, who made no other
"use

" use of art, than to imitate nature, in
" the most pleasing, and expressive
" manner; each stroke of his pencil
" was equally perfect, full of invention,
" and of new ideas, his genius was in-
" exhaustible. The model of sacred mu-
" sic, and in the theatre inimitable! a
" man who commanded our affections,
" not only by his talents, but by his
" virtues, of friendship, probity, and
" patriotism; no man was ever so uni-
" versally lamented by the whole nation,
" from the king, to the lowest of his
" subjects * ."

Now, to reverse the medal; it is denied, by the other party, that Graun
was the creator of his own taste, which
is the taste of Vinci; they deny, that he
is ever pompous or terrible, but say, that
an even tenor runs through all his works,
which never reach the sublime, though

* Kritische Briefe über die Tonkunst. I. Band.
Berlin 1760.

the tender and graceful are frequently found in them; they are equally unwilling to subscribe to his great invention, or the originality of his ideas; and think that still more perfect models of sacred music may be found in the chorusses of Handel, and the airs and duos of Pergolese and Jomelli: nor can they well comprehend, how that composer can be called *inimitable*, who is himself an *imitator*.

The concert-master, John Gottlib Graun, brother to the opera-composer, his admirers say, " was one of the greatest performers on the violin of his time, and most assuredly, a composer of the first rank; his overtures and symphonies are majestic, and his concertos are masterpieces, particularly those for two violins, in which he has united the most agreeable melody, with all the learning that the art of counter-point can boast; he has likewise frequently set the *Salve Regina*, and composed masses, which are rendered

grand

grand and noble by simplicity and good melody, even in the most laboured parts."

But less quarter is granted to this master, by the admirers of more modern music, than to his brother; they often find his overtures and symphonies too like those of Lully, and too full of notes to produce any other effect, when played at Berlin, than that of stunning the hearers; and in his concertos and church music, when that is not the case, the length of each movement is more immoderate, than Christian patience can endure.

Perhaps the truth may lie between these two opinions; and with respect to the chapel-master Graun, it should be remembered, that he was seldom allowed to follow the bent of his own genius.

It was not at first my intention to detain my reader so long in Berlin, and its environs; but the musical performances in his Prussian majesty's dominions, have been so much celebrated during his reign, that

that they merited a particular investigation; it is now, however, time to sum up the evidence, and it would be the highest injustice to deny, that Berlin has long had, and still has, a great number of *individuals* among the musical professors, whose abilities are great and striking; but, with respect to the *general* and *national* style of composition and performance, it seems at present, to be formed so much upon *one model*, that it precludes all invention and genius. Perhaps, it would be equally rational to suppose, that the blood of a Quantz or a Graun, if injected into the veins of another composer, would circulate better than his own, as to imagine, that *their* ideas and thoughts, when he has adopted them, will suit him better than those which he has received from nature.

Of all the musicians which have been in the service of Prussia, for more than thirty years, Carl. P. E. Bach, and Francis Benda, have, perhaps, been the only two,

two, who dared to have a ſtyle of their own; the reſt are imitators; even Quantz and Graun, who have been ſo much imitated, formed themſelves upon the works of Vinci and Vivaldi. M. Quantz is an intelligent man, and talks well concerning muſic; but talking and compoſing are different things; when he wrote his book, more than twenty years ago, his opinions were enlarged and liberal, which is not the caſe at preſent; and Graun's compoſitions of thirty years ago, were elegant and ſimple, as he was among the firſt Germans to quit fugue and laboured contrivances, and to allow, that ſuch a thing as melody exiſted, which, harmony ſhould ſupport, not ſuffocate; but though the world is ever rolling on, moſt of the Berlin muſicians, defeating its motions, have long contrived to ſtand ſtill.

Upon the whole, my expectations from Berlin were not quite anſwered, as I did not find that the ſtyle of compoſition, or manner of execution, to which his

Prussian majesty has attached himself, fulfilled my ideas of perfection. Here, as elsewhere, I speak according to my own feelings: however, it would be presumption in me to oppose my single judgment to that of so enlightened a prince; if, luckily, mine were not the opinion of the greatest part of Europe; for, should it be allowed, that his Prussian majesty has fixed upon the Augustan age of music, it does not appear that he has placed his favour upon the best composers of that age. Vinci, Pergolese, Leo, Feo, Handel, and many others, who flourished in the best times of Graun and Quantz, I think superiour to them in taste and genius. Of his majesty's two favourites, the one is languid, and the other frequently common and insipid,—and yet, their names are *religion* at Berlin, and more sworn by, than those of Luther and Calvin.

There are, however, schisms in this city, as elsewhere; but heretics are obliged

liged to keep their opinions to themselve, while those of the establishment may speak out: for though a universal toleration prevails here, as to different sects of christians, yet, in music, whoever dares to profess any other tenets than those of Graun and Quantz, is sure to be persecuted.

The music of this country is more truly German than that of any other part of the empire; for though there are constantly Italian operas here, in carnival time, his Prussian majesty will suffer none to be performed but those of Graun, Agricola, or Hasse, and of this last, and best, but very few. And, in the opera house, as in the field, his majesty is such a rigid disciplinarian, that if a mistake is made in a single movement or evolution, he immediately marks, and rebukes the offender; and if any of his Italian troops dare to deviate from strict discipline, by adding, altering, or diminishing a single passage in the parts
they

they have to perform, an order is sent, *de par le Roi*, for them to adhere strictly to the notes written by the composer, at their peril. This, when compositions are good, and a singer is licentious, may be an excellent method; but certainly shuts out all taste and refinement. So that music is truly stationary in this country, his majesty allowing no more liberty in that, than he does in civil matters of government: not contented with being sole monarch of the lives, fortunes, and business of his subjects, he even prescribes rules to their most innocent pleasures.

HAMBURG.

The entrance into this city, is free from examination, or custom-house embarrassments, the name only of a traveller being demanded at the gates. The streets are ill built, ill paved and narrow, but crowded with people who seem occupied with their own concerns; and there is an air of chearfulness, industry, plenty, and liberty, in the inhabitants of this place, seldom to be seen in other parts of Germany.

The city of Hamburg has long been famous for its operas, and it seems, from Mattheson's list of them in his *Musical Patriot*, that those performed there, during the latter end of the last century, and the beginning of this, exceeded, in number, those of every other city in the German empire.

The first musical drama, to be found in the annals of the Hamburg stage, is *Orontes*, set by the chapel-master, Theil, 1678; but this, and most of the operas performed here till the beginning of the present century, were in the German language.

The compositions of Keiser, Matthefon, Handel, and Telemann, for this theatre, are the most renowned; of Keiser, some account has been already given, vol. I. p. 346, to which I shall only add, that

that he composed a hundred and seven operas, chiefly for the Hamburg stage; that he was born in 1673, and died 1739.

Of Mattheson, it will be necessary to be somewhat more particular, as he was not only a native of Hamburg, but one who long figured there in the triple character of singer, composer, and theorist. It was his boast, before his death, in 1764, at the age of eighty-two, that he had printed as many books, on the subject of music, as he had lived years; and that he should leave to his executors an equal number, in manuscript, for the use of posterity.

In 1761, he published a translation of the Life of Handel, from the English, with additions and remarks, which are neither very candid nor liberal. But how should the author of that book expect quarter from him, in which it is asserted, that " Mattheson was no great singer, and only " employed occasionally." In refutation

of

of which he assures us, that he constantly sung the principal part in the Hamburg operas, during fifteen years, and with such success, that he could command the passions of his audience, by exciting in them, at his pleasure, joy, grief, hope, and fear. And who shall venture to doubt of his having possessed these powers, when their effects are thus attested *by himself?*

Indeed, this author was not only captious and minute, in his criticisms upon the writers under his consideration, but perpetually quarrelling with his readers: however, he was diligent in finding, and exact in stating facts.

Whoever wishes to be acquainted with the particulars of Handel's younger years, before his arrival in England, or journey into Italy, will find them in the writings of M. Mattheson: indeed, tradition has preserved so many anecdotes concerning his performance at Hamburg, that many musical people, who came into the world too late to hear him, think they have lived in vain.

It was in this city, likewise, that Handel began his career, as a composer, though, upon his first arrival, he was only employed in the orchestra, as a performer on the violin, upon which he played the second *ripieno* part.

He then pretended to know nothing though he used to be very arch, and had always, says M. Mattheson, a dry way of making the gravest people laugh without ever laughing himself; it was upon occasion of the harpsichord player at the opera happening to be absent, that he was first persuaded to take his place; but he then shewed himself to be a great master, to the astonishment of every one, except Mattheson, who had accidentally met with him at an organ in one of the Hamburgh churches in 1703; at which time, he was nineteen, and Mattheson twenty-two years of age.

After

After this he used frequently to dine with Mattheson, at the house of his father, and he then, according to his own confession obtained, from Handel a knowledge in modulation, and a method of combining sounds, which no one else could teach him. These young performers had at this time frequent contests together, for pre-eminence on keyed instruments; and in their several trials Handel had constantly the advantage on the organ, though Mattheson sometimes was thought to equal him on the harpsichord.

Upon a vacancy in an organist's place at Lubec, they travelled thither together, and in the wagon composed several double *fugues, da mente,* say Mattheson, not *da penna*. Buxtehude was then at Lubec, and an admirable organ-player; however, Handel's powers on that instrument astonished even those who were accustomed to hear that great performer.

Handel

Handel and Mattheson were prevented from becoming candidates for the place of organift at Lubec, by a condition that was annexed to the obtaining that office, which was no other than to take with it, a wife, whom their conftituents were to nominate; but thinking this too great an honour, they precipitately retreated to Hamburg.

About this time was performed there an opera compofed by Mattheson, called Cleopatra, in which he acted the part of Anthony himfelf, and Handel played the harpfichord; but Mattheson being accuftomed, upon the death of Anthony, which happens early in the piece, to take the harpfichord, in the character of compofer, Handel refufed to indulge his vanity, by relinquifhing to him this poft; which occafioned fo violent a quarrel between them, that at going out of the houfe, Mattheson gave him a flap on the face, upon which both immediately drew their fwords, and a duel a duel enfued, in the market-place, before the door of the opera-houfe: luckily, the fword of Mattheson was broke againft a metal button upon Handel's coat, which put an end to the combat, and they were foon after reconciled.

Such is the account, which, long before the death of Handel, Matthefon himfelf publifhed*, concerning the difference that happened between them, during their youth, at Hamburg.

Handel remained five or fix years in this city, and compofed here, in 1705, his firft opera of *Almira*, which being greatly approved, he next year produced his fecond opera of *Nero*. From this time, till 1708, when he fet two other operas, *Florino*, and *Daphne*, he furnifhed nothing for the ftage, though he compofed harpfichord pieces, fingle fongs, and cantatas innumerable; but, according to Matthefon, who is not addicted to

* Grundlage einer Ehren-Pforte. Hamburg, 1740.

flattery, without taste or delicacy, though excellent with respect to harmony: indeed, during the last century, harmony was so much attended to by composers, that melody was utterly neglected.

During his residence at Hamburg, Matthefon allows, that Handel improved his style greatly, by his constant attendance at the opera, and says, that he was even more powerful upon the organ, in extempore fugues, and counterpoint, than the famous Kuhnau of Leipsic, who was, at this time, regarded as a prodigy.

Telemann, born at Magdeburg, in 1681, succeeded Keiser as opera composer at Hamburg, for which city he produced thirty-five operas. His compositions for the church and chamber, are said to be more numerous than those of Alef. Scarlatti; in the year 1740 his overtures amounted to six hundred. This author, like the painter Raphael, had a first and second *manner*, which were extremely different from each other. In the first, he was hard, stiff, dry, and inelegant;

elegant; in the second, all that was pleasing, graceful, and refined. This varied and voluminous composer, died at Hamburg, 1767, in the eighty-sixth year of his age.

And now, having dispatched the four principal musicians of past times, whose works have been the delight and ornament of this city, I shall proceed to give an account of what it contains most remarkable in music at present.

The first visit I made in this city, was to my worthy friend and correspondent, M. Ebeling, with whose conversation I was now as much captivated, as I had been before by his letters. As this gentleman had been previously apprized of my intention to take Hamburg into my tour, and was a perfect judge of the nature of my enquiries, he had collected all his musical curiosities, of which he is in possession of a great number, and laid them ready for my inspection.

Though this city has been so famous for its opera in times past, it is a species of exhibition that has been discontinued here for some years. Indeed, I saw no serious opera while I was in Germany. But this drama being usually supplied by Italians, I did not regard it as the principal objects of my present tour, which was to enquire after music, and musicians, purely German.

Hamburg is not at, present, possessed of any musical professor of great eminence, except M. Carl Philip Emanuel Bach; but he is a legion! I had long contemplated, with the highest delight, his elegant and original compositions; and they had created in me so strong a desire to see, and to hear him, that I wanted no other musical temptation to visit this city.

M. Ebeling having been so kind, before my arrival, as to communicate the translation, which he has done me the honour to make in German, of my Italian Tour, and to acquaint him with my intention of coming to Hamburg, undertook to introduce me to him, the morning

ing of my arrival. M. Bach received me very kindly, but said that he was ashamed to think how small my reward would be, for the trouble I had taken to visit Hamburg. "You are come here, "said he, fifty years too late."

He tried a new *piano forte*, and in a wild, careless manner, threw away thoughts and execution upon it, that would have set up any one else. He desired me to fix a time for coming again, and said, that he must have me for a whole day to himself, which would not be half sufficient for the exchange of our ideas. He offered to accompany me to every church in Hamburg, where a good organ was to be found; said he would look out for me some old and curious things; and told me, at my departure, that there would be some poor music of his, performed in St. Catherine's church, the next day, which he advised me not to hear. His pleasantry removed all restraint, without lessening that respect and veneration for him, with which his works had infpired me at a diftance.

After quitting M. Bach, I fpent the reft of the day, in delivering letters, viewing the town, and in vifiting bookfellers, of which, there is a great number in Hamburg. Among thefe, I muft make my acknowledgments to M. Bode, an eminent printer and publifher, and a good mufician, who rendered me many fervices.

In the evening, M. Ebeling, after fhewing me part of his excellent collection of mufic, and mufical writers, did me the favour of introducing me to M. Büfch, profeffor of mathematics, at whofe houfe, and with whofe family, I fpent a moft agreeable evening; which, indeed, was productive of no mufical event, or new difcovery; for I had long been convinced, that there is no harmony more enchanting, than that arifing from the coincidence of hearts, and accord of fentiments in fociety.

M. profeffor Bufch, and M. Ebeling are at the head of the *academy of commerce,*

merce, eſtabliſhed at Hamburg, in 1768, an inſtitution admirably calculated for the education of young perſons, intended for merchants, in the ſeveral parts of the world, where the German, Engliſh, French, Italian, and Dutch languages are required; with which the pupils are taught book-keeping, geography, and hiſtory, as far as it is connected with the commercial intereſts of the ſeveral inhabitants of the globe *.

* Meſſieurs Büſch and Ebeling are aſſiſted in this undertaking, by nine different maſters, two of whom are experienced merchants, ſkilled in every branch of trade. I viſited the young ſtudents while they were receiving their inſtructions from the ſeveral maſters, and never before ſaw ſo much order, decorum, and application among young perſons, who ſeemed under ſo little reſtraint. The ſociety at preſent is numerous, and conſiſts of young gentlemen from Spain, France, England, Holland, Ruſſia, and different parts of Germany; two years only are required for completing the courſe of their mercantile ſtudies, at the end of which, with a tolerable genius, they will have acquired a ſufficient knowledge in languages and traffic, to be uſefully employed in a compting-houſe. The ſame care that is taken in forming

Saturday, 10th October, Dr. Mompſon, an eminent phyſician, as well as a perſon of refined taſte in literature, and the arts, to whom I was honoured with a letter from England, obligingly carried me this morning to the celebrated poet, Klopſtock, who is called, the Milton of Germany. I had the pleaſure of converſing with him, and ſeveral perſons of learning and diſcernment, for a conſiderable time; during which, many curious ſubjects were ſtarted and diſcuſſed. I am unable to ſpeak of M. Klopſtock's poetical abilities; but it is the opinion of his countrymen, that he has left all other bards far behind him: his Meſſiah, which is but lately finiſhed, is the firſt poem of the Germans as the Iliad is of the Greeks.

theſe young perſons for commercial concerns, is likewiſe beſtowed in preparing them for the commerce of the world, by rendering them intelligent and amiable members of ſociety; ſeventy pounds a year, includes every expence of lodging, board, and inſtructions.

They

They speak of his odes, as of a *novum atque inauditum scribendi genus*; and say, " that old Greece and Rome might de- " cide about the force, sublimity, truth, " and harmony of these poems; the " numbers are sometimes taken from the " Greek; but many are of his own " invention. Klopstock's merit in the " German language, will be best known " to future ages; his odes require a rea- " der of good natural sense, well ac- " quainted with the history of his own " country, its language, antiquity, and " the harmony of verse; the more they " are studied, the more they will please; " they are by many reckoned unintelli- " gible, merely because they are analo- " gous to no other species of writing".

After this visit, M. Bach accompanied me to St. Catherine's church, where I heard some very good music, of his com- position, very ill performed, and to a congregation wholly inattentive. This man was certainly born to write for
great

great performers, and for a refined audience; but he now seems to be out of his element. There is a fluctuation in the arts of every city and country where they are cultivated, and this is not a bright period for music at Hamburg.

At church, and in the way home, we had a conversation, which was extremely interesting to me: he told me, that if he was in a place, where his compositions could be well executed, and well heard, he should certainly kill himself, by exertions to please. " But " adieu music! now, he said, these are " good people for society, and I enjoy " more tranquility and independence " here, than at a court; after I was " fifty, I gave the thing up, and said, " let us eat and drink, for to-morrow " we die! and I am now reconciled to " my situation; except, indeed, when I " meet with men of taste and discern- " ment, who deserve better music than " we can give them here; then, I blush
" for

"for myself, and for my good friends, "the Hamburghers."

After this, when our conversation turned upon *learned music*, he spoke irreverently of canons, which, he said, were dry and despicable pieces of pedantry, that any one might make, who would sacrifice his time to them; but it was ever a certain proof to him, of a total want of genius, in any one that was fond of such wretched studies, and unmeaning productions.

He asked, if I had found many great contra-puntists in Italy; and upon my answering in the negative, he replied, nay, if you had, it would have been no great matter; for after counterpoint is well known, many other more essential things are wanting to constitute a good composer. He said, he once wrote word to Hasse, that he was the greatest cheat in the world; for in a score of twenty *nominal* parts, he had seldom more than three *real* ones in action; but with these

he

he produced such divine effects, as must never be expected from a crowded score; upon this occasion I observed, that as it is the part of a wise man in conversation, to wait for an opportunity of saying something to the purpose before he speaks; so a good composer should do in writing accompaniments; and not, like those eternal praters, who have a rage for saying something, when there's nothing to be said, stun an audience with worse than unmeaning notes, which destroy all melody and expression in music; as a large company speaking all at once destroys conversation; and instead of reason, good sense, and good humour, makes social intercourse consist of nothing but clamour, impertinence, and noise: to this he entirely assented.

In the evening, M. Ebeling was so kind as to collect together all the Hamburg performers and lovers of music, he could muster, in order to treat me with a concert; and M. Bach was there to preside,

preside. I have great reason to be thankful for the pains that were taken in order to entertain me on this occasion. Several of M. Bach's vocal compositions were performed, in all which great genius and originality were discoverable; though they did not receive the imbellishments, which singers of the first class might have given to them. M. Bach has set to music, a *Paſſione*, in the German language, and several parts of this admirable composition were performed this evening. I was particularly delighted with a chorus in it, which for modulation, contrivance, and effects, was at least equal to any one of the best chorusses in Handel's immortal Messiah. A pathetic air, upon the subject of St. Peter's weeping, when he heard the cock crow, was so truly pathetic as to make almost every hearer accompany the saint in his tears.

Several symphonies and detached airs with an accompanied harpsichord *sonatina,*

tina, confisting of a very curious mixture of pathetic and *bravura*, were performed, in which the band had very hard duty, and though they are not in such constant practice as to be under exact discipline, yet they executed several very difficult pieces, with a reasonable degree of accuracy.

I mention M. Bach's vocal and miscellaneous compositions, in order to prove the ductility of his genius; but it is not on these that I would rest his reputation, so much as on his productions for his own instruments, the clavichord, and *piano forte*, in which he stands unrivalled; of these I shall have occasion to speak hereafter; as to the rest, perhaps as good songs, chorusses, and symphonies, have been made by others: for though his genius is equal to every thing in music, yet he has not had the practice, the experience, nor the fingers, or orchestra, to write for, which others have had before him: however, each candid observer and

hearer,

hearer, muſt diſcover, in his ſlighteſt and moſt trivial productions, of every kind, ſome mark of originality in the modulation, accompaniment, or melody, which beſpeak a great and exalted genius.

October 11th. I ſpent this day in a moſt agreeable manner, at the villa of John Hanbury, eſq. in the neighbourhood of Hamburg, where true Engliſh hoſpitality reigns. I was carried thither by Mr. Mathias, his majeſty's Reſident, to whom I had letters, and who countenanced and honoured me with the ſame notice as his majeſty's miniſters had beſtowed upon me in other parts of Germany.

At my return to Hamburg, in the evening, on the Altena ſide of the city, there were ſuch crowds of people walking and ſauntering up and down the road, it being Sunday, that carriages could, with infinite difficulty, approach the gates. It gave me a great idea of the populouſneſs of Hamburg: and, upon enquiry, I was aſſured

assured that it contains 120,000 inhabitants, within the walls, and 80,000 without. The common people were to-day clean, and looked free from want; a sight not very frequent in the other parts of Europe through which I had lately passed.

At night I was carried to a concert, at the house of M. Westphal, an eminent and worthy music-merchant. There was a great deal of company, and the performers, who consisted chiefly of *dilettanti*, were very numerous. This kind of concert is usually more entertaining to the performers than the hearers; however, there were many young musicians of this party, who had promising hands upon their several instruments, and who, with pains and experience, would become excellent performers, But in these meetings, more than others, anarchy is too apt to prevail, unless the whole be conducted by an able and respectable master.

Monday, 12th. This was one of the busiest days of my German tour; I spent the early part of the morning among the musical curiosities of my friend M. Ebeling, and the rest of it, at M. Westphal's musical warehouse. As M. Westphal is in correspondence with all the great printers and publishers of music in Europe, his catalogue is not merely local, and confined to Hamburg, or even the German empire; but is general, and that of all Europe: besides compositions that are printed and engraved, he has a great collection of manuscript music, which he disposes of, at a very fair and reasonable price. I was now unable to examine half the contents of his catalogue, before it was time to go to M. Bach, with whom I was engaged to dine and spend the day.

But, previous to the making my readers more intimately acquainted with the talents and character of this excellent musician, I shall present them with a few a few particulars relative to his life, which will be rendered more interesting, by a lift of his works, than by his adventures.

If a narration of the ftill, but fuccefsful efforts of genius in the clofet, could render a book equally entertaining with the public tranfactions of the field; the life of a philofopher, a man of fcience, or an artift, would be read with as much avidity, as that of a Cæfar, or an Alexander.

But though the day, and hour, are carefully configned to pofterity, when towns have been facked, and armies defeated; yet the exact time is feldom enquired, when difcoveries the moft ufeful to human nature have been made, or the greateft productions of genius conceived.

He would, therefore, be thought a moft contemptible biographer, who, in the life of a mufician, fhould circumftantially relate the year, the day, the hour when, and place where, a particular
fonata

sanata was composed, though, by its excellence, it should bid fair for delighting the lovers of music, as long as the present system of harmony shall subsist.

And yet an historian will be read with a kind of savage satisfaction, who in the course of events, tells us, when Kouli-kan, or any other tyrant, made dispositions for a battle, in which such carnage ensued, as will make humanity shudder with horror, as long as the recital of it shall blacken the annals of mankind.

Carl Philip Emanuel Bach, second son of Sebastian Bach, music-director at Leipsic, was born at Weimar, in Upper Saxony, and territory of Thuringia, 1714. In his youth he studied the law, both at Leipsic, and at Frankfort on the Oder, having been intended for a civilian; but his father discovering in him such a strong propensity to music, as would prevent his applying sufficiently to any other art, indulged his natural inclination, and suffered him to make it his profession.

It was at Frankfort upon the Oder that he first turned his talents to account, by composing and directing the music, at the academy, as well as at all other public exhibitions in that city, even while he continued his studies at the university.

In 1738 he went to Berlin, not without expectation that the prince royal of Prussia, who was then secretly forming a band, would invite him to Ruppin; he was not disappointed, the fame of his performance soon reaching this prince's ears, his royal highness sent for him to his court, and heard him with so much satisfaction, that he afterwards frequently commanded his attendance; but from the circumscribed power of the prince at that time, he did not take him into actual service till his accession to the throne, in 1740, and then M. Bach had alone

the

the honour to accompany his majesty upon the harpsichord in the first flute-piece that he played at Charlottenberg, after he was king.

During his residence at Berlin, M. Bach does not seem to have enjoyed that degree of favour to which his merit entitled him; for though music was extremely cultivated by his Prussian majesty, who supported operas with great expence and magnificence, and who had in his service musicians of the first abilities, yet he honoured the style of Graun and Quantz more with his approbation, than that of any other of his servants, who possessed greater originality and refinement; but his majesty having early attached himself to an instrument which, from its confined powers, has had less good music composed for it, than any other in common use, was unwilling, perhaps, to encourage a boldness and variety in composition, which his instrument would not allow him to participate.

But

But though Bach's ſtyle did not inſinuate itſelf into favour at the court of Berlin, it has been imitated and adopted by the performers upon keyed inſtruments in every other part of Germany. How he formed his ſtyle, where he acquired all his taſte and refinement, would be difficult to trace; he certainly neither inherited nor adopted them from his father, who was his only maſter; for that venerable muſician, though unequalled in learning and contrivance, thought it ſo neceſſary to crowd into both hands all the harmony he could graſp, that he muſt inevitably have ſacrificed melody and expreſſion. Had the ſon choſen a model, it would certainly been his father, whom he highly reverenced; but as he has ever diſdained imitation, he muſt have derived from nature alone, thoſe fine feelings, that variety of new ideas, and ſelection of paſſages, which are ſo manifeſt in his compoſitions.

The

The works which he produced, during his residence at Berlin, are so numerous, and, in general, so unknown in England, that I shall specify the principal of them here, for the satisfaction of those who may wish to procure them.

I. *Six Sonatas for the Harpsichord*, dedicated to the King of Prussia. Published by Schmidt, at Nuremberg, 1742.

II. *Ditto*, dedicated to the duke of Würtemberg, published the same year, and in the same city, by Windter. Many of his admirers look upon upon this as the best of his works.

III. *Two Trios for Violins, and a Base,* with remarks by the author. Printed by d°. In these pieces, the composer has endeavoured to support a dialogue between two persons of different characters.

IV. *Three Harpsichord Concertos.* Printed separately, by d°.

V. *An Essay on the Art of Playing the Harpsichord,* with examples, and twenty-six copper-plates, written in the German language, and printed for the author, 1753.

VI. *Ten Sonatas for the Harpsichord*, printed by Hafner, at Nuremberg, in his Miscellanies; from 1755, to 1765.

VII. *Two Sonatas for the Harpsichord*, with some detached pieces, and a *Fugue*, in Brietkopf's Collection, Leipsic, 1757.

VIII. *Melodies to Gellerts Hymns*, by Winter, at Berlin, 1759.

IX. *Twelve short Pieces, for two and three Voices*, in a pocket form. d°.

X. *Six Sonatas, with his own Graces*, book first: this work has been printed in London, by the late Mr. Walsh.

XI. *Second Part of* d°. 1761.

XII. *Essay upon the Art of Playing the Harpsichord*, vol. II. which treats of accompaniment, and voluntary playing, Berlin, d°.

XIII. *A Collection of Odes*, d°.

XIV. *Six Sonatas for the Harpsichord*, d°, 1762.

He has likewise composed a great number of symphonies, many of which have been printed separately. The whole of his works, include thirty trios for the harpsichord, and other instruments; eighteen solos, for different instruments;

ments; twelve sonatines, of which some are for two harpsichords, with accompaniments; forty-nine concertos for the harpsichord; a hundred and seventy lessons for the harpsichord; besides smaller pieces, and single fugues.

* * * *

It must be owned, that the style of this author is so uncommon, that a little habit is necessary for the enjoyment of it; Quintilian made a relish for the works of Cicero the criterion of a young orator's advancement in his studies; and those of C. P. E. Bach may serve as a touchstone to the taste and discernment of a young musician. Complaints have been made against his pieces, for being *long, difficult, fantastic,* and *far-fetched.* In the first particular, he is less defensible than in the rest; yet the fault will admit of some extenuation; for *length*, in a musical composition, is so much expected in Germany, that an author is thought barren of ideas, who leaves off
till

till every thing has been said which the subject suggests.

Easy and *Difficult*, are relative terms; what is called a hard word by a person of no education, may be very familiar to a scholar: our author's works are more difficult to *express*, than to *execute*. As to their being *fantastical*, and *far-fetched*, the accusation, if it be just, may be softened, by alledging, that his boldest strokes, both of melody and modulation, are always consonant to rule, and supported by learning; and that his flights are not the wild ravings of ignorance or madness, but the effusions of cultivated genius. His pieces, therefore, will be found, upon a close examination, to be so rich in invention, taste, and learning, that, with all the faults laid to their charge, each line of them, if wire-drawn, would furnish more new ideas than can be discovered in a whole page of many other compositions that have been well received by the public.

Though

Though M. Bach continued near thirty years at Berlin, it cannot be supposed that he spent his time there very happily. A style of music prevailed, totally different from that which he wished to establish; his salary was inconsiderable, and he ranked below several that were greatly inferior to him in merit.

Frequent opportunities offered, during this period, for his establishing himself very advantageously elsewhere, some of which he wished to accept; but he could not obtain his dismission: however, his salary, after many years service, was augmented.

Indeed, as M. Bach was not a subject of Prussia, it seems as if he might have quitted Berlin whenever he pleased; but as he had married during his residence there, and had issue by that marriage, it is supposed that his wife and children, being all subjects of his Prussian majesty, could not retire out of his dominions without his permission.

But

But in 1767, being invited to succeed Telemann, as music-director at Hamburg, after repeated solicitations and petitions, he was allowed to go thither with his family, where he has continued ever since.

* * *

When I went to his house, I found with him three or four rational, and well-bred persons, his friends, besides his own family, consisting of Mrs. Bach, his eldest son, who practises the law, and his daughter *. The instant I entered, he conducted me up stairs, into a large and elegant music room, furnished with pictures, drawings, and prints of more than a hundred and fifty eminent musicians: among whom, there are many Englishmen, and original portraits, in oil, of his father and grandfather. After I had looked at these, M. Bach was so

* He has two sons, the youngest of whom studies painting, at the academies of Leipsic and Dresden.

obliging

obliging as to sit down to his *Silbermann clavichord*, and favourite instrument, upon which he played three or four of his choicest and most difficult compositions, with the delicacy, precision, and spirit, for which he is so justly celebrated among his countrymen. In the pathetic and slow movements, whenever he had a long note to express, he absolutely contrived to produce, from his instrument, a cry of sorrow and complaint, such as can only be effected upon the clavichord, and perhaps by himself.

After dinner, which was elegantly served, and chearfully eaten, I prevailed upon him to sit down again to a clavichord, and he played, with little intermission, till near eleven o'clock at night. During this time, he grew so animated and *possessed*, that he not only played, but looked like one inspired. His eyes were fixed, his under lip fell, and drops of effervescence distilled from his countenance. He said, if he were to be set to work frequently, in this manner, he should grow young again. He is now fifty-nine, rather short in stature, with black hair and eyes, and brown complexion, has a very animated countenance, and is of a chearful and lively disposition.

His performance to-day convinced me of what I had suggested before from his works; that he is not only one of the greatest composers that ever existed, for keyed instruments, but the best player, in point of *expression*; for others, perhaps, have had as rapid execution: however, he possesses every style; though he chiefly confines himself to the expressive. He is learned, I think, even beyond his father, whenever he pleases, and is far before him in variety of modulation; his fugues are always upon new and curious subjects, and treated with great art as well as genius.

He played to me, among many other things, his last six concertos, lately published

lished by subscription, in which he has studied to be easy, frequently I think at the expence of his usual originality; however, the great musician appears in every movement, and these productions will probably be the better received, for resembling the music of this world more than his former pieces, which seem made for another region, or at least another century, when what is now thought difficult and far-fetched, will, perhaps, be familiar and natural.

There are several traits in the characters of the younger Scarlatti and Emanuel Bach, which bear a strong resemblance. Both were sons of great and popular composers, regarded as standards of perfection by all their cotemporaries, except their own children, who dared to explore new ways to fame. Domenico Scarlatti, half a century ago, hazarded notes of taste and effect, at which other musicians have but just arrived, and to which the public ear is but lately

lately reconciled; Emanuel Bach, in like manner, seems to have outftript his age.

M. Bach fhewed me two manufcript books of his father's compofition, written on purpofe for him when he was a boy, containing pieces with a fugue, in all the twenty-four keys, extremely difficult, and generally in five parts, at which he laboured for the firft years of his life, without remiffion. He prefented me with feveral of his own pieces, and three or four curious ancient books and treatifes on mufic, out of his father's collection; promifing, at any diftant time, to furnifh me with others, if I would only acquaint him, by letter, with my wants.

Tuefday 13th. This morning was entirely employed in vifiting churches, and hearing organs, to which M. Bach was fo kind as to conduct me. The firft inftrument we heard, was at the new church of St. Michael, which is an elegant and magnificent building.

The

The late Mr. Mattheson, who was secretary of legation many years to the English Resident at Hamburg, and who has written so many treatises on music, bequeathed all his possessions to that republic, on condition that an organ should be built for this church, such as he described in his will. It has not been long finished, and is, I believe, the largest and most complete in Europe. It cost upwards of 4000 l. sterl. was built by Hildebrand, is of thirty-two feet, has four sets of keys, long compass, up to F in altissimo, and with the pedals goes down to double double C. The keys are covered with mother of pearl, and tortoise-shell; the front is curiously inlaid, and the case richly ornamented, though it is not, I think, of the most elegant form.

There are sixty-four stops in this instrument, among which the German flute is composed of as many real flutes as there are notes. The other stops are good of the kind, and the chorus is the most noble that can be imagined; but it is more striking by its force, and the richness of the harmony, than by a clear and distinct melody, which fashion makes it necessary to load with a crowd of accompaniments in all the German churches. M. Hartmann, a *dilettante*, was so obliging as to play on this instrument a considerable time, in order to let me hear all its powers. M. Bach has so long neglected organ-playing, that he says he has lost the use of the pedals, which are thought so essential throughout Germany, that no one can pass for a player worth hearing, who is unable to use them. A swell has been attempted in this instrument, but with little effect; only three stops have been put into it, and the power of *crescendo* and *diminuendo* is so small with them, that if I had not been told there was a swell, I should not have discovered it.

M. Matthefon's picture is placed in the front of the organ, and in the front of the

the gallery there is a fine old fashioned Latin inscription, giving an account of his benefaction: this good man had more pedantry and nonsense about him, than true genius. In one of his vocal compositions for the church, in which the word *rainbow* occurred, he gave himself infinite trouble to make the notes of his score form an *arch*. This may serve as a specimen of his taste and judgment, with respect to the propriety of musical expression and imitation.

By his last will and testament, an anthem was performed, which he had composed himself for the occasion; but it was fairly laughed at, when heard in its old fashioned guise. However, he possessed a large share of musical erudition, and was of great use to his countrymen, in his younger days, by bringing them acquainted with the music of other parts of the world, and by introducing a better style among them than their own: he was less fond of fugues than his cotemporaries,

poraries, but in his latter days he became a mere theorist, without taste or feeling.

Hamburg has no less than five organs of thirty-two feet; three of them made by Splitger, about the latter end of the last century, which are excellent for well-toned pipes, and noble choruffes: thefe are to be found in the churches of St. John, St. Nicholas, and St. James.

The organ of St. Peter's church is the most ancient in the town; it is not known when it was originally built, but the two last manuals, it has four, were made at Hartzogenbuch, in Brabant, by *Mister Nargenhof*, in 1548, and sent hither by sea: this, the organist, M. Pfiffer, told me, is upon record. Some of the stops are excellent, particularly the *vox humana*, which, though not like a human voice, resembles, in tone and in sweetness, a better kind of clarinet. M. Pfiffer is in years, but must have been a very brilliant performer in his youth, and he
still

still retains his powers of execution, both with hands and feet, beyond any one I ever heard, at his time of life.

In the afternoon, I was introduced to Signor Anfani, a first rate Italian singer, who had been two or three years at Copenhagen, and was now going to Amsterdam. He has an excellent tenor voice; is tall, thin, and of a good figure; he accompanied himself on the harpsichord, in several songs, in which he manifested not only great taste and expression, in slow movements, but great neatness in the quick; for he is able to execute, in *bravura* airs, the most rapid passages. His style is serious, and I never heard a better singer of his sort. He has a great compass of voice, with much strength and sweetness; his shake is a little too close, otherwise I should venture to pronounce him, a *perfect* tenor singer.

Having been assisted in my musical enquiries, at Hamburg, with such friendly zeal, and treated with so much kindness and hofpitality, it gave me great concern that I was unable to remain longer in that city; but the time being elapfed, which I had allotted myfelf for vifiting thofe parts of Germany where music has been moft cultivated, I was now under a neceffity of turning my face towards England.

BREMEN.

In my way from Hamburg to Amfterdam, I ftopt only a few hours in this city, as it contained no mufical incitements fufficiently powerful to encourage a longer refidence.

However, I vifited the Thumkirche or cathedral, belonging to the Lutherans, where I found the congregation finging a difmal melody, without the organ. When this was ended, the organift gave out a hymn tune, in the true dragging ftyle of Sternhold and Hopkins. The inftrument is large, and has a noble and well-toned chorus, but the playing was more old fafhioned, I believe, than any thing that could have been heard in our country towns, during the laſt century. The interludes between each line of the hymn were always the ſame, and of the following kind:

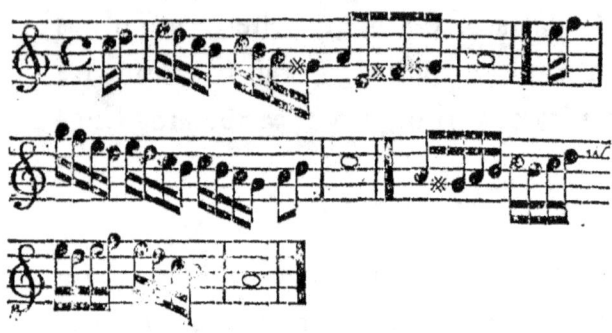

After hearing this tune, and theſe interludes, repeated ten or twelve times, I went to ſee the town, and returning to the cathedral, two hours after, I ſtill found the people ſinging all in uniſon, and as loud as they could, the ſame tune, to the ſame accompaniment. I went to the poſt-office, to make diſpoſitions for my departure; and, rather from curioſity than the love of ſuch muſic, I returned once more to this church, and, to my great aſtoniſhment, ſtill found them, vocally and organically performing the same ditty, whose duration seems to have exceeded that of a Scots Psalm, in the time of Charles I.

This may give some idea how necessary a quality *length* is, in the musical performances of some parts of Germany. In this city, as there is neither court nor theatre, it is natural to suppose that music cannot have been much cultivated.

LOW COUNTRIES.

GRONINGEN.

I little expected to find any thing interesting here concerning music; but, upon enquiry after the organist of the principal church of St. Martin, I was told, that his name was Lustig; I then remembered to have seen, many years ago, some suites of lessons by one of that name, for the harpsichord, full as good as any of the time; and at Antwerp I had purchased a musical treatise tife in Dutch, with the fame name prefixed to it; but I little fufpected thefe to have been the productions of the organift of Groningen. However, upon my calling at his houfe, to beg his permiffion to fee the organ, I foon difcovered that he was author of the above, and of feveral other works, of which he not only furnifhed me with a catalogue, but made me a prefent of a new edition of his treatife.

The organ of St. Martin's church was originally built by the famous Rodolpho Agricola*; but it has received feveral additions fince; however, that part which was of his conftruction is far the beft, particularly feveral reed ftops. The *vox humana* is very fweet, but refembles a

---

* Rodolpho Agricola, was born at Bafflon, a village near Groningen, 1442; if we may believe his hiftorian. Melch. Adami, Agricola was poffeffed of univerfal knowledge; he does not, however, tell us, that he was an *organ builder*, though he makes him an excellent mufician. *Canebat voce, flatu, pulfu.* Vitæ Philof.

fine

fine hautbois or clarinet, more than a human voice; there are four sets of keys, with 54 stops, a few pipes of the pedals are 32 feet long, and, upon the whole, it is one of the most pleasing instruments I ever met with.

M. Lustig, who is a Hamburgher, and was a scholar both of Mattheson and Telemann, has been 44 years organist of this church; he is an intelligent wellbred man, and has been a very useful professor; he still retains his hand, and, a few allowances made for change of taste, he is a very able and good organist.

Here I again found myself in a country of *carillons*; I had indeed heard some slight attempts made at Bremen, but in this place every half hour is measured by chimes.

AMSTERDAM.

In my way from Groningen hither, having crossed the Zuider-Zee, I approached this city by water, which affords one of the finest spectacles that can
be

be imagined; such a noble port, and so crowded with ships of all sizes and countries I had never before seen at one glance; I entered the town in great tranquility, without a single question concerning myself or baggage. The streets through which I passed to the Bible, in the Warmor-straat, were narrow, but clean, and well-paved, with a brick foot-path, though not raised, as in London; the shops were well furnished, and there was all the appearance of a brisk commerce, and an affluent people.

Upon the day of my arrival, October 20, I went to the new church, just at the time when the afternoon service was begining; the building is lofty and noble; the organ which is partially gilt, has a fine appearance, but no other use of it was made now, than to accompany the congregation in two long and tiresome Psalms, without either prelude or interlude, nor was the Psalm given out, as is usual in other places.

The

The chorus and tone of this instrument are very fine; it is well kept in tune, but no reed-stops were used this evening. I could not only distinguish the *bordun*, or double base stop in the pedals, but, in the treble parts; which, though it enriched the harmony, gave a heaviness, and, if I may so call it, a clumsiness to the melody, that should predominate, and had the same effect, as if the treble part in a concert were played by double bases, with violins and violoncellos. It is the custom here for the male part of the congregation to keep their hats on during the whole service, except when the Psalm is singing.

There has been no theatrical exhibition in this city, since the play-house was burnt down, except at the fair, in an occasional booth; nor is the theatre likely to be soon rebuilt, as the ground is not yet fixed upon, where it is to be constructed. Perhaps the fatal accident by which the former playhouse was burnt

burnt down, is regarded by the magistrates, as a *warning*; for, many years ago, when the steeple of the New Kerk was destroyed by lightning, before it was near finished, supposing that heaven was averse to steeples, they would never resume the work.

The inhabitants at present seem to have no places of amusement in the evening, except their shops and counting-houses; but as I had neither of my own, I went to those of the famous bookseller, Rey, and the music-seller Hummel, where, having lightened my purse, and loaded my servant, I retreated to the first bed which I had seen since my departure from Hamburg.

This is truly the country of chimes; every quarter of an hour a tune is played by them at all the churches, but so indistinctly, on account of the confluence of sounds, that I was seldom able to discover what was playing.

M. Renard, his majesty's agent, to whom I am indebted for all the information I acquired during my residence in this city, did me the favour to carry me to the organist of the Old Kerk, M. Pothoff, who is blind; he was deprived of his sight, at seven years old, by the small pox; and this misfortune first suggested to his friends the thought of making music, which hitherto had afforded him no pleasure, his profession; and it afterwards became his darling amusement.

The organ of the Old Kerk was completed twelve years ago, by Batti, of Utrecht, after having been begun in 1725, taken down in 1738, and attempted to be finished by several bunglers, without success: it is only what is called a sixteen feet instrument. It is very full of work, and of stops, to the amount of sixty-four. It has three sets of keys, from double C to c, *in alt*. both in the manuals and pedals, with nine pair of bellows.

M. Pot-

M. Pothoff was organist of the Wester Kerk twenty-two years before he obtained this place; his hand, taste, and abilities in every particular, are truly astonishing; the touch of this instrument is the heaviest that I ever felt, each key requiring almost a two-pound weight to put it down; and, to play it full, there is a spring of communication, by which the keys of the great and choir organ are moved, at the same time, which likewise adds very much to the stiffness of the touch; however, such is the force of M. Pothoff's hand, that he plays this organ with as much lightness and rapidity, as if it were a common harpsichord.

This admirable organist was never out of Amsterdam except for a few days at the Hague, many years ago; and yet his taste is of the best modern kind; his *appogiaturas* are well taken, and admirably expressed, his fancy is extremely lively, and though he plays very full, seldom in less than five parts, with the manuals

als and pedals together, yet, it is neither in the dry nor crude way, which I had so frequently heard in Germany. He discovered, though not injudiciously, by many of his passages, that he was a harpsichord player; but so well is he acquainted with the different genius of the organ, that his most rapid flights, of which he had many, occasioned none of those unpleasing vacuities of sound, which so commonly happen, when this instrument is touched by *mere* harpsichord players.

M. Pothoff played two fugues in a very masterly manner, the subjects of which he reversed, and turned to a thousand ingenious purposes; they were something like the following:

He received inſtructions, when young, from Vetvogle and Unhoorn, both organiſts at Amſterdam; but his taſte is of ſo delicate a kind, that I could not eaſily imagine it to have been acquired in a place where little other muſic is encouraged or attended to, than the jinging of bells, and of ducats. However, he told me, that Locatelli, the famous violin player, who lived many years in this city, and died here about eight years ſince, uſed to give him inſtructions, and to encourage his muſical ſtudies by allowing him the advantage of being always a hearer at his public concerts, as well as private performances. This, in ſome meaſure, helped me to account for his taſte and fancy, for Locatelli was poſſeſſed of a great deal of both; and though he delighted in capricious difficulties, which his hand could as eaſily execute as his head conceive, yet he had a fund of knowledge, in the principles of harmony, that rendered

dered such wild flights agreeable, as in less skilful hands, would have been insupportable.

M. Pothoff seems not only to have greatly profited from the instructions and example of Locatelli, but to have kept pace, in point of taste and refinement, with more modern performers; however, neither imitation nor study could form such a musician as M. Pothoff, who is possessed of a large portion of that divine enthusiasm, which alone can transport an artist beyond the bounds of mediocrity, and, by making him feel strongly himself, can enable him to communicate his feelings to others.

He is married, and has children; and though not young and totally blind, he runs up and down the narrow steps of the organ loft, as nimbly as if he were but fifteen, and had the perfect enjoyment of his sight: he likewise pulls out, and puts in the stops of the organ himself,
with

with wonderful dexterity, which, from their being so numerous, would be a difficult task, and require practice, in one that could see.

When he was a candidate for the organ, at the *Wester Kerk*, he obtained a victory over twenty-two competitors, who all played against him*. Upon this occasion, in order to preclude all partiality in the judges, who were professors, they were not allowed to know who had played, till they had given their opinion of each performance, in writing; a precaution which is thought necessary at Amsterdam, lest compassion, friendship, or powerful recommendation should warp the judgment of those that are invested with the power of determining the question. If this method were

* Our Stanley, in 1726, at the age of fourteen, was in like manner elected organist of St. Andrew's church, Holborn, in preference to near as many candidates.

always practised on such occasions, there would not be so many bad organists, or such a number of good performers unemployed; but, in general it is in vain to play for a place, be a candidate's talents ever so great, as the matter is often determined before it comes to a hearing, and almost always by incompetent judges.

Friday, 23d of October. At nine o'clock this morning, I went by appointment, to the *Wester Kerk* to hear the organ; it is not so large as that of the *Aute Kerk*, but greatly superior in tone; the *vox humana* is the worst stop in this instrument: the rest are sweet, even, and mellow; the touch, though by no means so light as that of the instruments made lately in England, is yet far less heavy and laborious to the performer, than that of the Old Kerk. M. Stechwech, the organist, is a neat performer; but not possessed of that fire and invention, which

which characterise the voluntaries of M. Pothoff. This inftrument was built in 1687; the organifts here have juft heard of fuch a thing as a fwell in an organ, but it is difficult to make them comprehend, by defcription, its conftruction, and effect.

At noon I attended M. Pothoff to the tower of the *Stad-huys*, or town-houfe, of which he is *carilloneur*; it is a drudgery unworthy of fuch a genius; he has had this employment however, many years, having been elected to it at thirteen. He had very much aftonifhed me on the organ, after all that I had heard in the reft of Europe; but in playing thofe bells, his amazing dexterity raifed my wonder much higher; for he executed with his two hands paffages that would be very difficult to play with the ten fingers; fhakes, beats, fwift divifions, triplets, and even *arpeggios* he has contrived to vanquifh.

He began with a Pfalm tune, with which their High Mightineffes are chiefly delighted, and which they require at his hands whenever he performs, which is on Tuefdays and Fridays; he next played variations upon the Pfalm tune, with great fancy, and even tafte: when he had performed this tafk, he was fo obliging as to play a quarter of an hour extempore, in fuch a manner as he thought would be more agreeable to me than plafmody; and in this he fucceeded fo well, that I fometimes forgot both the difficulty and defects of the inftrument; he never played in lefs than three parts, marking the bafe and the meafure conftantly with the pedals. I never heard a greater variety of paffages, in fo fhort a time; he produced effects by the *pianos* and *fortes*, and the *crefcendo* in the fhake, both as to loudnefs and velocity, which I did not think poffible upon an inftrument that feemed to require little other

other merit, than force in the performer.

But surely this was a barbarous invention, and there is barbarity in the continuance of it; if M. Pothoff had been put into Dr. Dominicetti's hottest human cauldron for an hour, he could not have perspired more violently than he did after a quarter of an hour of this furious exercise; he stripped to his shirt, put on his night-cap, and trussed up his sleeves for this *execution*; and he said he was forced to go to bed the instant it was over, in order to prevent his catching cold, as well as to recover himself; he being usually so much exhausted, as to be utterly unable to speak.

By the little attention that is paid to this performer, extraordinary as he is, it should seem as if some hewer of wood, and drawer of water, whose coarse constitution, and gross habit of body, required frequent sudorifics, would do the bufinefs, equally to the fatisfaction of fuch unfkilful and unfeeling hearers.

I have defcribed the kind of keys to *carillons,* and manner of playing them, in fpeaking of thofe at Ghent; thefe at Amfterdam, have three octaves, with all the femitones complete, in the manual, and two octaves in the pedals: each key for the natural found, projects near a foot; and thofe for the flats and fharps, which are placed feveral inches higher, only half as much. All the keys are feparated from each other, more than the breadth of a key, which is about an inch and a half, to enable the player to avoid hitting two at a time, with one hand.

Befides thefe *carillons à clavier,* the chimes here, played by clock-work, are much celebrated. The brafs cylinder, on which the tunes are fet, weighs 4474 pounds, and has 7200 iron ftuds fixed in it, which, in the rotation of the cylinder,

give

give motion to the clappers of the bells. If their High Mightinesses' judgment, as well as taste, had not failed them, for half the prime cost of this expensive machine, and its real charge for repairs, new setting, and constant attendance, they might have had one of the best bands in Europe: but those who can be charmed with *barrel music,* certainly neither want, nor deserve better. There is scarce a church belonging to the Calvinists, in Amsterdam, without its chimes, which not only play the same tunes every quarter of an hour, for three months together, without their being changed; but, by the difference of clocks, one has scarce five minutes quiet in the four and twenty hours, from these *corals for grown gentlemen.* In a few days time I had so thorough a surfeit of them, that in as many months, I really believe, if they had not first deprived me of hearing, I should have hated music in general.

The

The *vox humana*, in the organ of the New Church here, has been so much celebrated by travellers, that I determined not to quit Amsterdam without hearing it; and the organist, M. Linzen, was so obliging as to satisfy my curiosity. This is one of the largest and most ancient instruments in the city. The chorus is a very noble one, as I had before observed, in hearing it during the church service, accompany the congregation in their psalmody. The *vox humana*, it must be owned, is one of the best stops, of that kind, which I have ever heard.

As every species of national music seemed to merit my attention, I went to the synagogue of the German Jews, in this city, to hear what the musical performance, during their religious rites, was, and how far it differed from that of other synagogues where I had heard singing in different parts of Europe. At my first entrance, one of the priests was chanting part of the ser-

service in a kind of ancient *canto fermo*, and responses were made by the congregation, in a manner which resembled the hum of bees.

After this, three of the sweet singers of Israel, which, it seems, are famous here, and much attended to by Christians as well as Jews, began singing a kind of jolly modern melody, sometimes in unison, and sometimes in parts, to a kind of *tol de rol*, instead of words, which, to me, seemed very farcical. One of these voices was a falset, more like the upper part of a bad *vox humana* stop in an organ, than a natural voice. I remember seeing an advertisement in an English newspaper, of a barber, who undertook to dress hair in such a manner as exactly to resemble a peruque; and this singer might equally boast of having the art, not of singing like a human creature, but of making his voice like a very bad imitation of one. Of much the same kind is the

merit

merit of such singers, who, in execution, degrade the voice into a flute or fiddle, forgetting that they should not receive law from instruments, but give instruments law.

The second of these voices was a very vulgar tenor, and the third a *baritono*. This last imitated, in his accompaniment of the falset, a bad bassoon; sometimes continued one note as a drone base, at others, divided it into triplets, and semiquavers, iterated on the same tone. But though the tone of the falset was very disagreeable, and he forced his voice very frequently in an outrageous manner, yet this man had certainly heard good music and good singing. He had a facility of running divisions, and now and then mixed them with passages of taste, which were far superior to the rest. At the end of each strain, the whole congregation set up such a kind of cry, as a pack of hounds when a fox breaks cover.

It was a confused clamour, and riotous noise, more than song or prayer. However, this is a description, not a censure of Hebrew music, in religious ceremonies. It is impossible for me to divine what ideas the Jews themselves annex to this vociferation, I shall, therefore, neither pronounce it to be good or bad in itself, I shall only say, that it is very unlike what we Christians are used to in divine service.

I must not quit Amsterdam, without observing, that though, on account of the theatre being burnt down, and the time of the year, there was now neither play nor concert to be heard, yet in winter there are, as I was informed, several public and private concerts in this city. Signor Raimondi, an Italian, and M. Esser, a Dutchman, have been the principal violins here, since the death of Locatelli. There is also an Italian merchant, Signor Sarti, who is said to be an

admi-

admirable performer on the German flute. The French company of comedians, who acted here while there was a theatre, are not yet dismissed, but are kept on half pay. Upon the whole, Amsterdam does not seem to be a very amusing residence for idle people; there is so little for them to see in the way of pleasure, and so much for the mercantile part of the inhabitants to do in the way of business, that they seem very unfit company for each other.

HAARLEM.

There were few things that I was more eager to see, in the course of my journey, than the celebrated organ in the great church of this city. Indeed, it is the *lion* of the place; but to hear this lion roar, is attended with more expence than to hear all the lions and tygers in the Tower of London. The fee of the *keeper*, or organist,

ganist, is settled at half a guinea; and that of his assistant keeper, or bellows-blower, at half a crown. Expectation, when raised very high, is not only apt to surpass probability, but possibility. Whether imaginary greatness diminished the real, on this occasion, I know not, but I was somewhat disappointed upon hearing this instrument. In the first place, the person who plays it is not so great a performer as he imagines; and in the next, though the number of stops amounts to sixty, the variety they afford is by no means equal to what might be expected. As to the *vox humana*, which is so celebrated, it does not at all resemble a human voice, though a very good stop of the kind: but the world is very apt to be imposed upon by names; the instant a common hearer is told that an organist is playing upon a stop which resembles the human voice, he supposes it to be very fine, and never enquires into the

pro-

propriety of the name, or exactness of the imitation. However, with respect to my own feelings, I must confess, that of all the stops I have yet heard, which have been honoured with the appellation of *vox humana*, no one, in the treble part, has ever reminded me of any thing human, so much as of the cracked voice of an old woman of ninety, or, in the lower parts, of Punch singing through a comb.

As this organ is not only said to be the largest, but the best in Europe, that is, in the world, I shall here insert a list of the stops it contains, with equivalent English names, to such as are used in England, and short explanations of the rest. But as technical terms will be unavoidable in this description, I advise my miscellaneous readers to pass it over, for it can interest none but organ-players, or persons not wholly unacquainted with the construction of that instrument.

CATA-

[305]

CATALOGUE *of the Stops in the great Organ at* HAARLEM, *built by* Müller, 1738.

Great Manual.

Nº.	Names.	Length of longest pipe.		English equivalents.
1.	*Preſtant,*	16 feet.		Open double diap.
2.	*Bourdon,*	16.		Stopt ditto.
3.	*Octave,*	8.		Open diapaſon.
4.	*Viol da Gamba,*	8.	A narrow pipe which imitates the whiſtling of the bow.	Uniſon with ditto.
5.	*Roer Fluit,*	8.	With a funnel, or ſmall pipe, upon the top.	Diap. half ſtopt.
6.	*Octave,*	4.		Principal.
7.	*Gem's-Hoorn,*	4.	A kind of flute, the pipes narrow at the top.	Uniſon with ditto.
8.	*Roer-Quint,*	6.		Twelfth half ſtopt.
9.	*Quint,*	3.		Fifth.
10.	*Tertian,*	2 ranks.		Tierce or 17th.
11.	*Mixture,*	6, 8, and 10 ranks.		Furniture, or mix-[ture.
12.	*Wood Fluit,*	2 feet.	Stopt pipe, uniſon with the	Fifteenth, or oc-[tave flute.
13.	*Trumpet,*	16. ⎫		⎧ Double trumpet.
14.	*Trumpet,*	8. ⎬ reed ſtops ⎨		Trumpet.
15.	*Trumpet,*	4.		Clarion.
16.	*Hautbois,*	8. ⎭		⎩ Hautbois.

VOL. II.　　　　　X　　　　　Upper

Upper Manual.

Nº.	Names.	Length.		English names.
1.	*Prestant,*	8 feet.		Open diapason.
2.	*Quintadeena,*	16.	Breaks into a 5th. which predominates.	Double diapason.
3.	*Gemshoorn,*	8.		Unis. with stopt [diap.
4.	*Baar pyp.*	8.	A muffled pipe used with the *vox humana.*	Bear pipe.
5.	*Octave,*	4.		Principal.
6.	*Flag Fluit,*	4.	Derivation unknown.	Flute.
7.	*Nassat,*	3.		Stopt twelfth.
8.	*Nagt-Hoorn,*	2.	Night-horn; but, why so called, no reason can be given.	Flute.
9.	*Flageolet,*	1 ½.		Octave twelfth.
10.	*Sesquialter,*	2 ranks.	Tuned octave and 12th to the diap.	Sesquialter.
11.	*Cimbaal,*	3 ranks.		Octave to mix- [ture.
12.	*Mixture,* 4 and 6 ranks.		A series of eight notes repeated through the instrument.	Mixture.
13.	*Schalmay,*	8.	Reed stop.	Bagpipe.
14.	*Dulcian,*	8.	A narrow delicate pipe, unison with the diap.	Dulcian.
15.	*Vox humana,*	8.	An imitation of the human voice.	

Positif,

Positif, or small Organ.

Lowest set of keys.

Nº. Names.	Length.	English names.
1. *Prestant*,	8 feet.	Open diapason.
2. *Holfluit*,	8.	Diapason half [stopt.
3. *Quintadeena*,	8.	Ditto.
4. *Octave*,	4.	Principal.
5. *Flute*,	4.	Flute.
6. *Speel Fluit*,	3.	Twelfth.
7. *Sesquialter*,	2, 3, and 4 Ranks.	
8. *Super-Octave*,	2 feet.	Fifteenth.
9. *Scherp*,	6 and 8 ranks.	High mixture.
10. *Cornet*,	4 ranks.	
11. *Cimbaal*,	3 ranks.	Octave mixture.
12. *Fagotte*,	16 feet.	Double bassoon.
13. *Trumpet*,	8	
14. *Regaal*,	8. Formerly a portable organ used in processions, was called a *regal*; the stop in this organ is entirely composed of reeds.	Regal.

Pedals.

Pedals.

Nº.	Names.	Length.		English names.
1.	*Principal,*	longest pipe 32 feet.		Octave below the [double diap.
2.	*Prestant,*	16.		Double diap. open.
3.	*Subbas,*	16.		Ditto, stopt.
4.	*Roer-Quint,*	12.		Fourth below the [diap. stopt.
5.	*Holfluit,*	8.		Diapason half stopt.
6.	*Octave,*	8.		Open diap.
7.	*Quint-Prestant,*	6.		Fifth.
8.	*Octave,*	4.		Principal.
9.	*Ruisch-Quint,*	3.		Twelfth.
10.	*Holfluit,*	2.		Fifteenth.
11.	*Bazuin,*	32.	By the Germans called *Posaune,* a reed stop.	Double Sacbut.
12.	*Bazuin,*	16.		Sacbut.
13.	*Trumpet,*	8.		Trumpet.
14.	*Trumpet,*	4.		Clarion.
15.	*Cink,*	2.	A cornet, horn, or shawm.	Octave Clarion.

This

This organ has 60 stops, 2 tremulants, 2 couplings, or springs of communication, 4 separations or valves to close the wind-chest of a whole set of keys, in case of a *cipher*, and 12 pair of bellows.

Upon the whole, it is a noble instrument, though I think that of the New Church at Hamburg is larger, and that of the Old Kerk, in Amsterdam, better toned; but all these enormous machines seem loaded with useless stops, or such as only contribute to augment noise, and to stiffen the touch.

LEYDEN.

In this city, which is one of the best built and most agreeable of the Low Countries, there is not only a celebrated university, but a theatre, where Dutch plays are exhibited two or three times a week. As there is no great commerce carried on here, it is the place to which the rich citizens of Amsterdam retreat, as well when their *plumb* is full grown, as when age and infirmities have deprived them of the power of longer purfuing the Mammon of unrighteoufnefs.

The plays and players of this theatre are not of the moft refined fort; farce has not yet quitted tragedy, nor has Punch quitted farce; however, thefe exhibitions amufe perfons, whofe tafte has not been formed upon refined models, and perhaps come more home to their bufinefs and bofoms, than the tragedies of Sophocles, or comedies of Menander, would do, if they were now to be reprefented in the original Athenian manner.

As to mufic, mechanical chimes, every quarter of an hour; *carillons* at noon, two or three times a week; and huge organs, coarfely played, to more coarfe pfalmody, conftitute all that Apollo and the Nine Mufes have given to this place, in the way of harmony and melody, as far as I was able to difcover.

However, I was told, that in this city, during term time, there is a very able performer on the violin, M. Vermeullen, who gives leſſons to the ſtudents of the univerſity, among whom there are frequent private concerts; but he was abſent when I was at Leyden, ſo that I had no opportunity of hearing him.

H A G U E.

Though Amſterdam is the capital of the United Provinces, yet this being the reſidence of the Stadtholder, and the place where his court is conſtantly kept, it ſhould, of courſe, be likewiſe the ſeat of the polite arts.

The muſical eſtabliſhment of his ſerene highneſs conſiſts chiefly of German muſicians. The chief director and compoſer, is M. Graaf, of whom ſeveral works are printed in France and Holland. The names of the reſt are Keller, Gundlach, Muller, Halfschmid, Rohling, Weis, Keller jun. and J. A. Dambach. Beſides theſe *fixtures*, there are meſſ^{rs}. Malherbe, of Liege, and Juſt, a young German, and ſcholar of Schwindl, who is author of some pretty pieces for the harpsichord. M. Schwindl himself, whose name is well known in the musical world, by his admirable compositions for violins, which are full of taste, grace, and effects, resided a considerable time at the Hague, but was gone from thence before my arrival.

M. Spandau, who has been since heard with such satisfaction in England, I found at the Hague. In his performance upon the French horn, he has contrived, by his delicacy, taste, and expression, to render an instrument, which, from its coarseness, could formerly be only supported in the open air, or in a spacious building, equally soft and pleasing with the sweetest human voice.

Here are two theatres, one for German, and the other for French plays, and comic operas. I saw the little opera of *Toinon et Toinette*, in the French theatre, which is small, as was the company, and the merit of the performers.

The

The Hague seems more calculated for birds of passage than natives. The want of variety in the company, and in the performers, makes them soon mutually tired of each other. It is common for German and Italian musicians, in their way to or from England, to visit, and stop a short time at the Hague, where, by concerts, they usually gain money sufficient to enable them to pursue their journey; but they seldom remain here longer than a ship which enters a port merely to wood and water.

Here are four churches, three belonging to the Calvinists, and one to the Lutherans, in all which there are large organs; but neither the instruments, nor those who perform upon them, are much celebrated.

If my musical acquisitions and discoveries received but small augmentation at the Hague, I was amply rewarded for the trouble of going thither, by the notice with which I was honoured by his excellency,

lency, Sir Joseph Yorke, and the pains he kindly took with design to render me service.

DELFT.

There are two handsome churches in this town, and organs in both. M. Berguys, the organist, and *carilloneur* of one of them, is, M. Pothoff excepted, the best performer I met with in Holland, particularly on the *carillons*, which he plays with astonishing dexterity.

ROTTERDAM.

M. Van Hagen, a German, who is the principal organist here, is likewise an excellent performer on the violin, of which he convinced me by playing one of his own solos. He was a scholar of Geminiani, and he not only plays, but writes very much in the style of that great master of harmony. His daughter has a fine voice, and sings with much taste and expression. His son has been under M. Honaür,

Honaür, at Paris. Except thefe particulars, the only difcovery which I was able to make, relative to mufic, in this large and populous city, was, that it contained nothing more to be difcovered: but this negative kind of knowledge is not without its ufe, as it affuages curiofity, and precludes all felf-reproach on the fcore of negligence.

* * * *

Here ends my fecond Tour. With refpect to Germany, if I have been unable to penetrate into feveral parts of it which were well entitled to my attention, or have omitted to mention muficians of abilities in others, I hope it will be remembered, that to have vifited every province, court, and city, of this vaft empire, and to have ftaid as long in each as would have been neceffary to hear *all* the beft performers, during carnival time, as was frequently recommended to me, would have required the life of a Patriarch.

arch. However, if the reader will take the pains to trace my route in a map, he will find that I visited almoſt every capital; and that, from my firſt landing on the continent, ſteering from weſt to eaſt, and from ſouth to north, I made an angle through Flanders, Brabant, and the German empire, of near two thouſand miles, before I entered Holland, in my way back to England.

To compenſate, however, in ſome degree, for the length of the way, and the ſhortneſs of my time, I ſhall here, as an appendix, ſubjoin a few particulars, which I have obtained from good authority, relative to the ſtate of muſic, in ſuch parts of Germany as it was not in my power to viſit.

Father Martin Gerbert, of the congregation of Benedictines, at the abbey of St. Blaiſe, in the Black Foreſt, near Friburgh, in Briſgaw, about thirty miles from Straſburg, publiſhed in 1763, the Plan of *a Hiſtory of Church Muſic*, from the

the firſt century, to the preſent time *. After this publication, he travelled thro' Germany, and a great part of France and Italy, in order to collect materials in the ſeveral convents and public libraries of thoſe countries; and in 1765 he printed his *Itinerary,* informing the public of the ſucceſs of his reſearches †.

When I arrived at Manheim, my curioſity was ſo much excited by a peruſal of this Itinerary, and the reports concerning the materials which M. Gerbert had been long accumulating for his projected Hiſtory, that I determined to viſit his convent, though it was ſituated very wide of my intended route; but after preparing for this deviation from my firſt plan, and obtaining the neceſſary infor-

* *De Cantu & Muſica Eccleſiaſtica a prima Eccleſiæ Ætate uſque ad preſens Tempus.*

† *Martini Gerberti Iter Allemannicum,* accedit *Italicum et Gallicum. Sequuntur Gloſſaria ex codicibus Manuſcriptis, a Seculo* 9 *uſque* 13. *Typis San-Blaſianus,* 1765.

mation

mation for finding my way thither, I had the mortification to hear, that this great and valuable collection of materials for the history of sacred music had been destroyed, not long since, by a fire, together with the convent in which they were deposited. I had nothing but patience to comfort me under this disappointment; however I was glad to hear, that the reverend and learned compiler of all these treasures of antiquity, had lately had the consolation of being exalted to the head of his society, under the denomination of *prince-abbot* of St. Blaise.

The duke and sovereign of Furstenburg, is a great musician and encourager of music; all the performers of Germany are sure of an asylum at his court, of being well heard, and, if excellent, well rewarded.

M. Riepel at Ratisbon is esteemed one of the best theorists, and most intelligent musicians of that place; I had formed the design of going thither from Munich,

Munich, in my way to Vienna, but was discouraged from putting it into execution, by hearing that M. Riepel, as well as all the chief muſicians of Ratiſbon, were then with the prince of Tour-Taxis at Tiſchengen. However, I ſhould have gone to Tiſchengen in ſearch of them, had not an excellent judge of muſic aſſured me, that he had often viſited the Prince of Tour-Taxis, for a month or ſix weeks at a time, both there and at Ratiſbon, but was never charmed by his concerts, though he had a numerous band; as the muſic was performed in an inelegant and inexpreſſive manner, with an almoſt total neglect of *piano* and *forte*, and of light and ſhade; ſo that the pieces which they executed, however good in themſelves, afforded him but very little pleaſure.

M. Riepel has written ſeveral ingenious tracts mentioned in Marpurg's and Hiller's collections; and, in a curious compoſition, much celebrated in Germany, he has found the means of imitating almoſt every ſpecies of military noiſe, by muſical inſtruments.

At GOTHA there is a good band, over which M. George Benda presides, as *maestro di capella*. The principal performers are M. Hattasch, on the violin; Kramer, on the harpsichord; and Boehmer on the bassoon. I have seen in different musical collections, some pleasing productions by M. Gräfe, a *dilettante* of this city. The chapel-master is author of a great variety of works for the church, stage, and chamber. His compositions are in general new, masterly, and learned; but his efforts at singularity, will by some be construed into affectation.

There was no place in Germany which I left unseen with more regret than BRUNSWIC, as that city seems to be in possession of several musicians of distinguished abilities. At the head of these must be ranked M. Schwanberger, who is author of several serious operas, which are composed in a most refined and pleasing taste; his melodies are graceful and natural,

natural, his accompaniments ingenious and judicious, and the clearness and facility with which he writes, manifest great experience, and a happy selection; his harpsichord pieces, as well as those written for violins, are full of pleasing effects, produced by fair and warrantable means.

M. Fleischer is another Brunswic composer of great merit, whose church-music, comic operas, and harpsichord lessons, are all written in an elegant and pleasing style.

The reigning duke's first violin and concert-master is M. Pesch, who is also author of several agreeable pieces for his instrument, which have been printed at Leipsic, by Brietkopf.

This city is at present likewise in possession of M. J. C. Frederic Bach, eldest son of the celebrated Sebastian Bach, and chapel-master of the court of Beckenberg; he is an able mathematician, and regarded as the greatest fugist, and most learned professor in Germany. He was born in 1710, and was several years organist and music-director at Hall, in Saxony, before he entered into the service of the court at Beckenberg.

Music is cultivated in few places more successfully than at Brunswic, to which the passion of the reigning duke for operas, and the taste and discernment of the hereditary prince, have greatly contributed.

The archbishop and sovereign of SALTZBURG is very magnificent in his support of music, having usually near a hundred performers, vocal and instrumental, in his service. This prince is himself a *dilettante*, and good performer on the violin; he has lately been at great pains to reform his band, which has been accused of being more remarkable for coarseness and noise, than delicacy and high-finishing. Signor Fischietti, author of several comic operas, is at present the director of this band.

The

The Mozart family were all at Saltzburg laſt ſummer; the father has long been in the ſervice of that court, and the ſon is now one of the band; he compoſed an opera at Milan, for the marriage of the arch-duke, with the princeſs of Modena, and was to compoſe another at the ſame place for the carnival of this year, though he is now but ſixteen years of age. By a letter from Saltzburg, dated laſt November, I am informed, that this young man, who ſo much aſtoniſhed all Europe by his infant knowledge and performance, is ſtill a great maſter of his inſtrument; my correſpondent went to his father's houſe to hear him and his ſiſter play duets on the ſame harpſichord; but ſhe is now at her ſummit, which is not marvellous; "and," ſays the writer of the letter, " if I may judge of the muſic " which I heard of his compoſition, in " the orcheſtra, he is one further in- " ſtance of early fruit being more extra- " dinary than excellent."

The music-shops of NUREMBERG are the most remarkable in Germany. It is in this city only, that musical compositions are engraved; in other parts of the empire, they are all printed with types. Hafner, Winterschmidt, and Schmid are proprietors of the principal shops. M. Agrel is the only musician residing at Nuremberg, who has distinguished himself as a composer; his pieces for the harpsichord were once in vogue, but though faultless as to counterpoint, they never, with respect to invention, seemed to surpass mediocrity.

At ZERBST, M. Heock, has the reputation of being a great performer on the violin; M. Krebs of ALTENBURG, scholar of Sebastian Bach, has been very much admired for his full and masterly manner of playing the organ, and M. Kunzen, whose performance must be still remembered with great pleasure by those who heard him in England, is at present the worthy organist of LUBEC.

Besides

Besides M. Hiller, four composers reside at Leipsic, with whom I had not time to cultivate a personal acquaintance; these are M. Doles, cantor, and composer of church music; M. Löhlein, a harpsichord player, and composer; M. Neefe, author of some pretty sonatas for that instrument, and M. Reichard, a composer of comic operas, by no means devoid of genius.

M. Rolle, music-director of MAGDEBERG, is a spirited and ingenious composer, who has distinguished himself by productions for the church; but I have seen some of his pieces for the harpsichord, which have pleased me more than his other works, particularly, in the Berlin collections, where there are lessons by this author, full of fire, and in which pleasing effects are produced, by the introduction of old passages, in a new manner.

M. Müller, the court-organist at DESSAU, is possessed of considerable abilities; his compositions discover taste, fancy, and a powerful hand; but his ambition to produce *new* passages, upon all occasions, renders his pieces frequently laboured, unnatural, and affected; and to this vice may be added, that, so common to his countrymen, of spinning his subjects and movements to a tiresome length.

M. Wolf, at WEYMER, is a natural and pleasing composer of comic operas, in the German language; a species of composition become very prevalent in the northern parts of the empire, since the year 1750, when M. Hiller set to music the first drama of that kind, which was brought upon the stage. It gained great applause against the opinion of the critics, by whom it was much decried, on account of the lowness of the subject, which was *the Merry Cobler*, imitated from our farce of the Devil to Pay. Before this period the Germans had only serious operas and *intermezzi*, in their own language, upon the stage; but the present rage

rage for burlettas is so strong, that persons of judgment think it will destroy all true taste for music of a higher class.

M. Richert, of KONINGSBERG, is a great voluntary-player on the violin, and particularly remarkable for the truth and facility with which he plays *double stops*.

M. Fr. Xav. Richter should have been distinguished among the musicians of Manheim; his works, of various kinds, have great merit; the subjects are often new and noble; but his detail and manner of treating them is frequently dry and steril, and he spins and repeats passages in different keys without end. The French have a term for this tediousness, which is wanting in other languages, they call it *Rosalie:* I know not whence this expression is derived; but it means a string of repetitions, either a note higher, or a note lower, of the same passage or modulation; which indicates a want of invention in a composer, as much as stammering

mering and hesitation imply a want of wit or memory in a story-teller.

Father Schmitt, a monk of the Cistertian order, at the abbey of Eberbach, in Rheingau, is author of trios for violins, that are not only full of taste and fancy, but composed with a boldness, spirit, and accuracy, which *dilettanti* seldom arrive at.

M. Johann Gottfried Müthel, of Riga, being by birth and education a German, deserves a place here, though he is at present established in a city which appertains to Russia. When a student upon keyed instruments has vanquished all the difficulties to be found in the lessons of Handel, Scarlatti, Schobert, Eckard, and C. P. E. Bach; and, like Alexander, laments that nothing more remains to conquer, I would recommend to him, as an exercise for patience and perseverence, the compositions of Müthel; which are so full of novelty, taste, grace, and contrivance, that I should not hesitate to rank them

them among the greateſt productions of the preſent age. Extraordinary as are the genius and performance of this muſician, he is but little known in Germany, and all I could gather there concerning him is, that he received inſtructions from Sebaſtian Bach, and lived ſome time at Schwerin, before he ſettled in Riga. The firſt of his works, which I can trace to have been publiſhed, were *Odes*, printed at Hamberg, 1759. The reſt, which are all for the harpſichord, appeared in the following order: three *Sonatas*, and *two Airs*, with twelve variations, Nuremburg, 1760. Two *Concertos*, printed by Hartknock, Riga, and Mittau, 1767. *Duetto* for two clavichords, two harpſichords, or two *forte pianos*. d°. Riga, 1771.

The ſtyle of this compoſer more reſembles that of Emanuel Bach, than any other. But the paſſages are entirely his own, and reflect as much honour upon his head as his hand. Indeed his writings abound with difficulties, which to common

mon hearers, as well as common players, must appear too elaborate; for even his accompaniments are so charged as to require performers, for each instrument, of equal abilities to his own, which is expecting too much, in musicians of this nether world.

If my leisure and abilities would have sufficed for so extensive a plan, I should have been glad to have made the journal of this tour, *the present state of arts and sciences, in general*; however, *poetry* is so nearly connected with *music*, that I could not help making some enquiries after the most eminent poets now living in Germany, and I shall here present my readers with what I found to be the general opinion there of men of taste and learning, with respect to their abilities.

M. *Klopstock* has been already mentioned, and Madame *Karsch*, the poetess of Berlin, may be ranked next to him for original genius. This lady is quite a meteor, and surprises the more by the elevation

levation and beauty of her poems, on account of her low-origin, she being descended from parents who were unable to afford her a liberal education, and married very young to a serjeant, in a regiment quartered at Glogau. When she arrived first at Berlin, a few of her verses were handed about, which were so much approved, that a subscription was opened for printing a collection of them: since that time she has supported herself with dignity, by the productions of her pen.

The works and character of *Wieland* are equally various: *aliusque & idem.* He spent his youth in piety and flights of enthusiasm, composing nothing but *Sympathies, Moral Tales, Letters from the Dead,* a poem *on Nature,* and *Christian Hymns* and *Psalms.* At a different period of his life, his muse passing to another extreme, he wrote tales of a different kind, which not only surpassed those of La Fontaine, in simplicity and beauty, but in loose-

ness

ness and immorality. He wrote two poems called *Idris* and *Amadis*, in stanzas, like those of Ariosto, with *Don Sylvio de Rosalva*, a romance, in the style of Cervantes; all full of wit and humour.

His master-piece is said to be *Agathon*, a romance in the ancient Greek manner. He is likewise author of a poem called *the Graces*; of *Musarion*, and *Diogenes*, the first a poem, the other written in prose, and with the humour of Sterne. His last work is called *the Golden Mirror*, and abounds with severe strictures on princes and priests.

This writer is a wonderful example of contradiction in human nature. His philosophy is calculated for persons in the great world. The Germans frequently compare his genius with that of Voltaire, and even carry their admiration so far, as to say, that he excells him in all but his dramatic pieces; both have written much, and both have repeated themselves.

M. *Lessing*.

M. *Lessing*, of Wolfenbuttle, is a man of universal knowledge and genius, having succeeded equally well in *Lyric Poems, Fables, Remarks on Critics, Satyrs, Dramas,* and *Discoveries in Antiquity.*

Haller's poems are chiefly on philosophical subjects. Those *On the Origin of Evil,* on *Reason, Infidelity, Superstition, The Vanity of Human Virtue, The Alps,* and an unfinished ode *On Eternity,* are accounted the best.

Rammler, of Berlin, holds a distinguished rank among German poets. His odes are said to have too much of Greece and Rome. *Glaucus* is his best poem.

Gleim, is called the Anacreon of modern times.

Gellert's Fables and Tales are much admired.

Gesner is a pastoral poet of great reputation.

Dr. *Cramer*'s *Odes on the Resurrection,* his *Luther,* and *Melancthon,* are very much esteemed.

Rabner

Rabner is a celebrated satyrist; and *Hagedorn, Utz, Gisecke, Gerstenberg, Schweibeler, Jacobi, Weise,* and *Lichtwehr,* are poets whose productions are much esteemed by their countrymen.

Germany contains thirty-six universities, of which there are seventeen catholic, seventeen protestant, and two, as those of Erfurt and Heidelberg, where students of both religions are admitted. If I were to enumerate all the men of learning and abilities, in these seminaries, who are labouring for the advancement of science, the list would doubtless be too considerable for my work: however, M. *Zacheriä*, of Brunswick, and M. *Krause,* of Berlin, are entitled to a place here for their musical talents.

M. *Zacheriä*, besides being a poet of the first rank, and celebrated for the wit and humour of his mock-heroic poems, is likewise a good practical musician, and an excellent theorist and critic of musical productions.

And

And *M. Krause*, of Berlin, who has acquired great reputation, by his admirable work upon the subject of *German Lyric Poetry*, is likewise author of several musical compositions, which are much esteemed by connoisseurs.

Having now laid before the reader such information as I have been able to obtain, concerning the present state of music in the countries through which I have travelled in this Tour, I have only to add, that, besides the many excellent musicians which I found in Germany, it has furnished almost every great city in Europe with professors of uncommon abilities; and it is hardly too much to say, that the best German musicians, of the present age, with a few exceptions, are to be found out of their own country. Indeed, it has been observed, that, from whatever cause, transplanted Germans, *cæteris paribus*, surpass, in most of the fine arts, those that remain in their original soil.

By travelling, muficians lofe, among other local partialities, that veneration for a particular ftyle, which fo much encreafes the number of imitators, and keeps them in fuch fubjection, that, like the writers of modern Latin, they dare not hazard a fingle thought for which claffical authority cannot be produced.

The muficians of almoft every town, and every band in the fervice of a German prince, however fmall his dominions, erect themfelves into a mufical monarchy, mutually jealous of each other, and all unanimoufly jealous of the Italians, who come into their country: for my own part, as a byftander, who had no fhare in thefe quarrels, and was not in the leaft interefted in the event, I thought I could fee prejudice operating ftrongly on both fides. As to the Italians, however, it muft be acknowledged that they are careffed, courted, and frequently rewarded with double the falary that is paid even to fuch natives as have

the

the claim of superior merit. The Germans, therefore, under such provocation, must not be too severely censured for under-rating the talents of many great Italian masters, and treating them with a contempt and severity which is due only to the grossest ignorance and stupidity.

My intention was neither to write a panegyric, nor a satire, on the music of Germany, but to describe its effects on my own feelings. I set out with a desire to be pleased; and if I have been sometimes dissatisfied, and my disappointment has produced censure, I hope it will not draw upon me the charge of wanting either impartiality or candour.

Praising all is praising none — and I have sometimes had my doubts concerning such ideal beauties of particular styles as are supported by exclusive admiration.

I will not say that the Germans have no national music; they have had many men of great abilities, who have never been

been in Italy, and who have difdained to pillage the works of their neighbours; but the prefent caft of German melody can as eafily be traced from the opera fongs of the Italians, as the tafte of moft German compofers and performers from that of the beft fingers of Italy.

Indeed, many favourable circumftances have contributed to facilitate their acquiring this tafte; particularly their intercourfe with the natives in the great poffeffions they have beyond the Alps; and even at home, the inhabitants of Vienna, Munich, Drefden, Berlin, Manheim, Brunfwick, Stutgard, and Caffel, where there is, and has long been, an Italian opera, have not liftened to Italian finging in vain.

Setting however, particular diftinctions afide, the refult of all my enquiries and obfervations, is the eftablifhment of two facts; the firft, that there is very little good finging by the natives, in any part of Europe, except Italy; the fecond, that

that though the Italians excel the people of all other nations in vocal mufic, yet the Germans, with a few exceptions, excel even the Italians in the conftruction and ufe of moft inftruments; and perhaps, it is not difficult to account for the different mufical excellence of thefe two nations. The language of the Italians is more favourable to mufic than that of any other people, and the cuftom of performing almoft continually, the moft refined and expenfive compofitions in their churches and theatres, cannot but produce a general rectitude of tafte among all ranks of people, and afford a moft perfect model of imitation, to all who have a diftinguifhing ear, and flexible voice. On the contrary, the language of the Germans is among thofe that are the leaft favourable to mufic; and very little vocal mufic is performed among them, except to Italian words, even in their operas: it was therefore natural, that inftrumental mufic should

should become the general object. The number of schools that have been mentioned in this Journal, where instrumental music is taught, increases the number of competitors; and the munificence of the German princes, who keep numerous bands of performers, not only for the service of the court, but the field, cannot but incite the most vigorous efforts to excel.

Upon the whole, with respect to the fine arts, it seems as if every school, and every country, had its peculiar vices, as well as virtues. In music, it has been shewn in my former tour, that the Lombard, Venetian, and Neapolitan schools, have characteristic distinctions; the same might be proved of the several styles of composition and performance in the principal cities of Germany; Vienna being most remarkable for fire and invention; Manheim, for neat and brilliant execution; Berlin, for counterpoint; and Brunswic, for taste. But, without

out opposing town to town, and state to state, it may be said of Germany in general, that the musical virtues of its natives, are *patience* and *profundity;* and their vices, *prolixity* and *pedantry*. The Italians are apt to be too negligent, and the Germans too elaborate; in so much, that music, if I may hazard the thought, seems *play* to the Italians, and *work* to the Germans. The Italians are perhaps the only people on the globe who can trifle with grace, as the Germans have alone the power to render even labour pleasing.

INDEX.

A.

ACADEMY of Commerce at Hamburg, some account of, 247.
Accompaniments, compared to conversation, 252.
Adam, M. musician at Dresden, 71.
Agrel, 324.
Agricola, M. composer at Berlin, 89, 204.
———— Signora, singer at Berlin, 93.
———— Rodolpho, 281.
AMSTERDAM, 282.
Ansani, Signor, an excellent tenor singer, 277.
Aotourou, 124.
Architecture, at Potzdam, 117. How encouraged there, 197.

B.

Bach, Sebastian, his great talents, 80. Challenged by Marchand, 81.
———— Frederic, 321.
Bach, Carl. Phil. Emanuel, at Hamburg, 244. His reception of the author, 245. His opinion of canons, 251. Sketch of his life, 259. List of his works, 263. Reflections on his style, 265. Excellence of his performance, 269. Flexibility of his genius, 270. Parallel drawn between him and Domenico Scarlatti, 271.
Backers, 146.
Band of the great opera at Berlin, 95.
Band, the much celebrated, under Hasse at Dresden in 1755, 51.
Benda, Francis, concert-master to the king of Prussia, 96, 118. His opinion of Giardini, 127. His affecting manner

manner of playing, 128. Sketch of his life, 129 to 140. Formed his style from good singing, ibid.
Benda, George, composer at Saxe-Gotha, 140.
—— Joseph, violin player at Berlin, 97, 218.
Berguys, organist and carilloneur at Delft, 314.
BERLIN, 86, 201. Great number of musical critics there, 224.
—————— musicians formed upon one model, 230.
Berselli, Matteo, his character as a singer, 175.
Bertuch, M. organist of St. Peter's, Berlin, 205.
Bezozzi, Signor, hautbois player at Dresden, 27, 45. Parallel between him and Fischer, 45.
Binder, M. organist at Dresden, 55.
Bode, M. an eminent printer at Hamburg, 246.
BOHEMIA, 1.
Bohemians, famous for musical talents, 3. Taught music at the common reading schools, 12, 14.
Borosini, singer, 180.
Braun, his character as a singer, 180.
Breitkopf, music seller at Leipsic, 73. Inventor of musical types, and of catalogues in notes, ibid. His printing-office, 78.
BREMEN, 278. Psalmody there, 279.
Bridge at Dresden, rule observed in passing it, 26.
BRUNSWIC, 320.
BUDIN, 16.
Buffardin, German flute player. 167, 170, 192.
Buononcini, 190.
Büsch, professor of mathematics at Hamburg. 246.
Buxtehude, famous organist, 239.

C.

Calori, Signora, singer at Dresden, 29.
Cantor, his office in Germany, 220.
Carestini, Giovanni, his character as a singer, 180.
Carillons, 282. At Amsterdam, 293. At Leyden, 310.
Chimes, played by clock-work, at Amsterdam, 296.
Church music, discouraged at Berlin, 91.
Comic operas, German, 326.

Concert-room of the new palace at Potzdam described, 144.
Concert, at Dresden, 44. At Sans-Souci, 151. At Berlin, 201. At Hamburg, 252, 256.
Concialini, Carlo, singer at Berlin, 98.
Conversations, with M. Dulsick, 5. With Benda, 127. With M. Quantz, 150. With C. P. E. Bach, 245, 250. With M. Klopstock, 248.
Cuzzoni, her character as a singer, 180.
Czarth, 101, 135.
Czaslau, 4.

D.

Delft, 312.
Domenico, his character as a singer, 179.
Doles, 325.
Dresden, 25.
Dubourg, 191.
Duel between Handel and Mattheson, 240.
Dulsick, Johann, organist and cantor at Czaslau, 4.

E.

Ebeling, M. 72. His translation of *the present State of Music*, 243. Introduces the author to M. C. P. E. Bach, 245. A great collector of musical curiosities, 246.
Elbe, passage down that river from Lobeschütz to Dresden, 20.

F.

Farinelli, 183.
Fasch, M. chamber-musician to the king of Prussia, 222.
Faustina, her portrait in the Dresden gallery, 41. Her character as a singer, 187.
Festing, 191.
Fischer, parallel drawn between him and Bezozzi, 45.
Fischietti, 322.
Fleischer, 321.
Foot-paths, peculiar to London, 197.

Fran-

Francifchello, 137.
Frauen-Kirche at Drefden, 30.
French mufic, its effect on a Greek lady, 123. On a native of Otaiti, 124. M. Quantz's opinion of it, 185.
Flute, German, improved by M. Quantz, 186, 194.
Fux, 178.

G.

Galatea, a paftoral opera, 225.
Gafparini, Signora a finger at Berlin, 97.
Gafparini, Signor, a Roman compofer, 182.
Gaffati, Pietro, 180.
Gellert, 333.
Geminiani, 191, 314.
Gefner, 333.
Gerbert, father, his plan of a hiftory of church mufic, 316. His materials deftroyed by fire, 318.
Giardini, 127.
Gleim, 333.
Götfel, M. German flute player at Drefden, 44.
Graaf, M. mufic director at the Hague, 311.
Grauel, M. violoncello player at Berlin, 218.
Graun, Charles Henry, 97. His works, 125. Two opinions concerning him, 227.
Graun, Joh. Gottlieb, 97. Praifed and cenfured, 228, 229.
GRONINGEN, 280.

H.

HAARLEM, 302.
Haarlem, organ, catalogue of its ftops, 305.
HAGUE, 311.
Haller, 333.
Hamburg, 234. Its populoufnefs, 255.
Handel, 190, 191. Began his career at Hamburg, 238. His great abilities upon the organ, 239, 242. His duel with Matthefon, 240.

Harpsichords made better in England by Germans than in Germany, 146.
Hasse, 50. His first theatrical composition, 183. Introduces Quantz to old Scarlatti, 184.
Heinichen, 171, 176.
Hiller, M. music director at Leipsic, 72.
Hoëckh, M. 135, 324.
Hohlfeld, constructor of a machine for writing down extempore pieces of music, 216.
Homilius, M. cantor and church composer at Dresden, 71.
Hunger, M. organist at Dresden, 48.
Hummel, music seller at Amsterdam, 285.
Hunt, M. violin player at Dresden, 44.

I.

Just, composer at the Hague, 311.

K.

Karsch, Madame, poetess at Berlin, 330.
Keiser, 83.
Kirkman, 146.
Kirnberger, musician at Berlin, 209. Scholar of Sebastian Bach, 210.
Klopstock, the Milton of Germany, 248. His countrymen's opinion of him, 249, 330.
Kone, chamber musician to the king of Prussia, 201.
KONINGSTEIN, 22.
Konyczek, 134.
Krause, 335.
Krebs, 324.
Kruch, first violin at Czaslau, 4.
Kunzen, 324.

L.

Landi, Abate, poet at Berlin, 98.
LEIPSIC, 71.

Length,

Length, neceſſary in German muſical compoſitions, 265.
Leſſing, M. 333.
LEYDEN, 309.
Lindner, M. 92, 201.
Linzen, M. organiſt of the new church at Amſterdam, 297.
Löbel, a blind Hebrew fidler, 134.
LOBESCHUTZ, 17.
Locatelli, 289.
Löhlein, 325.
Lotti, 173.
Luſtig, organiſt at Groningen, 280.

M.

Machine for writing down extempore pieces of muſic, conſtructed at Berlin, 213. Deſtroyed by fire, 214.
Maladie du pais, 125.
Marble gallery at Potzdam, 146.
Marchand challenges Sebaſtian Bach, 81.
Mara, M. violoncello player at Berlin, 208.
Marpurg, M. at Berlin, 105. His muſical writings, 106, 206, 212.
Marriage Jubilee, 140.
Mattheſon, 235. Printed as many books as he lived years, 236. Conteſt for ſuperiority over Handel, 239. Quarrel and duel with ditto, 240. Bequeaths an organ to the new church at Hamburg, 273. Its excellence, 274.
Metaſtaſio, his opinion of German ſinging-ſchools, 23.
Miſliwiceck brought up in Bohemia, 13.
Mingotti, her portrait in the picture gallery at Dreſden, 41.
Modern muſic always to be abuſed, 157.
Monticelli, 51.
Mozart family, 322.
Mumſſon, Dr. at Hamburg, 248.
Müller, 325.
Muſic, its effects moſt powerful in hot climates, 3. By what means become ſo general in Bohemia, 4. Injured
by

by time, 153. Stationary at Berlin, 195, 234. Requires paſſion and enthuſiaſm, 224.
Muſic ſchools in Bohemia, 4. At Teechenbrod, 4. At Janich, ibid. At Bömiſchbrod, ibid. At Czaſlau, 5. At Budin, 16. At Lobeſchütz, 17. At Köningſtein, 23. At Pirna, ibid. At Dreſden, 63.
Muſic ſhops at Leipſic, 73. Hamburg, 257. Amſterdam, 285, and Nuremberg, 324.
Muſical writers at Berlin, 88.
Müthel, great player and excellent compoſer, 328. Account of his works, 329.

N.

Naumann, *maeſtro di capella* at Dreſden, 34.
Neefe, 325.
Nicolai, a learned bookſeller at Berlin, 89.
Night-watch at Berlin, 89.
NUREMBERG, 324.

O.

Organs at Czaſlau, 5. At Prague, 8, 9. At Lobeſchütz, 17. At the Frauen-Kirche, Dreſden, 30. Elector's chapel, Dreſden, 54. Garriſon church, Berlin, 103. St. Peter's, Berlin, 204. St. Mary's, Berlin, 206. New church, Hamburg, 272. St. Peter's, Hamburg, 276. At the cathedral, Bremen, 278. St. Martin, Groningen, 280. New church, Amſterdam, 283. Old church, Amſterdam, 286. The great church at Haarlem, 302.
Organiſts, method of chuſing them at Amſterdam, 291.
Orſini, Gaetano, 131. His character as a ſinger, 179.
Orontes, an opera by Theil, 235.

P.

Palace, new, at Potzdam, deſcribed, 143.
Pantaleone, 58, 167.
Parade at Potzdam, 195.

Paſſione, of C. P. E. Bach, 253.
Peſch, 321.
Picture gallery at Dreſden, 39, 52.
PIRNA, 23.
Piſendel, 167, 172, 192.
Pfiffer, M. organiſt of St. Peter's, Hamburg, 276.
Poets, German, ſome account of, 330.
Poor ſcholars at Dreſden, their origin, 63. Divided into troops, 68. Their dreſs, 70.
Porporino, ſig. firſt ſerious ſinger at Berlin, 98.
Poſtillions, 20, 84.
Pothoff, M. blind organiſt at Amſterdam, 286. His great abilities on the organ, 287. An ingenious fugiſt, 288. His aſtoniſhing execution as carilloneur, 293.
POTZDAM, 114. Its beautiful buildings, 177.
Poutaveri, his mimickry of the French opera, 124.
PRAGUE, 6. Why not abounding in great muſicians, 10.

Q.

Quantz, John Joachim, chamber muſician to the king of Pruſſia, 150. Sketch of his life, 161 to 194. His improvement of the German flute, 186, 194.

R.

Racks, aboliſhed at Dreſden, 61.
Rabner, 334.
Rammler, 333.
Reflections on the muſical talents of the Bohemians, 3, 10. On different ſtyles in muſic, 157. On the neceſſity of contraſt in muſic, 202. On the ſinging at Leipſic, 76. On the comparative muſical merit of the Germans and Italians, 337.
Reichard, 325.
Richert, 327.
Richter, 101, 327.
Riedt, M. flute player at Berlin, 201, 204. His fondneſs for calculations, 223.

Riepel,

Riepel, M. musician at Ratisbon, 319.
Ringk, M. organist of St. Mary's, Berlin, 206.
Rode, four monumental paintings by him, at Berlin, 104.
Rolle, 325.
Rosalba, her portraits in the picture gallery at Dresden, 41.
Rosalie, what, 327.
ROTTERDAM, 314.
Rück, M. 204.

S.

SALTSBURG, 322.
Sans-Souci, palace, 113, 147, 148.
Sarti, Signor 301.
Scarlatti, Alessandro, his opinion of wind instruments, 184.
——— Domenico, ibid. and 271.
Schale, M. 223.
Schmeling, Mademoiselle, first singer at Berlin, 97. Her amazing powers, 108, 111, 206.
Schmidt, 169, 171.
Schmitt, father, 328.
Schüler, M. 204.
Schwanberger, 320.
Schwindl, M. 312.
Seger, organist at Prague, 13.
Senesino, 174. His character as a singer, 176.
Shudi, 145.
Silbermann, 48.
Singing at Leipsic, 76. At Bremen, 278. At the German Jews synagogue, 299.
Snetzler, 102, 146.
Spandau, 312.
Stamitz, brought up in the common school at Teuchenbrod, 12. His great and original genius, 13.
Stechwech, organist of the Wester Kerk at Amsterdam, 292.
Street musicians at Prague, 10.

Strosil,

Strofil, a musical instrument, 70.
Sulzer, M 208.
Swell, not to be found in German organs, 102.
Synagogue, German Jews, at Amsterdam, 298.

T.

Telemann, a most voluminous composer, 242. His first and second manner, 243.
Tesi, Vittoria, 176.
Theatres, small one at Dresden, 29. Great one at ditto, 50. At Leipsic, 74. At Berlin, 94.
Thum-Kirche, at Bremen, 278.
Tunnerstick, Dr. his experiment, 35.

V.

Van Hagen, organist at Rotterdam, 314.
Vivaldi, his concertos studied by Fran. Benda, 133. By Quantz, 165.
Vox humana, stop, 303.
Universities, German, 334.

W.

Wagner, 103.
Weidemann, 191.
Weidner, M. 135.
Weiss, 167, 177, 192.
Westphal, an eminent music merchant at Hamburg, 256.
Wieland, a German poet, 331.
Wolf, M. organist at Prague, 8.
Wolf, at Weymer, 326.

Z.

Zachariä, 226, 334.

FINIS.

Titles published by Travis & Emery:

Bathe, William: A Briefe Introduction to the Skill of Song
Bax, Arnold: Symphony #5, Arranged for Piano for Four Hands by Walter Emery
Burney, Charles: An Account of the Musical Performances in Westminster-Abbey
Burney, Charles: The Present State of Music in France and Italy
Burney, Charles: The Present State of Music in Germany, The Netherlands …
Crimp, Bryan: Solo: The Biography of Solomon
Hawkins, John: A General History of the Science and Practice of Music (5 vols.)
Herbert-Caesari, Edgar: The Science and Sensations of Vocal Tone
Herbert-Caesari, Edgar: Vocal Truth
Mainwaring, John: Memoirs of the Life of the Late George Frederic Handel
Malcolm, Alexander: A Treaty of Music: Speculative, Practical and Historical
Mellers, Wilfrid: Angels of the Night: Popular Female Singers of Our Time
Mellers, Wilfrid: Bach and the Dance of God
Mellers, Wilfrid: Beethoven and the Voice of God
Mellers, Wilfrid: Caliban Reborn - Renewal in Twentieth Century Music
Mellers, Wilfrid: François Couperin and the French Classical Tradition
Mellers, Wilfrid: Harmonious Meeting
Mellers, Wilfrid: Le Jardin Retrouvé, The Music of Frederic Mompou
Mellers, Wilfrid: Music and Society, England and the European Tradition
Mellers, Wilfrid: Music in a New Found Land: … … American Music
Mellers, Wilfrid: Romanticism and the Twentieth Century (from 1800)
Mellers, Wilfrid: The Masks of Orpheus: …… the Story of European Music.
Mellers, Wilfrid: The Sonata Principle (from c. 1750)
Playford, John: An Introduction to the Skill of Musick.
Purcell, Henry et al: Harmonia Sacra … The First Book, [1726]
Purcell, Henry et al: Harmonia Sacra … Book II [1726]
Rastall, Richard: The Notation of Western Music.
Simpson, Christopher: A Compendium of Practical Musick in Five Parts
Tans'ur, William: A New Musical Grammar; or The Harmonical Spectator
Tosi, Pier Francesco: Observations on the Florid Song.
Van der Straeten, Edmund: History of the Violoncello, The Viol da Gamba …

Travis & Emery Music Bookshop
17 Cecil Court, London, WC2N 4EZ, United Kingdom.
Tel. (+44) 20 7240 2129